# The Didactic Muse

WILLARD SPIEGELMAN

# The Didactic Muse

Scenes of Instruction in Contemporary
American Poetry

PRINCETON UNIVERSITY PRESS
Princeton, New Jersey

Library of Congress Cataloging-in-Publication Data

Spiegelman, Willard.
  The didactic muse : scenes of instruction in contemporary American poetry / Willard
Spiegelman.
    p.  cm.
  Includes index.
  ISBN 0-691-06799-6 (alk. paper)   ISBN 0-691-01460-4 (pbk.)
    1. American poetry—20th century—History and criticism. 2. Didactic poetry,
American—History and criticism. 3. Classicism—United States. I. Title.
PS309.D53S65   1989
811'.0509—dc20        89-32283

This book has been composed in Linotron Baskerville

Printed in the United States of America
by Princeton University Press,
Princeton, New Jersey

FOR KENNETH BLEETH

". . . quel condotto che speranza mi dava e facea lume"

# CONTENTS

## ACKNOWLEDGMENTS

This book was begun and finished under the most pleasant circumstances imaginable. Thanks to a fellowship from the Rockefeller Foundation, I spent the 1985–86 academic year as a Scholar-in-Residence at the Poetry Center of the Ninety-second Street YMHA in Manhattan, where so many twentieth-century literary lights have appeared to the public that any critic of poetry would have to be dazzled and illuminated in equal measure. The courtesies of Shelley Mason and Karl Kirchwey, the former and present directors of the Center, as well as those of the staff of the Performing Arts division, made life at the "Y" a constant pleasure. Stephen Tapscott, the other Rockefeller beneficiary, became an amiable companion and a sounding board for many ideas. Evelyn Bleeth, and Jo and Willem Brans, offered considerable hospitality during the year in New York. In 1987–88, as a visiting professor at Williams College, I enjoyed the natural beauty of the Berkshires, and profited from the stimulation provided by my students and my lively colleagues in the English department, the word-processing advice of Miriam Grabois, and the freedom from administrative responsibility that enabled me to complete this book.

The attentions of W. S. Di Piero, John Hollander, and Alan Wilde have helped assure the book's appearance in the world. Garrett Stewart and Theodore Weiss read the complete work and made important recommendations for changes and expansions. I continue to be grateful for the encouragement and financial backing of my department heads at Southern Methodist University and of the deans of Dedman College. Susan Meyn has offered so much computer advice in time of trouble that I think that this book could literally never have appeared without her intervention. At Princeton University Press, Robert Brown and Beth Gianfagna have supervised the editing and production of the book with consummate efficiency and reliability. Megan Benton, with an eye for both nuance and accuracy, performed the copyediting speedily and sensitively.

Portions of chapters 2, 4, and 5 appeared in a different form in the *Southwest Review* and *Salmagundi*; an earlier version of my discussion of Robert Pinsky was published in *Dictionary of Literary Biography: Yearbook* (Gale Publishing, 1982). An earlier version of one section of chapter 6 is used by permission of the publisher and reprinted from my "Breaking the Mirror: Interruption in Merrill's Trilogy," in *James Merrill: Essays in Criticism*, edited by David Lehman and Charles Berger. Copyright © 1983 by Cornell University Press.

For permission to quote from the poets contained in these pages, I wish to make the following acknowledgments:

Selections from A. R. Ammons, *Tape for the Turn of the Year*, W. W. Norton, 1965; *Collected Poems, 1951–1971*, W. W. Norton, 1972; and *Sphere: The Form of a Motion*, W. W. Norton, 1972, are reprinted by permission of the author.

W. H. Auden, "New Year Letter," reprinted by permission of Curtis Brown, Ltd., copyright © 1941 by W. H. Auden.

"Sandpiper" and excerpts from "North Haven" from *The Complete Poems 1927–1979* by Elizabeth Bishop. Copyright © 1962, 1978 by Elizabeth Bishop. Reprinted by permission of Farrar, Straus and Giroux, Inc.

Excerpts from *Collected Poems 1947–1980* by Allen Ginsberg. Copyright © 1984 by Allen Ginsberg. Reprinted by permission of Harper & Row, Publishers, Inc.

Selections from the poetry of Anthony Hecht are reprinted with permission of Atheneum Publishers, an imprint of Macmillan Publishing Company, from *A Summoning of Stones*, copyright © 1954, and renewed 1982 by Anthony E. Hecht; from *The Hard Hours*, copyright © 1967 by Anthony E. Hecht; from *Millions of Strange Shadows*, copyright © 1977 by Anthony E. Hecht; and from *The Venetian Vespers*, copyright © 1979 by Anthony E. Hecht.

Selections from the poetry of James Merrill are reprinted with permission of Atheneum Publishers, an imprint of Macmillan Publishing Company from *The Changing Light at Sandover*, copyright © 1976, 1978, 1980, and 1982 by James Merrill.

Selections from *The Collected Poems of Howard Nemerov*, University of Chicago Press, 1977, are reprinted by permission of the author.

Excerpts from Robert Pinsky, *Sadness and Happiness*, copyright © 1975 by Princeton University Press, and *An Explanation of America*, copyright © 1979 by Princeton University Press.

Selections from Adrienne Rich, *Poems Selected and New, 1950–1974*, W. W. Norton, 1974; *Adrienne Rich's Poetry*, W. W. Norton, 1975; and *The Fact of a Doorframe: Poems Selected and New, 1950–1984*, W. W. Norton, 1984, are reprinted by permission of the author.

Selections from *Axe Handles*, copyright © 1983 by Gary Snyder. Published by North Point Press and reprinted by permission; selections from *Left Out in the Rain*, copyright © 1986 by Gary Snyder. Published by North Point Press and reprinted by permission.

Although it would seem natural for the author of a work on didacticism to mention his own teachers, I have already done so in an earlier book, on Wordsworth. Nevertheless, I must acknowledge three other debts to individuals from whom I've learned: when J. D. McClatchy suggested that I apply for the Rockefeller grant, I never knew where his recommendation might lead. Thanks to him, I conceived of the project out of which this entire book grew. Critic, poet, editor, and informal adviser, he has been as generous to me as he has been to many others. Second, I wish to signal my respect for the late David Kalstone who, although never officially my teacher, was a model of professional kindness, critical acumen, and personal liberality that one might well emulate but never match. Finally, I have dedicated this book to the person for whom I find even Dante's words of praise insufficient.

# The Didactic Muse

# Introduction:
# W. H. Auden's "New Year Letter"

Aut prodesse volunt aut delectare poetae
aut simul et iucunda et idonea dicere vitae.
quidquid praecipies, esto brevis, ut cito dicta
percipiant animi dociles teneantque fideles:
omne supervacuum pleno de pectore manat.
ficta voluptatis causa sint proxima veris.

(Poets aim either to benefit, or to amuse, or to utter words at once both pleasing and helpful to life. Whenever you instruct, be brief, so that what is quickly said the mind may readily grasp and faithfully hold: every word in excess flows away from the full mind. Fictions meant to please should be close to the real.)          —HORACE, *Ars Poetica*

From Horace to Robert Frost ("a poem begins in delight and ends in wisdom") the major current of Western poetics has flowed from the wells of pleasure to the depths of instruction. That poetry serves pedagogy seemed as unarguable in the classical and early modern worlds as it may appear untenable in the contemporary one. Poets traditionally held their mirrors up to nature not simply to reflect it but to occasion reflection and right action in their readers. Poet as teacher, reader as student: the roles are clear from Horace's obiter dicta, maxims, and specifically literary advice (e.g., in *Epistles* 1.2 he applauds Homer's models of behavior, like Ulysses as *utile exemplar* of wisdom) to Wordsworth's remark to Sir George Beaumont that "every great poet is a Teacher—I wish to be considered as a teacher or as nothing."[1] Poets have appropriated to themselves the sacred obligation of preparing a citizenry, a prince, an individual conscience for life in this world. As a still earlier example, Aristotle might be considered the first defender of the role that mimetic poetry can play in the education of future leaders. And although didacticism has had a bad press at least since Keats ("we hate poetry that has a palpable design upon us") and Shelley ("didactic poetry is my abhorrence; nothing can be equally well expressed in prose that is not tedious and supererogatory in verse"),[2] the younger Romantics nevertheless proclaimed their intention of "doing the world some good" (Keats) and implied a hope, in a para-

3

phrase of Shelley's *Defence of Poetry*, that eventually it might acknowledge their legislating prophecies. To "teach the adverting mind," what Shelley hopes that Mont Blanc will do, is likewise his own anticipated accomplishment.

Horace's remarks from *Ars Poetica* are a positive rejoinder to the condemnation by Plato and his like-minded successors of poets who misuse art's mimetic powers. The lines also dramatize a dialectic of instruction *within* poetry itself: Horace replaces a simple dichotomy ("aut prodesse . . . aut delectare") with a complex synthesis of simultaneity ("aut simul et iucunda et idonea") that I shall use as a starting point for the following reflections. Pleasure and instruction, far from occupying opposing ends of a logical or aesthetic spectrum, sit squarely together in both the poet's intention and the audience's reception of his work. Brevity is not only the soul of wit but also the sine qua non of instruction: the very concision of verse, even in forms fuller and more discursive than epigram and lyric, allows it privileges that might be denied to the wordier wanderings of prose.

In the panorama of literary culture, it increasingly appears that modernism was an aberration. Or, at the very least, many of its formulaic injunctions, if not its practices, were. Ezra Pound's command, "Go in fear of abstractions," and William Carlos Williams's preference for a direct, sensuous apprehension through images to any lengthier speculation are understandable responses to the excesses of late Victorian preaching and the mindless music of Swinburne's opulent periphrases, but the altar of symbolism at which the great moderns worshiped seems in retrospect to have been a temporary and perhaps fragile structure.[3] Since 1945 American poets have increasingly rejected the major principles of Yeats and Pound even as they have absorbed their lessons, in favor of more didactic stances in their poetry. Frank Kermode's *Romantic Image*, which identified the iconic centers of modernism and relied on Pound's insistence that the "image" is not, and is always antithetical to, an idea, cannot be taken as a guide to the poetic heirs, especially the American ones, of the modernist giants.[4] Equally aberrant is the deliberate turning away from traditional aesthetics in Charles Newman's condemnation of postmodernism, a diatribe that purports to deny the traditional wisdom but has trouble finding a substitute for it: "What we finally want from literature is neither *amusement* nor *edification* but the demonstration of a real authority which is not to be confused with sincerity, and of an understanding which is not gratuitous."[5]

The much bedeviled matter of "edification" or didacticism deserves more detailed treatment than it has received; perhaps it should simply be acknowledged that "didactic" is one poet's opprobrious term for another's work not to his liking. To call something didactic is to call it bad, superficial, preachy. Yet all the principal remarks of the major nineteenth-century poets, even before they ossified into Ancient Sages, suggest the fundamental identity of teaching with writing and of learning with reading. Modernism suppressed both sentimentality and direct instruction, replacing them with an "erotics of the image,"[6] but discursiveness, as Robert Pinsky defines it in *The Situation of Poetry*, has re-entered the pages of much important contemporary American poetry.[7] Perhaps this tendency reflects a gradual retrenchment, a poetic equivalent of political conservatism (this is another way of defining what Robert von Hallberg refers to as the "suburban" nature of some of the best postwar American poetry),[8] or perhaps it indicates the desire of many poets to speak in the honest, sometimes unironic tones of conversation, and to imbue their work with the virtues of good prose. Thus, the label "discursive," whether taken as "wandering" or "explanatory" (the complementary terms are Pinsky's), may be applied to recent American poetry in predominantly longer forms as well as to the epigrammatic, witty, and deliberately condensed lyrics of J. V. Cunningham and the mock-pedagogy of John Ashbery. Like discourse, both philosophy and pedagogy have returned beneath the poetic mantle. Poets have resumed their historically sanctioned, or at least self-proclaimed, roles as teachers. This role-taking may be only the inevitable effect of their literal presence, in great numbers, within the confines of the academy and their new jobs as teachers of "creative" writing (a distinctly postwar phenomenon), although I suspect a cultural cause deeper than that of a mere vocational rearrangement. Acts of informative teaching have produced a new rhetoric of instruction within our poetry, and poets as various and *un*didactic as Robert Hass (*Field Guide*), Tess Gallagher (*Instructions to the Double*), and Annaliese Wagner (*Hand Work*) have been giving us recipes, templates, guides, and treatises for several decades. Reading through the titles of individual poems in representative volumes by other essentially lyric poets also yields a survey of instructional motifs: witness Maxine Kumin's "How to Survive Nuclear War" in *The Long Approach* (1985) and, from David Wagoner's *Collected Poems* (1976), "The Lesson," "The Singing Lesson," "The Breathing Lesson," "Advice to the Orchestra," "A Police Manual," and "Do Not Proceed Beyond This Point Without a Guide." The list could be extended.

"Education by poetry is education by metaphor," said Frost in a famous pronouncement. Elsewhere he seems to prepare an audience for the very points I assert in this book: "School and poetry come so near

being one thing . . . it is but an extension from the metaphors of poetry out into all thinking, scientific and philosophic."9 Frost preferred
to construe both poetry and its constituent metaphors as living things;
reaffirming a Coleridgean organicism, he condemns those people as
lost who would dare to think of their material without the saving, organizing grace of a "gathering metaphor." Metaphor is "a very living
thing," he asserts, and poetry educates us to think metaphorically,
thereby enabling us to work through and with the metaphors of other
disciplines. Living before Thomas Kuhn, Frost anticipated Kuhn's
thesis that science works intuitively to effect its major revolutions.10
Frost himself suspects as much: "Poetry is simply made of metaphor.
So also is philosophy and science, too." If one agrees with Frost that
metaphor, which is usually said to separate poetic from scientific language, in fact forms the basis of all kinds of knowing, then one should
also reverse the standard dichotomy between science and poetry from
the other direction, in order to allow poetry to contain within itself the
kinds of methodology usually deemed "scientific." Literary analysis is
a curious two-way street. A poem, of course, is the solution to a set of
formal and intellectual problems that one must try to reconstruct
when attempting to understand it, but it is also a piece of empirical
evidence from which one moves forward to an inductive conclusion.
One proceeds from data to conclusion, and at the same time attempts
an archaeological act of reconstruction, from the poetic conclusion to
the original hypothetical set of problems from which it derives. Poetry
is not discourse, but it may be discursive without undermining its poetic status.

It is necessary to attend more closely to the relationship between
styles of teaching and poetic technique, to the implied roles of our
poets as well as to their metaphors. The polemics of Adrienne Rich,
the sometimes vatic looniness and political obsessiveness of Allen Ginsberg, and the cracker-barrel stances of A. R. Ammons and (with some
added layers of Talmudic sagacity) Howard Nemerov are all pedagogic strategies. Our poets are wearing many of the same cloaks that
teachers have traditionally chosen for themselves, those of Socratic *ei-
ron*, Eastern guru, soapbox orator, parent, and psychotherapist.

In much of the poetry discussed in this book, the pedagogy is in-
flected with irony, wit, self-deprecation, and skepticism, all of them
modernist stances as well as the legacy of an ingrained American common sense. In other words, it combines direct preaching with the "indirection" associated with modernism in early Eliot and Auden, as well
as in their novelistic contemporaries. Thus, Ammons in "Uh, Philoso-

phy" (*Northfield Poems*, 1967) pretends to dismiss his subject offhandedly, even while delving more deeply into it:

> I understand
>     reading the modern philosophers
> that truth is so much a method
>         it's perfectly all
> right for me to believe whatever
>     I like or if I like,
> nothing:
>     I do not know that I care to be set that free:

Later in the same poem, Ammons disavows the power of abstract ideas
in favor of an updating of Yeats's enterprise of nakedness: "philosophy is . . . / something to knock people down with:/ . . . the philosophy
gives clubs to / everyone, and I prefer disarmament." And yet in no
other recent poet do ideas, scientific principles, and philosophical abstraction collide so gracefully with the facts of ordinary perception
and the habits of daily routine. Ammons charms readers disarmingly,
making what Richard Poirier terms the standard American "association of heroic action with denudation," but he always carries plenty of
defensive scientific equipment on his field excursions.[11]

In combining plain speaking, explanation, scientific examination,
and playfulness, Ammons meanders down one discursive path. In addition to following this path, this book surveys those of Nemerov,
Ginsberg, Pinsky, Rich, and of Anthony Hecht and James Merrill, all
poets born between 1920 (Nemerov) and 1940 (Pinsky). These constitute a generation for which World War II was the central historical
fact and whose first major works (with the exception of Pinsky) were
published during the supposedly arid decade of the 1950s. Merrill is
central to the argument because he incorporates scientific themes,
philosophical language, and the expectation of instruction into increasingly capacious poetic forms. He is the first poet since Yeats to
have seriously defined a universe or created a system, and to have re-
created, in *The Changing Light at Sandover*, not only a scene of instruction and revelation but also a textbook for a spiritual and physical understanding of the universe.

At the start of his career Merrill angered some reviewers who called
him a mere miniaturist, making poems about and into glittering na-
creous objects, the elegant impedimenta from a life of lustrous privilege. Then, in his "sacred" books, when he answered a call for "poems
of science," other critics dismissed as simplistic or irrelevant his efforts
to include subatomic particle physics, genetics, and doctrines of rein-

carnation into a cosmic theodicy. Whether Merrill's explanations of the universe originated from his own imaginings or in those disembodied voices speaking to him from a crackpot mechanism and a board game is moot. He met the demands of his spirits and, having learned a lesson, became, in his turn, a teacher to his readers. *The Changing Light at Sandover* stands as the most complete object in a field littered with Romantic and post-Romantic *disiecta membra*; it challenges too-easy categorical distinctions between lyric and narrative and judgments about the tones, subjects, and processes appropriate to each. As an epic poet, Merrill has sought to teach—through the discourses of his spirits and the other dramatic characters who enter his mind or the room of his instruction, now inscribed within the pages of his text.

Whereas Ammons courts "abstraction" with polysyllabic, latinate diction and his own preferred, key words ("saliences," "peripheries," "radiances") in essentially lyric structures, Merrill's abstractions owe less to a signature vocabulary. Employing the widest range of diction available to any living poet, he gives primers in scientific principles, manners, world history, art appreciation, and family relations, registering the lessons in appropriate speech. Mixing lectures, narrative, dramatic encounters, extractable lyric moments, and even some Poundian illustrations ("In a work this long, / Madness to imagine one could do / Without the apt ideogram or two"), *The Changing Light at Sandover* gives new meaning to the term "georgic."

As poets of instruction, all of the writers dealt with in this book are, in fact, georgic, whether explaining, lecturing, delivering opinions, or more generally sharing enthusiasms with a specific or implied audience. "What we have loved, / Others will love, and we will teach them how," proclaimed the confident Wordsworth at the end of *The Prelude*: another name for the instruction proffered by our poetic teachers is love, bestowed hopefully and received gratefully in the exchange between them and their readers.

I begin with some commentary on a paradigmatic poem by the preachiest of postwar poets, the one who most clearly bridges the gap between the modernist generation and the contemporary Americans I label "didactic." W. H. Auden's "New Year Letter" marks a turning point for its author, and is a fitting introduction to certain styles in contemporary poetry. Combining instruction with wit, philosophy with chattiness, it announces Auden's arrival in this country, and it divides his earlier, English work, with its political engagements and youthful ironies, from his return to religion and the increasingly avuncular, fussy, and cozy tones of his later poetry.

"New Year Letter" exemplifies what I referred to earlier as the dialectic of instruction; it embodies as well the two kinds of discursiveness that Robert Pinsky has formulated.[12] Its immediate personal source is Auden's affection for Elizabeth Mayer, friend and hostess, to whom it is addressed, and for the civilized harmony represented by her domestic establishment in (aptly named) Amityville, Long Island. Its occasion is both the traditional time of stock taking and Auden's awareness of impending world catastrophe. Grappling with political, ethical, and at last religious questions gives Auden cogent thematic direction and a serious didactic purpose. Still, as Edward Callan has noted, "the verse letter espouses coherences and dialectical tension as approaches to truth, and attacks all one-sided claims to the whole truth, whether these be Darwinian, Freudian, or Marxist, without denying each some truth, or even a good measure of it."[13]

The verse epistle addresses a figure within a private realm and examines a public one; seeking an explanation for personal and world crises, it must also discover apposite languages for each. For this reason, the "letter's" closest affinities are not, as many critics feel, with Kierkegaard (because of the organization of its themes into aesthetic, ethical, and religious areas) but with Wordsworth's *Prelude*, another, though longer, verse epistle that measures the public realm by its effects on the personal life, and that creates a new speech out of Miltonic epic and ordinary conversation, appropriate to historical analysis, philosophical speculation, and personal reminiscence. Although neither Auden's answers nor all of his stylistic habits are Wordsworth's, his dilemma is: in both cases a poet confronts world disaster, the one retrospectively and the other immediately, and looks for a vantage point from which to make a closer examination without jeopardizing personal sanity or poetic potency.

In rhythmically varied octosyllabic couplets, the medium of those other "master[s] of the middle style" (Auden's label for Dryden) whose voices he is partly borrowing—Marvell, Swift, Yeats—Auden announces his affiliation with poets who entertain the rival demands of private happiness and civic obligation. Since he says toward the start of the poem that "order" is "the task / Both Eros and Apollo ask," he seems to be pledging himself in creative apprenticeship to both libidinal and rational principles, or personal and public ones. Even in the apparently easy lines at the beginning, his stylistic choices reflect the synthetic nature of the order that he seeks:

Under the familiar weight
Of winter, conscience and the State,

> In loose formations of good cheer,
> Love, language, loneliness and fear,
> Towards the habits of next year,
> Along the streets the people flow,
> Singing or sighing as they go:
> *Exalté, piano*, or in doubt,
> All our reflections turn about
> A common meditative norm,
> Retrenchment, Sacrifice, Reform.
>
> $(1-11)^{14}$

The occasion is ordinary and annual (the poem is dated 1 January 1940), presented in a rhythm that recalls the banalities of urban life in T. S. Eliot's early comic verse (the "flowing" people suggest the crowds flowing over London Bridge in *The Waste Land* as well as the women talking of Michelangelo in "Prufrock"). It is also generalized; the poet opens with the language of abstraction, which builds in the form of a list (Auden's legacy from Byron and Pope) to the still grander personifications of the end of the passage. From the specific and the "familiar," to the typical, to the general—such is Auden's strategy for moving toward larger sightings.

The poem continually repeats this progression, as in the very next passage, which moves from narrative reminiscence ("Twelve months ago in Brussels I / Heard the same wishful-thinking sigh") to personified abstraction ("There crouched the presence of the Thing"). Part 2 begins the same way, with a description of place and time, the end of the decade; it continues with a lengthier investigation of a symbolic landscape and with an intimation of a human figure petrified like Lot's wife:

> And now and then a nature turns
> To look where her whole system burns
> And with a last defiant groan
> Shudders her future into stone.
>
> (337–40)

It reaches at last a moral lesson based on what has come before:

> How hard it is to set aside
> Terror, concupiscence and pride,
> Learn who and where and how we are,
> The children of a modest star.
>
> (341–44)

Both of the first parts prepare readers for part 3, the poem's longest and most important; it, too, begins with a visible scene, runs swiftly to abstractions, and then juxtaposes public and private realms with an image of a "privileged community" (as it is called in line 856), Auden's vision of Edenic moments of Being in the ordinary course of Becoming:

> Across East River in the night
> Manhattan is ablaze with light.
> No shadow dares to criticize
> The popular festivities,
> Hard liquor causes everywhere
> A general *détente*, and Care
> For this state function of Good Will
> Is diplomatically ill:
> The Old Year dies a noisy death.
> Warm in your house, Elizabeth,
> A week ago at the same hour
> I felt the unexpected power
> That drove our ragged egos in
> From the dead-ends of greed and sin
> To sit down at the wedding-feast,
> . . . . . . . . . . . . .
> And GLUCK and food and friendship made
> Our privileged community
> That real republic which must be
> The State all politicians claim,
> Even the worst, to be their aim.
>
> (834–48, 855–59)

The power of Auden's didacticism stems from his mingling of particular detail ("Across the East River") with easy personification (Care, Good Will, the noisy Old Year); of simple statement confined to single couplets (834–37) with enjambment cunningly employed (838–40); of tempting accumulations of anaphora ("And GLUCK and food and friendship") with the unexpected power of run-ons and rhythmic variation ("That drove our ragged egos *in* / From the dead-ends"). Everywhere personal, the poem is nowhere confessional: the technique gives the illusion of coziness kept within public bounds, of angst observing decorum.

"New Year Letter" might have been called "The Quest," a title given to twenty Rilkean sonnets that followed it in the original edition. All of the poem's figurative devices, its rhetorical agencies and religious

speculations, are tropes of exploration (not pronouncement), efforts
to discover "a way" to deal with public and private turmoil. That the
end of the poem points to the religious orthodoxy of much of Auden's
late work should in no way prevent one from looking closely at the
wide range of poetic as well as thematic instruments with which he
examines his path.

At the age of thirty-two Auden made a literal ocean crossing that
would have permanent personal and creative consequences for him.
Not surprisingly, at work on the poem while he passed his symbolic
thirty-third birthday, Auden begins his "Letter" with a self-appraisal.
All of part 1 deals with the general province of art (Kierkegaard's aesthetic realm)—what it is and does—and with Auden's specific version
of the test to which any artist puts himself, an imaginary judgment
from a tribunal of precursors, those dead poets at whose "feet," in the
colloquial and technical senses, he has studied. As it happens, the inefficacy of language becomes a major fear in the poem, almost in direct proportion to Auden's famous technical facility. In the beginning
of part 2, for example, he significantly imagines a landscape in which
a Wordsworthian nature has obscured the written signposts that might
lead one out of darkness. The poem portrays contemporary disaster
in terms of a linguistic displacement, as the written word has been oc-
culted in favor of the spoken logos. Even the earlier urban scene has
been replaced by a barren heath:

> Tonight a scrambling decade ends,
> And strangers, enemies and friends
> Stand once more puzzled underneath
> The signpost on the barren heath
> Where the rough mountain track divides
> To silent valleys on all sides,
> Endeavoring to decipher what
> Is written on it but cannot,
> Nor guess in what direction lies
> The overhanging precipice.
> Through the pitch-darkness can be heard
> Occasionally a muttered word,
> And intense in the mountain frost
> The heavy breathing of the lost.
>
> (319–32)

Writing deceives and disappears in an emblematic setting reminiscent
of Wordsworth's "Michael" or Frost's "Directive." For one who believes
that "poetry makes nothing happen," as Auden confessed less than a

year before in his elegy to Yeats, the struggle to read and decipher the languages of nature and politics dovetails with an effort to find a "civil" speech that will represent and allay personal anxieties and measure up to the standards by which Auden would choose to be judged by his masters. The particular duplicities of poetry, through the heightening of ordinary language, have captured the accomplished writer, who sees them both as a collection of devious satanic instruments and as handles to salvation.

Auden's appearance before the tribunal of his betters in part 1 follows a section in which he acknowledges the relative successes and failures of the general artistic enterprise. Eros and Apollo demand an order that can never be entirely willed by the individual creator, but a single life, the basis of artistic creation, is "the unique [that] serves to typify" the general, and becomes "an algebraic formula, / An abstract model of events." As a fait accompli art is not life, although it has a mimetic origin in its attempted fidelity to observed detail. Once it is done it "cannot tell men how to be," even though the model may work analogically (cf. Wordsworth's rhetorical question in *The Prelude* when he suggests a possible defense of personal confession: "What one is / Why may not many be?"). To Auden, artists can only "challenge, warn and witness" (127).

Having asserted, one hundred lines before, the conventional wisdom about the order created by art ("Where nothing but assent was found, / For art had set in order sense / And feeling and intelligence, / And from its ideal order grew / Our local understanding too" [51–55]), Auden now complicates the commonplace with a skeptical intimation that artists, surviving their own "soiled, shabby, egotistic lives," are merely weak vessels, unworthy in themselves and also when compared with their predecessors. It is significant that the art that had set sense, feeling, and intelligence in order was music: the passacaglia of Buxtehude (48) represents, as music does everywhere in Auden's work, an agency of redemption, precise because unlinguistic. It is Gluck (855), not Goethe, who gives access to an ideal community. This stock-taking poem examines guilt and weakness and begins by specifically considering poetic unworthiness. The apparent price Auden pays for his own ease is his doubt of its worth.

The mingled modesty and pride in the imagined scene of judgment are a striking, preparatory confirmation of the influence studies of Harold Bloom (whose appraisals of exactly who influences whom are often as surprising as Auden's roll call of favorite poets) and, more important, a model for the reading scene with which James Merrill ends *The Changing Light at Sandover*. Both episodes derive ultimately from the charge put by Longinus in his advice to would-be poets, to consider "how Homer would have said this same thing," and to measure oneself against the standard of one's predecessors: "to undergo such a trial is, really, a great thing: to establish such a jury and a theatre for our speeches and writings and to play at placing what we have written under the audit of such heroes as our judges and witnesses."[15] The even greater question, for which the prior one is anticipatory, is "how will succeeding generations hear our writings?" but it is always easier to measure against the past than against a speculated future. Whereas Merrill's spirits gather for a combination reading-party-trial (the constituents, really, of the modern phenomenon of the campus reading) to hear a performance of the great work in which most of them have figured, Auden's tribunal meets in preparation for the rest of a poem in which they play no organic part. Merrill's epic is circular, ending with its own performance on the word that began it (a gentle "Admittedly . . ."); Auden's "perpetual session" of judges, a list of his own devising, gathers to receive the praise of the self-accused. Auden is instructing his readers, in other words, by telling them which spirits occupy his own thoughts: Dante first (no accident that Merrill also selects "that lean hard-bitten pioneer" as his "influential ghost" throughout the sacred books, or that Howard Nemerov, the other most Audenesque American poet, has spent a lifetime studying the *Commedia*), and then Blake, Rimbaud, Dryden, Catullus, Tennyson, Baudelaire, Hardy, Rilke, and Kipling.

The list (163–232) pays explicit homage, and it also implicitly directs an understanding of the meditation that follows it; it is not gratuitous. From Dante, Auden has learned how to see the world as whole and rational, governed by an all-powerful Love; from Blake, the "choleric enthusiast," he has inherited an unwillingness to accept "the Newtonian Universe" and a happy mysticism that enables him to hear "inside each mortal thing / Its holy emanation sing"; with Rimbaud, he shares a sense of guilt (as well as a homosexual preference), and a skill quick at "strangl[ing] an old rhetoric." These are the presiding justices, the others occupying lower places at court.

And what do the judges decide? Auden may tickle us with his list (who else would call Rilke "him *die Dinge* bless, / the Santa Claus of loneliness"?), but lightly reminds us in advance that the genial, "quiet attentive crowd," which makes an "intense interrogation," will "pass no sentence but our own." His masters are projections of his own will and conscience, and when he finally acknowledges his own poetic faults, the judgment is entirely his own, not theirs:

> For I relapse into my crimes,
> Time and again have slubbered through
> With slip and slapdash what I do,
> Adopted what I would disown,
> The preacher's loose immodest tone.
>
> (218–22)

Self-knowledge enters the poem looking like a combination of confession and critical acuity: asserting with his wonted ease and musical deftness ("slubbered . . . slip and slapdash") the breeziness that was always his stylistic hallmark, Auden confesses a didactic zeal that is itself part of his didactic program.

Having made his private and vocational statements, Auden can move gracefully into a lengthy description of "the situation of our time" (233) as a scene from a detective novel (one of his favorite genres, and itself a formal, discursive model). We have a corpse, he says, as evidence of a crime in which it turns out that all are implicated. Once again he balances the individual with the general, using the first (his own poetic plight, then the appearance of "the body half-undressed") as a ground for larger assertions about our common fate. What the poem has already stated directly ("Art in intention is mimesis / But, realized, the resemblance ceases" [76–77]), it proves dramatically by spiralling from particularity to generality as from inductive evidence, through hypothesis, to a sound conclusion:

> Yet our equipment all the time
> Extends the area of the crime
> Until the guilt is everywhere,
> And more and more we are aware,
> However miserable may be
> Our parish of immediacy,
> How small it is, how, far beyond,
> Ubiquitous within the bond
> Of an impoverishing sky,
> Vast spiritual disorders lie.
>
> (257–66)

Auden's easy speech disguises the tightness of a method beneath a voice that seems to be meditating at random. But the coherence of imagery (the entire section beginning with the detective motif at line 233 and ending at line 294 after a long list of contemporary historical disasters is filled with envisioned corpses and cries of pain) and the modulation of expression (one may feel, before one notices, the balance in the lines above between items of expansion and images of pettiness and diminution) grant the poem a persuasiveness that more spectacular or, to use Auden's later designation in "The Horatians," "foudroyant" harangues would lack.

The speaker's disavowal of real power takes us into his confidence as he concludes part 1 with a modern version of the classical modesty *topos*. The teacher shakes his head, wondering at the possible fecklessness of his enterprise:

> Though language may be useless, for
> No words men write can stop the war
> Or measure up to the relief
> Of its immeasurable grief,
> Yet truth, like love and sleep, resents
> Approaches that are too intense,
> And often when the searcher stood
> Before the Oracle, it would
> Ignore his grown-up earnestness
> But not the child of his distress,
> For through the Janus of a joke
> The candid psychopompos spoke.
>
> (294–305)

Even here the dramatic quality of the discursive couplets gives them appreciable authority. By beginning reluctantly and ending with a modified assertion, Auden asks readers to consider even the limited power of language as an unqualified good. Additionally, his wit, clever but not arch, undermines his initial skepticism: the repetition of "measure" in "immeasurable," and its reminder of the poem's own constrained "meter," represent the very joking duplicity that already makes language a privileged lever to truth. Although the lines imply that the poetic Oracle speaks with an approach *less* intense, they everywhere prove just the opposite. Under the guise of a supple wit that prefers game to earnestness, Auden shows how "the good offices of verse" (310) may succeed where political diplomacy fails. At the end, he prays for a public resolution through private means:

> May an Accord be reached, and may
> This *aide-mémoire* on what they say,
> This private minute for a friend,
> Be the dispatch that I intend.
>
> (311–14)

The praying voice of the private citizen sounds more persuasive than that of the politician, as Auden, like his early model E. M. Forster, implicitly knows. The intimacy of an epistle, with its combination of private revelation and public commentary, provides an analysis of world catastrophe and solace for its approaching horrors.

The linguistic preoccupations of part 1 continue in part 2, now augmented by a witty, ethical consideration of duplicity as the province of Satan. One may regard the entire "letter" as an experiment in self-consciousness, based on two self-contradicting pairs of theses: first, that "the intellect in each / Can only think in terms of speech" (454–55) but that speech is always unsatisfactory; second, that the private life is superior to the public one but that the restraints of the individual consciousness thwart most efforts at sympathy or community.[16] The Drydenic clarity of Auden's "middle speech" is undone by his own wit, the Janus-like openings of words and transitions, and by his greater sense, prefiguring those of Theodor Adorno and George Steiner, that world horror undoes the need for, as well as the potency of, all art. An acceptance of human puniness should ideally result in religious modesty, the first step toward salvation (the implication of lines 341–44, quoted earlier); it also, in this poet's case, might explain his choice of a style. Auden's poetic dilemma is not just the conventional Romantic one of finding, in those words of Horace that Coleridge appropriates as epigraph to his "Reflections on Having Left a Place of Retirement," *sermoni propiora*. Rather, Auden wishes to adopt a style that will enable him to avoid the pitfalls of blank verse—he wants to sound like neither Milton nor Wordsworth—however simplified a syntax he might construe. The rhymed octosyllables give the sounds of colloquialism, but their light musicality, peppered with occasional allegorical figures and punning gestures, raises them frequently to the level of high wit.

And wit, by the hypothesis of part 2, may be suspect. Satan, "the Spirit-that-denies" (384), the first great psychologist and schismatic, is the father of all doubleness, the one who "inspired [Creation] with the wish to be / Diversity in unity" (562–63). Wit speaks with a forked tongue that shuns or bifurcates what Keats called the true voice of feeling, because the devil, like Janus, is everywhere double, in rhetoric, in language, and in a theology that seeks "to be both god and dualist":

> For, if dualities exist,
> What happens to the god? If there
> Are any cultures anywhere
> With other values than his own,
> How can it possibly be shown
> That his are not subjective or

> That all life is a state of war?
> While, if the monist view be right,
> How is it possible to fight?
> If love has been annihilated
> There's only hate left to be hated.
>
> (573–83)

Simple statement, language that gives immediate access to feeling, now seems a theological as well as a psychological impossibility. Our small, paralyzed, inaccessible egos ("If in this letter that I send / I write 'Elizabeth's my friend,' / I cannot but express my faith / That I is Not-Elizabeth" [450–53]), the monads of existence, are themselves atomically divisible. The inner world possesses a Lucretian economy that is also pathetic: "the hard self-conscious particles / Collide, divide like numerals" (514–15). And just as individuality admits neither of external entry nor of genuine integrity but divides itself into constituent subparticles, so also language, like Satan, tempts readers with a dream of perfectability that can never be realized.

A poem, then, is a kind of desperate voyage, doomed to founder upon the rocks of its own imagined goal because its instruments are inept, its measurements inaccurate. The dangers are, by analogy between parts 1 and 2, religious as well as vocational, since Auden has already demonstrated his allegiance to the tricks of the trade, the Janus-like stance of Delphic oracle rather than ex cathedra pronouncements. The joke is another version of Satan's temptation:

> To say two different things at once,
> To wage offensives on two fronts,
> And yet to show complete conviction,
> Requires the purpler kinds of diction,
> And none appreciate as he
> Polysyllabic oratory.
>
> (584–89)

That last line participates with delight in the very Satanic appreciation that it defines and thus places the poet in Satan's party. But this section of the poem ends with a partial, hopeful solution to its implied question: how is it possible to retain the singularity of truth and truthful expression while disclaiming allegiance to the prince of lies (and poems) who controls the "either-ors," "the moral asymmetric souls"? The answer, mirabile dictu, is the logical denial of all dichotomy, and an implicit proof that in art, as opposed to logic, self-contradiction is not self-denial. From dichotomy comes synthesis:

Yet time and memory are still
Limiting factors on his will;
He cannot always fool us thrice,
For he may never tell us lies,
Just half-truths we can synthesize.
So, hidden in his hocus-pocus,
There lies the gift of double focus,
That magic lamp which looks so dull
And utterly impractical
Yet, if Aladdin use it right,
Can be a sesame to light.

(823–33)

The "mongrel halves / Who find truth in a mirror" (821–22) can know only the half-truths of both mimesis and the devil, but the mirror can become a lamp, illuminating truths previously hidden. Auden's "gift of double focus" is the equivalent of Horace's synthesis with which this chapter began. Just as words can be pleasing and helpful *at once* for Horace, so, to the twentieth-century Horatian, half-truths may bloom into fuller revelations when properly employed. The rest of Auden's poem seeks to explain to his Aladdins the right use of his magic lamp.

Explanation is part of the controlled mania in the "Letter." The extensive notes to the poem, eliminated after the first edition, function not only as a gloss on the poem's subject but also as a commonplace book, offering glimpses into the associative and reflective dimensions of the poet's mind: everything is grist for his mill in a poem that makes encyclopedic as well as discursive maneuvers. The notes to part 2, especially, cast an interesting retrospective light on Auden's affiliations with both Wordsworth and Blake, the first in his concern with self-consciousness and the relationship between inner and outer worlds, the second in his moral insistence on the negative existence of evil (what he calls "hindering" in his marginalia to Lavater) and on moral good as "an act" (Auden's word), a rearrangement of existence that lessens or removes a disharmony. If "New Year Letter" answers a need of Auden's comparable to that served by Wordsworth's *Prelude*, it also extends Blake's correlations of the theological-cosmic, the imaginative-sexual, and the political-moral realms throughout the Prophetic Books. Auden's rhetorical techniques, if not strictly speaking his poetic language, show his absorption of his Romantic precursors.

That he is always thinking of language, however, is proved by an important citation from Kierkegaard's journals, included as an annotation of line 514:

> The life of mankind could very well be conceived as a speech in
> which different men represented the various parts of speech. . . .
> How few are substantives, verbs, etc.: how many are copula . . .
> There are people in life whose position is like that of the inter-
> jection, without influence in the sentence. They are the hermits
> of life and at the very most take a case, e. g. *O me miserum.*

As defined by his language, the speaker of this poem is hardly an an-
chorite. In fact, the colloquialism of the middle style assures him a
social place—to continue Kierkegaard's fancy—among the more active
parts of speech. But he is anxious to remind his audience of its collective smallness, and in this he has deflected the egotistical sublimity of
his Romantic forebears while echoing their concerns. The startling
commentary on line 453 ("I is Not-Elizabeth"), concerning the origin
of self-consciousness, is a variant of Wordsworth's passage on the development of the imaginative faculty, "Blest the Infant Babe" (*Prelude*
2.232–65), and on the child's relationship to earth, his sustaining fos-
termother, in the Intimations ode. What for Wordsworth, however,
defines the beginning of self-love and self-reliance becomes for Auden
a premonitory intimation of later psychological dependency and religious humility:

> But the boy comes soon enough
> To the limits of self-love,
> And the adult learns how small
> Is the individual.
>                    (Notes, *DM*, 98)

Natural humility, as the counter to a great poet's natural pride, has
evolved as an inevitable goal in the poem's moral scheme. It is ironic,
actually, that a poem that strives successfully to maintain a distinctive
"speaking voice" should also lament the very singularity that allows for
individual utterance.

   This part of Auden's legacy to contemporary American poets is nowhere more striking than in the similar pronouncement made by Merrill in *The Changing Light at Sandover*.[17] At the end of the penultimate
section of "The Book of Ephraim" there is an elegiac moment that
compares the growth of the hero to the fate of the parents of his
friend David Jackson, who have grown old, quarrelsome, and querulous:

> And here was I, or what was left of me.
> Feared and rejoiced in, chafed against, held cheap,
> A strangeness that was us, and was not, had
> All the same allowed for its description,

And so brought at least me these spells of odd,
Self-effacing balance. Better to stop
While we still can. Already I take up
Less emotional space than a snowdrop.
My father in his last illness complained
Of the effect of medication on
His real self—today Bluebeard, tomorrow
Babbitt. Young chameleon, I used to
Ask how on earth one got sufficiently
Imbued with otherness. And now I see.

(CL, 89)

Merrill extends this updating of Keats's metaphor of the chameleon poet in *Mirabell*, the second part of the trilogy, when one of the spiritual voices who speak through the capital letters of the Ouija board reminds him of the complexity but ultimate smallness of any individual artist:

THINK WHAT A MINOR
PART THE SELF PLAYS IN A WORK OF ART
COMPARED TO THOSE GREAT GIVENS    THE ROSEBRICK MANOR
ALL TOPIARY FORMS & METRICAL
MOAT ARIPPLE!

(CL, 262)

The speaker here? W. H. Auden, naturally, Merrill's avuncular tutor and the enshrined poet among his heavenly guides. As Auden himself says at the end of "New Year Letter" (1649–50): "the powers / That we create with are not ours."

Like Auden's other heirs, Merrill has learned the full force of the Blakean aphorism in Auden's notes: "The Devil, indeed, is the father of Poetry, for poetry might be defined as the clear expression of mixed feelings. The Poetic mood is never indicative" (*DM*, 116). Clear teaching, complex truths: such is Auden's pedagogic manner, honed during his American years and passed on to students as diverse as Merrill, Howard Nemerov, and Adrienne Rich. Nemerov, especially, might be said to have profited from Auden's quatrain on the discrimination of truth from fiction:

Whether determined by God or their neural structure, still
All men have one common creed, account for it as you will:
The Truth is one and incapable of self-contradiction;
All knowledge that conflicts with itself is Poetic Fiction.

(DM, 116, commentary on line 829)

Mixed feelings and self-conflicting knowledge are the subjects of poetry; the Janus-of-a-joke and the self-delighting, self-tempting duplicities of a satanic muse participate in the pedagogy that these poets have adopted.

The last and longest section of "New Year Letter" extends the poem's earlier dichotomies and focuses on possible theological solutions to the moral-historical crisis of 1940. Echoing Forster's "What I Believe," Auden pictures a double order, public and private, for each person, who must guess his own "true Socratic sign," discover his own "athlon," distrust demagogues, and try to serve ends other than the state's: we "can love the *polis* of our friends / And pray that loyalty may come / To serve mankind's *imperium*" (998–1000). The political arena occupies a middle realm between individual or private life and a genuine commonweal that expands from ideal personal relations. Later on Auden makes a comparable extension of private to public realms when he acknowledges that in the face of political dissolution, "true democracy begins / With free confession of our sins" (1633–34).

Auden's didactic and poetic technique has included, to this point, devices of wit and wandering: duplicity in pun and metaphor, historical and rhetorical figures of dialectic, the incisiveness of pithy epigram, and the expatiation of list making. At the end, having specifically considered the problem of the freedom of the will in its existential alienation ("Aloneness is man's real condition" [1542]), Auden adds another element to his teaching strategy. As he has addressed his letter personally to Elizabeth Mayer—friend, hostess, civilized muse—he now invokes a Christianized spirit in a combination of his two styles, the pointed and the discursive. To the simplicity of direct address that is appropriate to lyric, or to those specifically lyric moments in longer forms, he adds the expansiveness of serial invocation. Like Shelley, ransacking his own language for appropriate apostrophes in "Epipsychidion," Auden refers to an unseen but remembered evanescent and transcendent form as, sequentially, Unicorn, "white childhood," dove, icthus, wind, voice, clock, and keeper, each of which encapsulates one or more of the poem's various subjects. Like a fugal stretto, these images revive earlier motifs for the benefit of the audience. A good orator, Auden sends his listeners (or his correspondent) off with a summary reminder of what they've heard, and with an Augustinian imprecation to the deity to

> Instruct us in the civil art
> Of making from the muddled heart
> A desert and a city where

The thoughts that have to labor there
May find locality and peace,
And pent-up feelings their release,
Send strength sufficient for our day,
And point our knowledge on its way,
*O da quod jubes, Domine.*

(1676–84)

The prayer asks for powers to create, to feel, and to know, the very powers, labeled by Kenneth Burke as *poiema, pathema,* and *mathema,* that constitute poetic truth.[18] It ranges neatly across the territories charted by the rest of the poem: the relationship of social achievement (a civil art) to inner identity (the muddled heart), and of various sorts of order (the task that both Eros and Apollo ask) to feelings either subverted or sublimated; it is the tautological request for God to grant what He has implicitly required.

The poem does not end at this point, however; the preacher has yet to utter a nunc dimittis. Turning aside from its sublime request of God and backing away from grandiose affirmations, it more humbly beseeches Elizabeth Mayer as a human embodiment of some of the virtues adumbrated earlier. It turns, in other words, back to the human from the divine, in language at once simply tender and grandly resonant (with overtones, as well, of Wordsworth's address to Dorothy at the end of "Tintern Abbey," as his "dear, dear" friend and sister). Mayer becomes the Shelleyan agent of "a warmth throughout the universe" (1695; cf. "Adonais," "That Light whose smile kindles the Universe" [478]) who will redeem ordinary secular mortals, such as all those celebrants of New Year's revels at the beginning, when "we fall down in the dance":

Dear friend Elizabeth, dear friend
These days have brought me, may the end
I bring to the grave's dead-line be
More worthy of your sympathy
Than the beginning; may the truth
*That* no one marries lead my youth
Where you already are and bless
Me with your learned peacefulness,
Who on the lives about you throw
A calm *solificatio,*
A warmth throughout the universe
That each for better or for worse
Must carry round with him through life,

A judge, a landscape, and a wife.
We fall down in the dance, we make
The old ridiculous mistake,
But always there are such as you
Forgiving, helping what we do.
O every day in sleep and labor
Our life and death are with our neighbor,
And love illuminates again
The city and the lion's den,
The world's great rage, the travel of young men.
                    (1685–1707, my emphasis)

Perhaps because the "that" in line 1689 may be either a conjunction or a relative pronoun, I think one can hear in these lines Auden's interest in Shelleyan matters. The reference to marriage, however one wishes to take it (perhaps as a recollection of Auden's political marriage to Erika Mann), seems to refer back to the "longest and weariest journey" that oppresses Shelley in the "Epipsychidion." The final triplet and pentameter line lend weight and dignity, probably with a punning echo of Virgil and Shelley again ("the world's great [r]age"), a reference to Auden's own exodus months before, and a refreshing reminder that the speaker of the poem is, indeed, still a young man. The letter has reproduced the voice of that young man, worried, striving, questing, and questioning, but also earnest, witty, learned, accomplished, and facile. The strategies of his instruction—direct pronouncement, incisive wit, meandering contemplation, cogent reductiveness, Yeatsian embodiments in images—even more than his prosodic variety are Auden's most important legacy to what Wordsworth in "Michael" called "my second self," those youthful poets, especially the American ones, who became his heirs.

# The Tempered Tone of Howard Nemerov

Howard Nemerov, by his own self-description a "teacherly" poet, has devoted a lifetime to three complementary activities: poetry, criticism, and pedagogy.[1] (Like John Berryman, and like most of the other poets whom I describe as "didactic," Nemerov has eschewed the teaching of "creative" writing in favor of more academic subjects. In his case these usually take the form of what he has been currently reading.) To these three interwoven strands his friend and teacher Kenneth Burke has suggested the analogies of power (poetizing), wisdom (theorizing), and spirit (the bond between the two as practiced in teaching),[2] and Nemerov himself, adopting the guises and tones of college lecturer, Mosaic sage, cracker-barrel philosopher, tribal shaman, tour guide, and parental explainer, everywhere dramatizes the moods, strategies, and assaults of the natural pedagogue. His essays contain epigrammatic nuggets about the interrelatedness of his various enterprises: "Poetry may be thought of as both pedagogic and therapeutic, exploring the whole realm of the possible, and part of the realm of the impossible as well"; "There is a real danger in teaching too well; that in time the lesson will actually be absorbed"; "The teacher loveth best what teachest [sic] best"; "Part of teaching ought to consist in making the familiar strange" (a lesson obviously absorbed from Coleridge's definition of the division of labors in *Lyrical Ballads*).[3] Nemerov has woven his life and his work into a unified design.

Nemerov adopted the language of the lecture hall and some of the virtues of good prose in his first volume of poetry, and successive books have only honed and distilled his essential temper. "In the Glass of Fashion" introduces some characteristic phrases: "I am asked why"; "Let me hypothesize an / Invasion of El Morocco"; "In the same way. . . ."[4] Hundreds of pages later in his *Collected Poems* occurs the same sort of thing: "This morning we shall spend a few minutes / Upon the study of symbolism, which is basic / To the nature of money" ("Money: an introductory lecture," 369); "Today we shall explain the mystery / Of points and lines moving over the void— / We call it paper—to imitate the world" ("Drawing Lessons," 496); "Prepare for death. But how can you prepare / For death? Suppose it isn't an exam, / But more like the Tavern Scene in Henry IV" ("Speculation," 500). In between, in verse and prose, Nemerov has sought patiently to discover and explain the way things are, the dependencies of mind and world, the reticulations within the natural order, and to contemplate the standard dualisms of western philosophy: multeity and unity, mind and body, nominalism and realism. This chapter explores his strategies of explanation, which devolve from a central feeling that all knowledge, and indeed all poetic truth, is ultimately tautological. The instructor constantly reminds us that we learn what we already know (there are echoes here, as in the work of Ammons, Ginsberg, and Merrill, of Plato, and in English literature of Pope, Wordsworth, and Keats): "The whole art of poetry . . . consists in getting back that paradisal condition of the understanding, the condition that says simply 'yes' and 'I see' and 'it is so.' Naturally enough, it doesn't happen often. But it does happen."[5] Nemerov's ongoing nostalgia is for prelapsarian wholeness, when word and thing were perfectly matched, before the collective fall into Babel and the opacities of language that made possible not just poetry but also all the duplicities of wit, irony, pun, and metaphor, the basic tricks in his own poetic dialect. In Nemerov's poetry one witnesses the contest of the plain speaker with the modernist to achieve an affable and persuasive style. Like his poems, Nemerov has become the master of statements that are "in the last degree uninformative and tautological . . . some nonsense we call wisdom" (*NSE*, 273). How he became our gentlest wit is a case study in the development of American poetry after Yeats and Auden extended their transatlantic influences.

The scope of this career, from *The Image and the Law* (1947) to *War Stories: Poems about Now and Long Ago* (1987), has taken Nemerov along a spectrum from Mosaic sage, old Testament prophet overseeing the rubble of postwar Europe and testifying to the collapse of Western civilization, to wry commentator, gradually adjusting vision and voice to smaller forms. Most American poets, he says in "Strange Metamorphoses of Poets," "start out Emily and wind up Walt" (451), but Nemerov has moved in the opposite direction. Epigram has replaced jeremiad, and riddle steps in for apocalypse. His changing sense of an audience has influenced his changing forms; becoming more teacherly in his tones, he begins to recognize the power of an economic couplet or a quatrain surrounded by silence. His lectures have become shorter, pithier, his wisdom condensed. Mary Kinzie explains the differences, beneath their similarities, between Auden and Nemerov, perhaps between the postwar British and American poetic characters: "Auden sounded, in both prose and poetry, as if he were writing for an audience; Nemerov seldom does. .... His prose pronouncements don't have the wallop of the 'famous poet' behind them as, in an accidental or inherited but undeniable way, Auden's do. Like most American men of letters, Nemerov sounds like a man who talks for his own edification."[6] I would disagree with Kinzie about the lack of audience; nevertheless, it has been Nemerov's style to speak to that audience almost offhandedly.

Whether addressed to himself or others, Nemerov's talk, his poetry, falls into certain overlapping categories to which he has laid the major claim among contemporary poets: he has also virtually redefined poetic genres by replacing lyric, ode, georgic, even pastoral and narrative (although he uses these all, in different ways) with the lesson, the explanation, the definition, and the exploration. Nemerov's poems, large and small, and his prose essays all share the questions adumbrated in "New Year Letter": How can poetry, in a time of strife, counter public horror? What kind of civil speech can poetry utter and remain faithful to the private and public realms? How can poetry reconcile duplicity and plain speaking in order to retain both the true voice of feeling and the sheer joy that comes from playing a game brilliantly? It might as well be Auden as Nemerov speaking: "Poetry is a way of getting something right in language" (*NSE*, 232); "I have devised and tried to obey the following instruction about writing: the saying as clear as you can make it—for that is your duty and your gift— ; the meaning as mysterious as may be. For the universe is so" (*NSE*, 207); "Writing means trying to find out what the nature of things has to say about what you think you have to say" (*NSE*, 12). Like all the poets I have labelled didactic, Nemerov self-consciously takes up a concern with language as a major subject in his poetry; perhaps alone among them, however, he does so to develop not a characteristic style or a stylistic character (both of which he had, almost ready-made, from the start) but a congruence with the rhythms of nature itself. Like Wordsworth's "discerning intellect," wedded to the goodly universe, Nemerov's mind everywhere seeks mirrors, reflections, complements; self, language, and world are tremulously poised as elements in a perfect ménage à trois.

Among his contemporaries, Nemerov has at once the most individual voice and the least personal, in the sense of confessional, manner. The poetry is perhaps self-absorbed as Kinzie suggests, but it is everywhere public. He once noted in an interview: "For a long time, it has seemed to me that writing poetry is a way of being interested in something other than yourself, and that was a happiness which we're lucky to have for a little while."[7] One short poem, selected almost at random, may stand as a paradigm for Nemerov's impersonal individuality and for his pedagogic procedures. From *Mirrors and Windows* (1958), an entire volume seeking out reflections, visions, and liminal access to truth, comes "Trees":

> To be a giant and keep quiet about it,                              1
> To stay in one's own place;
> To stand for the constant presence of process
> And always to seem the same;
> To be steady as a rock and always trembling,
> Having the hard appearance of death
> With the soft, fluent nature of growth,
> One's Being deceptively armored,
> One's Becoming deceptively vulnerable;
> To be so tough, and take the light so well,                        10
> Freely providing forbidden knowledge
> Of so many things about heaven and earth
> For which we should otherwise have no word—
> Poems or people are rarely so lovely,
> And even when they have great qualities
> They tend to tell you rather than exemplify
> What they believe themselves to be about,
> While from the moving silence of trees,
> Whether in storm or calm, in leaf and naked,
> Night or day, we draw conclusions of our own,                      20
> Sustaining and unnoticed as our breath,
> And perilous also—though there has never been
> A critical tree—about the nature of things.
>
>                                           (141)

"Trees" is an updating of an ancient genre, the riddle, to which Nemerov has turned even more vigorously in recent years. Without the title, we might imagine the poem as withholding its main subject (until line 18 when it names the trees) in order to provoke us into considering its questions: What is a quiet giant? What is tough and trembling at the same time? Just as it hides its subject delicately, so the poem also wears its erudition lightly. The very modesty pinpoints the politeness of Nemerov's speculative instruments; lucid, untechnical, his language adduces the grandest philosophical issues. It makes a nod toward the catch phrases of literary criticism (16) and of existentialism (8–9), taking those last terms less heavily than Auden did in "New Year Letter"; it probably wants us to think of Joyce Kilmer (in line 14 as well as the title) and, more seriously, of Hamlet (12); at last it an-

nounces conclusively but unobtrusively its real debt, to Lucretius' insistence on a cosmos in which stasis and movement are twinned opposites. The "nature of things" is everywhere to be double, to seem
strong and fragile, still and moving, one and many, obdurate and
yielding, silent and instructive.

Nemerov has always been interested in the poetic as well as the philosophical dimensions of dichotomy. Even his seeming simplicity in this
catalogue of riddles is deceptive and significant. A grammatical trick
resolves an initial inconclusiveness: the poem consists largely of infinitive phrases, gradually lengthening until we have perhaps forgotten
that neither a grammatical subject nor a predicate really exists. It begins with two phrases of one line each, followed by a couplet, and then
two longer units of five and four lines. The break at the end of line 13
is the major rupture in the poem, but it is also a hinge between the
first section, a description, and the second part, an application. But
without grammatical wholeness, the poem exists as glittering, separate
fragments, united only by the moving eye and mind that dart from
world to brain and back again, first observing, then *making* observations. The central paradox—people tell, while inanimate nature exemplifies—is resolved, through the Janus-of-a-joke, Auden might say,
by the poem's own method. It partakes of the human-creative and the
natural-silent realms precisely by embodying as well as explaining the
paradoxes it attributes to trees. All verbless incompletion, it moves forward to an end that satisfies the need for closure. We are left, against
our better judgment perhaps, grammatically hanging but intellectu-
ally fulfilled, owing to the poet's sleight of hand. "Trees" exemplifies
as much as it tells about the perilous, sustaining nature of universal
and mental things.

These perils derive from the seeming discontinuities, ruptures, and
divorces between word and meaning, or between perception and reality, that Nemerov finds everywhere; the sustenance is provided by
his continual self-assurance and wonder that unity exists, even if
darkly. Things belong together, especially language and its subjects:
"How lovely, and exact the fit between / The language and the thing
it means to say" ("Translation," in *CP*, 499). Without opening an Ae-
olian bag of countless windy permutations on nominalist and realist
theories of language, one can at least say that Nemerov, like Ammons,
is a poet of names. He could not walk through an arboretum and enjoy the trees unless he first looked at their labels. How can one know
what a thing is until one knows what it is called? "Learning the Trees"
(*CP*, 486) embodies Nemerov's belief that language, contrary to one
popular view, is not "a system of conventional signs for the passive

reception of experience, but an unknowably large part of a material world whose independent existence might be likened to that of the human consciousness."[8] The language of trees comes from a book ("which now you think of it / Is one of the transformations of a tree"); having learned it, the student may proceed outside to "see how the chaos of experience / Answers to catalogue and category." "Confusedly," he replies. Nemerov isn't so stolid that his orderly universe is without quirks, sputters, false leads, and oddities. On the contrary, one learns slowly, often in spite of nature's apparent reality. (Remember how in Frost's "Directive" nature "only has at heart your getting lost"? Nemerov has a touch of Frost's Yankee orneriness, his tongue-in-cheek pedagogy: one false move and nature has us trapped.) Language reveals and falsifies, "competing with / Experience while cooperating with / Experience, and keeping an obstinate / Intransigence, uncanny, of its own." Cooperation is the key to the harmony in Nemerov's poetic and natural worlds; competition the source of his bracing tonic, skepticism. After all, one can learn both trees and their language, "but their comprehensive silence stays the same." Readers are the critics, trees the poems. Indeed, both of the tree poems give a new twist and new force to the clichés of Joyce Kilmer.

In spite of his leanings toward philosophical realism, Nemerov is too urbane and secular to assent to universals; a city dweller for a good part of his life, he is too urban to find and read the *liber naturae* that he nostalgically seeks. Writing is all around him, but it is all, to paraphrase a line from "The View from Pisgah," alphabeting in the void:

> But I could think only, Red sun, white moon,
> This is a natural beauty, it is not
> Theology. For I had fallen from
> The symboled world, where I in earlier days
> Found mysteries of meaning, form, and fate
> Signed on the sky, and now stood but between
> A swamp of fire and a reflecting rock.
>                     ("The Loon's Cry," *CP*, 158–59)

> Miraculous. It is as though the world
> were a great writing. Having said so much,
> let us allow there is more to the world
> than writing: continental faults are not
> bare convoluted fissures in the brain.
> Not only must the skaters soon go home;
> also the hard inscription of their skates

is scored across the open water, which long
remembers nothing, neither wind nor wake.
                    ("Writing," *CP*, 203)

As he says beautifully in "The Blue Swallows," only the spelling mind
imposes meaning and "weaves up relation's spindrift web," cogent but
also unreal. Seeing in the swallows' tails the nibs of invisible pens is an
elegant fiction, admissible only after it has been stripped from the
mind as a surrogate for reality. At the end of the poem, Nemerov
assumes a middle position between discovery and invention, pragma-
tism and solipsism:

> O swallows, swallows, poems are not
> The point. Finding again the world,
> That is the point, where loveliness
> Adorns intelligible things
> Because the mind's eye lit the sun.
>                     (*CP*, 398)

There is a nostalgic hope for a return to Edenic wholeness in these
lines, but also a sense that we are forever fallen from the symboled
world. With a deliberate echo of the great Romantic poem of fall and
abundant recompense, Wordsworth's Intimations ode, Nemerov
closes by asserting the primacy of the perceiving self; at the end of his
ode, Wordsworth suggested that "the clouds that gather round the setting sun / Do take a sober coloring from an eye / That hath kept watch
o'er man's mortality." In "The Blue Swallows," likewise, mind comes
first as illuminating principle. It is a hope always entertained in Nemerov's poetry but not often as confidentially asserted as it is here.

"A Day on the Big Branch" (*CP*, 147–50) glances toward Wordsworth's (and Frost's) natural epiphanies, and to Dante's tropes of
atonement and purgation. Nemerov undercuts his models even when
affirming them in a minor key. This is one of his few narrative poems,
but even here the teacherly instinct infers lessons from his adventures.
After a boozy all-night poker game, winners and losers climb a wilderness hill that is both a refreshing pastoral retreat and "the desert,
empty places of our exile." It is nature looking like art, a waiting room
or perhaps a purgatory for some paradise to come. The men bathe
and sun themselves,

> dried out on the rocks
> like gasping trout (the water they drank
> making them drunk again), lit cigarettes and lay back

waiting for nature to say the last word
—as though the stones were Memnon stones,
which, caught in a certain light, would sing.

Made drunk again (a perverting of Frost's restorative waters in "Directive"), the men are ready for a vision but what they get is a silence, pregnant with natural sounds but not with otherworldly meanings. Still, Nemerov's steady tone combines jaded academic wisdom, the slightly hung over feeling of middle age, and a sophisticated eagerness for simplicities in nature and sermons in stones. Too smart to think a revelation will be made, Nemerov is too honest to turn one down when it offers itself. The old rocks *do* seem to induce purgatorial ideas, lessons about humility and patience, because they are either a page in the text of the world or a projection of the speaker's literary mind. Whether the ideas correspond to a real purgatory is beside the point. In fact, thinking back to the relatively easy days of youth and war, the various men are moved to stillness by the water and stones, which "entered our speech; the ribs and blood / of the earth, from which all fables grow, / established poetry and truth in us," and resolutions, however self-deceiving, are made at last. Returning home, and noticing how three bridges had been splintered by the floods of the stream, the men are struck by the previously unnoticed, massive spectacle of artifacts hurled and smashed by a natural force:

> this was a sight
> that sobered us considerably, and kept us quiet
> both during the long drive home and after,
> till it was time to deal the cards.

Something has been learned, perhaps (how "sobered" are they?); still, life goes on to the next poker game. Nemerov's modest relativism sounds a lot like Ammons's, especially at the end of his "Corsons Inlet" (*Collected Poems*, 1972), an equivalent poem:

> I see narrow orders, limited tightness but will
> not run to that easy victory:
>     still around the looser, wider forces work:
>     I will try
>     to fasten into order enlarging grasps of disorder, widening
> scope, but enjoying the freedom that
> Scope eludes my grasp, that there is no finality of vision,
> that I have perceived nothing completely,
>     that tomorrow a new walk is a new walk.

(151)

This comparison suggests that, with whatever cause and effect, an important voice in contemporary poetry is one of gentleness that is not self-effacement. Skeptical but still hopeful of major revelations (of scope, if not Emersonian Scope), Nemerov and Ammons speak softly, often bringing the cliché up to new levels of grandeur (Kilmer's "I think that I shall never see . . ." or Scarlett O'Hara's "tomorrow is another day"). Restricting themselves to the curves of ordinary speech, they occasionally ascend to higher levels. The prosaic is their greatest sin and temptation, as it was for Wordsworth, whom they resemble in their commitment to the mundane. One arrives at the sublime via the commonplace. More self-conscious and less apocalyptic, without Wordsworth's messianic fervor at the end of *The Prelude*, Ammons and Nemerov are both down-home schoolmasters. Here is Nemerov blushlessly remarking both the futility and necessity of formal graduation exercises with their banal rituals, and shamelessly punning to prove that poetry can imitate, yet surpass, its origin in common language:

> emptiness alone
> Has generality enough to send
> Yet one more generation to the world,
>
> And platitudes become the things they are
> By being uninformative and true:
> The words that for the hundredth time today
> Bounced off the sunlit stone into the past
> Have made the silence deeper by degrees.
>                 ("After Commencement," *CP*, 427)

From "generality" and "generation," through the two senses of "become" and the ambiguous adverbial "today," to the last, chuckling "degrees," Nemerov always gets away with it, because he knows just how far to go.

The personal note in poetry of this sort stems from the assurance of the voice but also from Nemerov's view of the world as an arena of reciprocities. William Pritchard, among others, has noticed that in certain passages in Eliot's poetry no one seems to be speaking to no one in particular: language itself is confronting something outside it.[9] This is similar but not quite identical to Mary Kinzie's depiction of Nemerov speaking like a man for his own edification; *his* stylistic decorum requires of him a sense of both audience and occasion or, more often, of self-knowledge. His language is accurate and clear, although sometimes double, and his syntax remains the most straightforward of any of Auden's poetic heirs, because the world, sometimes crazy and perverse, can be clarified. The quotation from Albrecht von Haller in *The Western Approaches* (1975) could stand as epigraph to the life's work: "Nature knits up her kinds in a network, not in a chain; but men can follow only by chains because their language can't handle several things at once" (471). True enough; but refined, multilayered poetic language is an equivalent of the simultaneity experienced in nature, just as lucid syntactic structures (the very opposite of those found in Merrill or Ginsberg, for example) give temporal, structural clarity. With mock-worldliness, Nemerov offers wickedly skewed advice to his son about education; one must learn certain things

> In order to become one of the grown-ups
> Who sees invisible things neither steadily nor whole,
> But keeps gravely the grand confusion of the world
> Under his hat, which is where it belongs.
>     ("To David, About His Education," *CP*, 269)

Beneath the Polonius-like sententiousness is an ironic hint that the world itself is not confused; only human understanding of it is. As Nemerov delights in pointing out in his prose, one never knows "the world," but only one's knowledge of it. Since "the mind includes what must the mind contain" (a line from Empson on which Nemerov meditates), all reality is a network of relations and interdependencies: "The Other is deeply meddled in this world. / We see no more than that the fallen light/ Is wrinkled in and with the wrinkling wave" ("This, That, & The Other," *CP*, 360). More intricate still are the convolutions and repetitions in "Equations of a Villanelle": "The breath within us is the wind without, / In interchange unnoticed all our lives. / What if the same be true of world and thought?" (*CP*, 477). The harmony has not gone unnoticed by the discerning poet who loves his riddles, gnomes, and puzzles because he already knows their answers.

What has always struck readers about Nemerov's characteristic tone is its temperateness. Although he has been moved by religious subjects, especially, like Auden and Merrill, by Dante, Nemerov's "middle" voice, like Auden's and Horace's, sounds predominantly secular. The poems are always mannerly, even when obscene. In an early poem to Paul Valéry, Nemerov defines mastery as "manners that can speak / Of excrement without offense" (*CP*, 20). In the title poem of his 1955 volume, *The Salt Garden*, reviving for a moment Marvell's pastoral octosyllables, Nemerov portrays the good breeding of breeding:

> Turnip and bean and violet
> In a decent order set,

Grow, flourish and are gone;
Even the ruins of stalk and shell,
The vine when it goes brown,
Look civil and die well.

(CP, 112)

In Lu Chi, author of a fourth-century prose poem on the art of letters, he finds a comrade:

your quiet voice is clear
About the difficulties and delights
Of writing well, which are, it seems, always
The same and generally unfashionable.

(CP, 198–99)

The words of both men are as "gentle as their substance is / Fastidious and severe." Not a member of what he calls the "Bleeding Hearts Association of American Novelists" (or poets), Nemerov rarely wears his heart on his sleeve; he likes, he says, "those masters better who expound / More inwardly the nature of our loss" (*CP*, 272), or those who, like Vermeer, can domesticate the inexorable and make it charming:

Taking what is, and seeing it as it is,
Pretending to no heroic stances or gestures,
Keeping it simple; being in love with light
And the marvellous things that light is able to do,
How beautiful! a modesty which is
Seductive extremely, the care for daily things.

(CP, 257)

One can hear in these excerpts Nemerov's characteristic manner and his genuinely Horatian tone (according to Auden's definition of looking at "this world with a happy eye / but from a sober perspective" ["The Horatians"]). Nemerov's *aurea mediocritas* steers between philosophical skepticism (one can never see things as the physicists say they are) and social satire on one side, and, on the other, an open-eyed, childlike appreciation of the world's miracles. Nemerov, growing old, becomes younger as he most adopts the manner of an ancient sage. Cynicism barely touches his voice; the occasional sardonic moments are offset by feeling and sympathy. It is no surprise that Montaigne is one of his favorite authors. *Nil admirari* is the password: admiring much, he is astounded and upset by little.

Although his style is incisive and discreet, Nemerov responds to the world with an indiscriminate excitement that imbues with new life the banalities of the everyday. Merely to list his unlikely subjects is to adduce Nemerov's intellectual variousness: suburbs, football, black holes, waiting rooms, pockets, Christmas shopping, Bach cello suites are all treated with the same courteous intelligence as larger scientific and aesthetic topics. Wordsworthian steadiness of perception coincides with Borgesian or Talmudic mystery: kabbalahs and alephs are dressed in New England homespun.

Nemerov's topical variety and tonal clarity derive from his holistic vision of a reality in which all is connected and in which a single object, even when transformed, is never lost. In the early, somber, postwar poems, he allows that "we may not pray for permanence." Later, he complements Ovidian change with the essential conservation of matter and energy: in "Ozymandias II" an old Cadillac, stripped and patched, moths in its upholstery, still runs: "it gets around, you see one on the street / Beat-up and proud, well, Jeezus what a country, / Where even the monuments keep on the move" (CP, 457). In the forties and fifties Nemerov was rabbinically fixated on sin and redemption. What was, early on, a source of prophetic despair ("Like melting wax we change, / Waiting the last shape of death at thy hand" [CP, 23]), inspires in the poems of his middle age intellectual energy, metaphysical delight, and emotional equilibrium. Nemerov's poetry makes sense because the world has come to make sense to him.

Although Nemerov was an accomplished poet from the beginning, it was not until his third volume, *The Salt Garden*, the first to represent fully his absorption by and into rural Vermont life, that he discovered the voice and methods that I label his characteristically didactic ones. Observing nature, he meets its ceremonies with his own courtesy; its simple, unrelenting order produces his own apposite poetic syntax. In natural organization the scholar finds a match for his categorizations, as in "The First Leaf," which deftly reads the *liber naturae* and sees the first leaf as "a Byzantine / Illumination of the summer's page / Of common text, and capital presage / For chapters yet to fall" (CP, 96). Three longer poems, the title piece, "The Sanctuary," and "The Pond," none a full success, all show how Nemerov injects his teacherly tones into two related genres, the lesson and the Wordsworthian nature encounter.

Structurally, "The Salt Garden" (CP, 112–14) is a before-and-after poem, its two complementary halves suggesting various oppositions: dream and waking, image and meaning, illusion and correction. As a dialectic construct, the poem moves to replace simple oppositions with complex syntheses. In the first part the speaker feels comfortable, almost complacent, with his amateur efforts at creating a seaside garden from what was "once the shore / And once, maybe, the ocean floor." The "decent order" of the surroundings maintains its civility even in decay. And the poet half-hopefully thinks, with a deliberate cliché that he soon corrects, that "here our life / Might be a long and happy one." This illusion is then punctured by the "ocean's wrinkled green / [that] Maneuvers in its sleep," and in a Yeatsian fashion the speaker questions the permanence of anything: "For what can man keep?" The Yeatsian line and the biblical sentiment are part of Nemerov's early poetic apparatus; the move from appearance and hope to melancholy skepticism is a standard Romantic trope.

The second half repeats and amplifies the first, centering its lesson on a figure from the air and sea rather than from land itself. A giant gull, wild, quiet, mantled in a "fierce austerity" that partakes equally of the sacramental and the savage, inspires the restless, early-awaking speaker to invest him with meaning and to see the landscape from a different angle of vision. The bird's inferred haughty dismissal of the salt garden as not worthy of his attention causes him to take flight:

> Noble, and not courteous,
> He stared upon my green concerns,
> Then, like a merchant prince
> Come to some poor province,
> Who, looking all about, discerns
> No spice, no treasure house,
> Nothing that can be made
> Delightful to his haughty trade,
> And so spreads out his sail,
> Leaving to savage men
> Their miserable regimen.

This wild beast rises rather than slouches, but Nemerov has had a vision comparable to Yeats's in "The Second Coming." The intellectual poet, receptive to learning and eager to perceive (and half-create) a metaphorical order, seems chastised and subdued by this emissary from an unhuman, ungeorgic realm:

> When he was gone
> I turned back to the house
> And thought of wife, of child,
> And of my garden and my lawn
> Serene in the wet dawn;
> And thought that image of the wild

Wave where it beats the air
Had come, brutal, mysterious,
To teach the tenant gardener,
Green fellow of this paradise,
Where his salt dream lies.

The poet-teacher has been instructed in the ambiguous relationship of wildness and order. Our little spot of earth, verdant and cultivable, affirms both civilization and acreage reclaimed from the sea, but Nemerov asserts its fragility, which comes from the realm of dreams and returns to it like the gull. Origins and destinations, dreams and their inevitable evaporation, are ultimately more enduring than human efforts at tenancy. The land, which we do not at any rate own but only rent, will always be reclaimed by sea, by bird, by primal forces that have no regard for pitiful human deceptions. Human greenness may mellow, at last, into the sere and yellow leaf of experience. Dreams, at the end, are put to rest (but to whom does the last "his" refer? Bird or man?) and are also revealed in their partial fraudulence, as one may hear in "lies" the very ring of untruth.

Another visionary encounter follows immediately in this volume. "The Sanctuary" (*CP*, 114) is a lyric that resembles one of Elizabeth Bishop's natural encounters (e.g., "At the Fishhouses," "Cape Breton," "The Bight") but although Bishop also learns lessons, more often than not her deliberate tact restrains her from doing anything more than implying them. Not for her the lecture (Bishop herself taught reluctantly and with difficulty),[10] or even the clear exposure of the thinking mind, but just the process itself. Nemerov reveals not only his thoughts but also his thinking about his thoughts. The action doesn't move merely from stimulus to response, or from perception to metaphor to conclusion: it tells us that it is doing so. Nemerov's true antecedent in this is neither Yeats nor Auden but the more totally self-conscious Wordsworth or the Shelley of "Mont Blanc," who applies his response to the external scene as deliberately as possible to his musings upon his mind, his musings *upon* his musings:

Dizzy Ravine! and when I gaze on thee
I seem as in a trance sublime and strange
To muse on my own separate phantasy,
My own, my human mind, which passively
Now renders and receives fast influencings,
Holding an unremitting interchange
With the clear universe of things around.

In "The Sanctuary," Nemerov focuses for seventeen lines on the delicate movement of trout gliding from shadow into sunlight, hinting
briefly at the larger meditations that will follow: the trout are "slow /
And so definite, like thoughts emerging / Into a clear place in the mind,
then going back, / Exchanging shape for shade." A single fish now
slides into the center and hangs alone and still. The poet, standing
equally immobile, observes the fish and affirms a connection:

> my life
> Seems to have been suddenly moved a great
> Distance away on every side, as though
> The quietest thought of all stood in the pale
> Watery light alone, and was no more
> My own than the speckled trout I stare upon
> All but unseeing. Even at such times
> The mind goes on transposing and revising
> The elements of its long allegory
> In which the anagoge is always death;
> And while this vision blurs with empty tears,
> I visit, in the cool pool of the skull,
> A sanctuary where the slender trout
> Feed on my drowned eyes.

The elaborate analogy appropriates the fish to the speaker's needs,
projecting upon it his sense of self-hovering in a constant holding pattern, but it also dissolves the speaker in his own Virgilian regrets (the
empty tears, *lacrimae inanes*), reducing his brain to a cold pond, itself
the image of the projected end, in which he foresees himself lying still
and dead.

The extended moment of contemplation and hypnotic wonder dies
when the fish breaks through the surface to snap up a fly, and the
speaker, finding "this world again in focus," reconsiders the fish and
the scene:

> This fish, a shadow dammed in artifice,
> Swims to the furthest shadows out of sight
> Though not, in time's ruining stream, out of mind.

"Dammed in artifice," the fish becomes Nemerov's equivalent of Keatsian figures annealed in art, or of Yeats's monuments of unaging intellect. "Dammed" is, of course, also "damned," as one hears the speaker's regret at what he has already admitted to be the anagoge of all
mental activity. Nemerov typically reserves the strongest, most outra-
geous puns for the end, as if to suggest that only linguistic doubleness

will resolve, or at least maintain, the frustrating doubleness he discovers in the world: the ruining stream of time replaces the expected "running" stream, and the cliché of the final couplet, invigorated and heard anew, like the "degrees" in "After Commencement," might suggest an originating rather than a concluding point for the poem. That is, the poem might have begun not so much with the narrative of observed detail but with an a priori decision to examine an old saw, as if Nemerov had challenged himself to conjure up an image, situation, or reflection, where "out of sight" is not "out of mind."

Against the relative tightness of these two self-conscious lesson poems might be placed the larger, looser narrative of "The Pond" (*CP*, 98–102). Where the first two show Nemerov trying to work in a Shelleyan manner, everywhere calling attention to the processes and conclusions of his own mind, here one finds an experiment in what Wordsworth labeled "Poems on the Naming of Places." This comparison also reveals the self-consciousness of Nemerov's procedure, which virtually challenges the audience to recall Wordsworth's poems that end with an act of naming that commemorates an event or person or else corrects a misperception.[11] But here the trick is, in part, that Nemerov performs *his* act of naming toward the beginning and then goes beyond the Wordsworthian model.

The loose blank verse hovers midway between Wordsworth's slow, stately rhythms and Frost's colloquial ones: the prosody tips readers off that Nemerov wants to pay homage to both of these teachers. The subject matter does the same, harking back to the skating episode of *The Prelude*, book 1, and to the Boy of Winander and the drowned man of Esthwaite in book 5; it also recalls Frost's rural tragedies, such as " 'Out, Out'—." But more central to Nemerov's poem than to anything by his predecessors is the lesson, the correction, the continual revision of moral as well as naturalistic detail. For all the traditional talk about Wordsworth's supposed preachiness, he normally leaves his message in poems of this sort implicit or mysterious. Nemerov, by contrast, extracts the message immediately and ponders it. It is not so much a conclusion as a point of departure, in the same way that "out of sight, out of mind" may be construed as a beginning rather than an end.

Nature has its own history, independent of but entwined with human lives, and Nemerov keeps a watchful eye on both worlds. Two local accidents overlap in this poem, and the observant poet, attending to appearances and disappearances, mysterious beginnings and uncertain endings, records them in a narrative that moves through a single annual cycle. Autumn rains have built up a pond at one end of a long meadow, and from the start the poem announces an interest in matters of depth and height, of the almost unnoticeable accumulations within a nature that one mistakenly thinks of as permanent and fixed, as opposed, one infers, to human transience. Names, like places, ought to signify permanence, knowability, familiarity:

> Where even if a stream runs dry in summer
> You have the stream-bed still to go by and
> The chartered name—Red Branch, and Henry's Creek,
> And Anthony's Race—for reassurance, though
> The reason of those names be sunken with
> The men who named them so, in the natural past
> Before our history began to be
> Written in book or map; our history,
> Or the settled story that we give the world
> Out of the mouths of crones and poachers
> Remembering or making up our kinship
> In the overgrown swamplands of the mind;
> And precious little reassurance, if
> You think of it, but enough about that.
>
> (99)

The locals think little of the pond, "whether it would go or stay," but by Christmas it has stayed long enough to solidify under a foot of snow "so you couldn't say / Except from memory where the water was / And where the land." But memory and all human measurements deceive, as does nature; the frozen pond claims as its first victim a young boy "skating in darkness all alone." Although the rural accents, the chattiness of diction, and the lilt of New England speech give the poem a Frostian ring up through the end of two long verse paragraphs, its framework and development are characteristically Wordsworthian. The town meeting votes to name the pond after the dead boy "when the next map was drawn: / *Christopher Pond*: if the pond should still be there" (100). The name suggests, perhaps too heavily, the weight of symbolic association.

The ominous aside ("if the pond . . .") has no analogy in Wordsworth's naming of places. The Lake District seems more stubbornly resistant to natural change than Vermont. Wordsworth urges readers to recall that in the country people may often be buried without tombstones, but as a corrective all local history builds itself from the associations of people with places in order to commemorate the former and humanize the latter. In Nemerov, even nature works against our hopeful wishes for permanence. Neither Wordsworth nor Keats ever

gave so clear a sense of the natural process of seasonal migration as
part of the ongoing mysteries of birth and death:

> Killdeer and plover
> Came and were gone; grackle, starling and flicker
> Settled to stay; and the sparrowhawk would stand
> In the height of noon, a stillness on beating wings,
> While close over the water swallows would trace
> A music nearly visible in air,
> Snapping at newborn flies. Slowly the pond
> Warmed into life: cocoon and bud and egg,
> All winter's seed and shroud, unfolded being
> In the pond named for Christopher, who drowned.
>
> (101)

The final subordinate clause ("who drowned") fits into the scheme of
things especially well: where logic might demand a pluperfect verb
("who *had* drowned"), the simple past tense suggests a virtual simultaneity of death with the ongoing procedures of recurrence and return.
The paradoxes of the passage ("seed and shroud") elicit a Keatsian
richness; the utter simplicity of the final reminiscence, a Wordsworthian acceptance.

Spring returns, life resumes, the dragonfly metamorphoses and
puts on its dazzling wings:

> Then day by day, in the heat of June, the green
> World raised itself to natural arrogance,
> And the air sang with summer soon to come.

And the poem, like the pond, reverses itself. The second half begins
with the personal experience of the speaker ("In sullen August . . . I
sat"), as if he now stands in for the dead but remembered boy. But the
pond itself has evaporated, in a midsummer plethora of activity that
contains as much death as life:

> life was choking on itself
> As though, in spite of all the feeding there,
> Death could not keep the pace and had to let
> Life curb itself: pondweed and pickerel-weed
> And bladderwort, eel-grass and delicate
> Sundew and milfoil, peopled thick the city
> Of themselves; and dragonfly and damselfly
> By hundreds darted among the clustering leaves,
> Striders by hundreds skated among the stalks

Of pitcher-plant and catkin; breathless the air
Under the intense quiet whining of
All things striving to breathe; the gift of life
Turning its inward heat upon itself.

(101–2)

Thoughtfully heeding as he enumerates the particles of place and
time in all their dappledness, Nemerov combines the poetic strategies
of Keats and Hopkins with his own modifications of the Wordsworthian inscription poem. Death is the child as well as the mother of
beauty: commemoration itself fails except in the artful constructions
of song:

So, Christopher, I thought, this is the end
Of dedication, and of the small death
We sought to make a name and sacrifice.
The long year has turned away, and the pond
Is drying up, while its remaining life
Grasps at its throat: the proud lilies wilt,
The milfoil withers, catkins crack and fall,
The dragonfly glitters over it all;
All that your body and your given name
Could do in accidental consecrations
Against nature, returns to nature now,
And so, Christopher, goodbye.

(102)

And again the poem seems to end, acknowledging the failure of human impositions on nature as well as the sullen ephemerality of natural landmarks.

Nemerov continues the poem, however, as the unfolding power of
sight inspires a movement beyond all apparent endings. Like beginnings, endings are deceptive and rarely, in fact, conclusive. The dragonfly returns to the poet's sight, prompting him to consider natural
history; the insect comes to symbolize natural metamorphosis (as the
gull in "The Salt Garden" represented nature's indifference to human
cultivation, or the trout in "The Sanctuary" an equivalent to flickering
human thought); formerly a larva on the pond's floor, now "taking a
lighter part" (in both senses of "light") in summer's pageant, the dragonfly inspires Nemerov's latest lesson:

I saw with a new eye
How nothing given us to keep is lost
Till we are lost, and immortality

Is ours until we have no use for it
And live anonymous in nature's name
Though named in human memory and art.
Not consolation, Christopher, though rain
Fill up the pond again and keep your name
Bright as the glittering water in the spring;
Not consolation, but our acquiescence.
And I made this song for a memorial
Of yourself, boy, and the dragonfly together.

Nature's name equals human anonymity; human memory and art, the
Wordsworthian and the Yeatsian commonplaces coming together, offer only partial compensation for our losses. Does the curt, monosyllabic "boy" imply a coldly anonymous fate, coming as it does after a
direct address to "Christopher"? Nemerov hesitates, uncertain of
whether art does offer consolation or whether human acquiescence to
inevitable disappearances requires relinquishing even *that* last infirmity of twentieth-century minds.

In these very uncertainties, "The Pond" may disappoint those readers who seek for clearer lessons, but it also points the way to Nemerov's later (I hesitate to call it "mature" because his poetry, like the
mind that created it, is mature in style and substance from the start)
works in *Mirrors and Windows* (1958), *The Blue Swallows* (1967), and *The
Western Approaches* (1975). Increasingly, human interpretation becomes what he calls it in "The Companions" (*CP*, 355), "the deep folly
of man / To think that things can squeak at him more than things can."
Waiting for an original response, in the Wordsworthian-Frostian manner, Nemerov teaches one how to respond to, and invent, the noises
of otherness. That in his later years he relies more noticeably on
gnomes, riddles, and epigrams means that he has reduced his lessons
to "squeaks," his own updating of Keats's spiritual, toneless "ditties."

The strongest part of what I have labeled Nemerov's didacticism
(and of the similar impulses in Ammons, Merrill, and Pinsky) is his
obsession with acts of reading or deciphering the objects of this world
as both signs and reflections of human inner language. For one who
has confessed that his knowledge of the world comes mostly from
books, it is no surprise that Nemerov should be the Linnaeus of poets,
classifying and defining. An instructive contrast may be made between
him and Elizabeth Bishop, who shares many of his concerns—a careful sighting of surrounding landscapes, a scrupulous effort to get
something right in language, an engagement of mind with nature. But
Bishop, unlike Nemerov, everywhere fills her subjects with a Keatsian

empathy or inwardness that Nemerov rarely thinks to develop. Clear
visualization, speculative suggestions, and delicacy of manner charac-
terize both poets' responses to the small sandpiper, but their techniques separate the essentially observant, reflecting (in both senses)
Nemerov from the imaginatively sympathetic Bishop.

Nemerov's "Sandpipers" (*CP*, 152) typically observes the species
rather than the individual. After a five-line look at the birds running
and eating, it makes a telling comparison:

> Small, dapper birds, they make me think
> Of commuters seen, say, in an early movie
> Where the rough screen wavers, where the light
> Jerks and seems to rain; of clockwork dolls
> Set going on the sidewalk, drawing a crowd
> Beside the newsstand at five o'clock; their legs
> Black toothpicks, their heads nodding at nothing.
> But this comedy is based upon exact
> Perceptions, and delicately balanced
> Between starvation and the sea.

Urban scenes, mechanical people or dolls, finally a hypothetical flourish ("this comedy is based upon"): this is the sociable view of an intellectual. The scene, as often in Nemerov, is a general one: he chooses
not to develop a fiction of immediacy although he retains the present
tense. The description exists in a theoretical present that forswears the
here and now. The bird, or the flock, is any single representative or
group within the species.

The last part of the poem returns again to the speaker's thoughts:

> Whenever a flock of them takes flight,
> And flies with the beautiful unison
> Of banners in the wind, they are
> No longer funny. It is their courage,
> Meaningless as the word is when compared
> With their thoughtless precisions, which strikes
> Me when I watch them hidden and revealed
> Between two waves, lost in the sea's
> Lost color as they distance me; flying
> From winter already, while I
> Am in August. When suddenly they turn
> In unison, all their bellies shine
> Like mirrors flashing white with signals
> I cannot read, but I wish them well.

This is self-concerned but hardly a version of the egotistical sublime. On the contrary, Nemerov's gentle manner and the touching pathos of his recognition of the distance as well as the similarities between a man with meaningful words and the birds with thoughtless beauty, precision, and instinct, keep readers from construing the observer the hero of his story. But of course he is, as he sadly acknowledges in the end, distancing himself and his limitations from the illegible beauty (what irony that even as a mirror the birds allow no self-knowledge!) that abandons him to the weakness of a cliché and the isolation of his contemplations. When looking at Bishop's wry presentation of the same bird in *Questions of Travel*, one can clearly distinguish between two temperaments and, accordingly, between lyric and georgic, immediacy and generalization, exclamation and explanation:

> The roaring alongside he takes for granted,
> and that every so often the world is bound to shake.
> He runs, he runs to the south, finical, awkward,
> in a state of controlled panic, a student of Blake.
>
> The beach hisses like fat. On his left, a sheet
> of interrupting water comes and goes
> and glazes over his dark and brittle feet.
> He runs, he runs straight through it, watching his toes.
>
> —Watching, rather, the spaces of sand between them,
> where (no detail too small) the Atlantic drains
> rapidly backwards and downwards. As he runs,
> he stares at the dragging grains.
>
> The world is a mist. And then the world is
> minute and vast and clear. The tide
> is higher or lower. He couldn't tell you which.
> His beak is focussed; he is preoccupied,
>
> looking for something, something, something.
> Poor bird, he is obsessed!
> The millions of grains are black, white, tan, and gray,
> mixed with quartz grains, rose and amethyst.[12]

Nowhere does a first person pronoun appear, yet the voice is distinct, even idiosyncratic. Just as Bishop focuses on a single bird on a specific beach, so she also characteristically miniaturizes the scene with her delicate personifications ("a student of Blake," "watching his toes"), and sympathetic identification ("Poor bird, he is obsessed"). Seeing a world in a grain of sand, like Blake himself, Bishop habitually reduces visionary encounters and inspired philosophical questions through the seemingly quaint delicacy of her tone, whereas Nemerov expands, opening out from observation. Similarly, her sentences here tend to the simple, the short, the detailed but clear listing of actions in order, whereas Nemerov spins more complex webs, articulating relationships in the elaborations of his lines.

The same contrast between temperaments and techniques can be made between the two poets' literary homages to recently departed poets, one a close friend, the other a distant teacher. Bishop's poignant elegy to Robert Lowell, "North Haven," uses as its central trope the mainstay of all pastoral elegy: the eternal return of nature versus the linearity of human life. Fluctuations, changes, seasonal shifts, personal death, even a flower procession, are all set against a backdrop of permanence ("the islands haven't shifted since last summer, / even if I like to pretend they have," she begins). The contrasts build to the strongly felt but understated last stanza:

> You left North Haven, anchored in its rock,
> Afloat in mystic blue . . . And now—you've left
> for good. You can't derange, or re-arrange,
> your poems again. (But the Sparrows can their song.)
> The words won't change again. Sad friend, you cannot change.
>
> (189)

This summing up looks backward ("anchored" and "afloat" repeat the central contrast) and accepts the finality of death as the failure of all temporary changes in the face of permanent change. The lesson of nature, metonymically standing for birds' song and human song ("Nature repeats herself, or almost does: / repeat, repeat, repeat, repeat; revise, revise, revise") conjoins but contrasts human efforts with the song of the sparrows. It is as if Bishop herself has updated Keats's listening to his nightingale, now inspired by a real rather than an imagined corpse. Perhaps the most delicate touch of all is the implicit duality of the last verb: it works with both transitive and intransitive force, subtly asking readers to remember that Lowell as the inveterate fusser with poems and as sentient human being has moved to the realm beyond revision and human sighting.

Nemerov himself has written a cogent explication of "For Robert Frost, in the Autumn, in Vermont" (see "The Winter Addresses of Kenneth Burke," reprinted in both *FT* and *NSE*). Even in an elegy, Nemerov retains his distance from his subject, preferring generalization to Bishop's specificity:

All on the mountains, as on tapestries
Reversed, their threads unreadable though clear,
The leaves turn in the volume of the year.
Your land becomes more brilliant as it dies.

The puzzled pilgrims come, car after car,
With cameras loaded for epiphanies;
For views of failure to take home and prize,
The dying tourists ride through realms of fire.

"To die is gain," a virgin's tombstone said:
That was New England, too, another age
That put a higher price on maidenhead
If brought in dead; now on your turning page
The lines blaze with a constant light, displayed
As in the maple's cold and fiery shade.

                              (*CP*, 405)

Frost is never mentioned ("your land" in line 4 is barely personal; "your turning page" a little more so, although it is an unnamed, living reader rather than a dead poet who is actually turning the page), his personality and even an intimation of relationship deflected in favor of a concentration on landscape. Having been absorbed by the land, the poet is now represented by it. Nemerov scants the personal, reacting instead like a satirist watching the puzzled pilgrims, witnessing their dying amid the dying year, and attending to the readability of scenery. As in Bishop's poem, the *liber naturae* and the *liber poetae* come together and then separate, Nemerov exploiting the image for all it is worth. And where Bishop listens closely to the strains of pastoral elegy, Nemerov makes the bold and completely successful decision to imbue his poem with larger associations. Frost shares his land with other dead New Englanders, who have lost their lives to gain them. The whole poem becomes a Dantean scene—beginning with the falling leaves and continuing through "realms of fire" and "fiery shade," the infernal rites of line 8, and implicit in the very analogy between reading and natural perception at first unclear and then fully legible in epitaph and poetic line. Grandly taking in the history of the oldest trope of all—"as leaves to the trees are the generations of men"—Nemerov places Frost amid the company of Homer, Virgil, Dante, and Milton. Where Bishop laments the end of revision (hers of Lowell, his of his lines), Nemerov seems to rejoice in the beautiful spectacle through which the world and Frost's pages have been clarified.[13]

Reading and naming, the twin acts of apprehension that are themselves a central trope in the poetry of the Romantic tradition from Wordsworth and Shelley through Whitman and Williams to Moore and Bishop, devolve in Nemerov upon his two prominent poetic techniques: labelling and punning. "Getting something right in language" means in part knowing what to call a thing or how to identify any inner or outer condition. The world is to be understood through a process of division, just as God's primal acts of creation involved the clarifying separation of darkness from light, earth from heaven, sea from land, and so on, down through the human repetition of God's action in Adam's naming the animals on parade. To poeticize is to separate, to define. In a touching, obviously autobiographical, late poem, "Beginner's Guide" (*CP*, 444–45), Nemerov looks wistfully back to the field guides, templates, and encyclopedias with which the young amateur attempted his first forays into understanding flowers, birds, and stars. Confusion defeated him before he reached mastery—there were too many flowers to be pressed, birds too quick to be spotted, stars so plentiful that numbers rather than names identified them. "Was it a waste?" he wonders of these efforts and the totemic books, "Remainders of an abdicated self / That wanted knowledge of no matter what." Remainders and reminders, too, since the self doesn't really change so much as it repeats its earlier behavior in a finer tone and in a deeper satisfaction with its failures:

> The world was always being wider
> And deeper and wiser than his little wit,
>
> But it felt good to know the hundred names
> And say them, in the warm room, in the winter,
> Drowsing and dozing over his trying times,
> Still to this world its wondering beginner.

"Trying" in its transitive and intransitive senses doubly implicates student and world, each trying the other and succeeding only in part. Likewise, self and world may actually be partners rather than the antagonists they initially seem: "The world was always *Being*" one may hear in the last sentence, an extension or heightening of normal human capacities rather than the sphere in which they are thwarted.

The puns in the ultimate lines point the way to an understanding of Nemerov's second obsessive method: his fascination with duplicities of language, whether in single words or in commonplace phrases given new punch and vim or, more generally, in the whole realm of metaphor, the most essentially duplicitous weapon in a poet's arsenal. Far from being mere academic bravado, an evasion of sincerity, true wit

offers Nemerov (and Auden, Merrill, and John Hollander) the surest
handle to appropriate emotions and to a fuller understanding of the
world's complexities. For all of the interest in dichotomies and antiphonal structures that he has obviously inherited from Yeats, Nemerov
usually adduces dualisms only to transcend them. Many poems come
to mind in which Nemerov develops his version of Blakean contraries.
Some end in resolution, others in stalemate. The early "Deposition"
(*CP*, 125), "Steps for a Dancer" and "The Dancer's Reply" (*CP*, 205–
6), and the minidramas "Endor" and "Cain" from *The Next Room of the
Dream* (1962) employ dramatic confrontation as a central organizing
principle, as do "Debate With the Rabbi" and especially "This, That &
the Other" in the same volume. Here, Nemerov revises Yeats's conversation between Hic and Ille, in "a dialogue of disregard" that is really
two simultaneous monologues about the relationship of "things below"
and "things above," of "All" and "the individual," of wave and particle,
of "Echo, reflexion, radar of all sorts." His two speakers conclude arbitrarily and in unison, with perhaps no real consolidation of their
ideas:

> The Other is deeply meddled in this world.
> We see no more than that the fallen light
> Is wrinkled in and with the wrinkling wave.
> (*CP*, 360)

A victory for both and neither, the harmony of the last line gives a
dappled compromise between extremes.

Compromises of this sort settle us into the heart of Nemerov's brand
of wisdom. Cracking, or almost, the nut of nature's puzzles enables
him to find coherence and pleasure through active engagement. One
understands his fondness for Stevens's aphorism: "The poem must resist / The intelligence, almost successfully." Without some struggle, no
understanding would be gratifying; without some degree of success,
no knowledge would ever be ours. Seeing patterns and bringing disparate phenomena into conjunction with one another provides an
analogy for artistic achievement as well:

> how privileged
> One feels to find the same necessity
> Ciphered in forms diverse and otherwise
> Without kinship—that is the beautiful
> In Nature as in art, not obvious,
> Not inaccessible, but just between.

It may diminish some our dry delight
To wonder if everything we are and do
Lies subject to some little law like that;
Hidden in nature, but not deeply so.
                    ("Figures of Thought," *CP*, 472)

By definition a pun must lie midway between the obvious and the inaccessible: if completely self-evident, it gives no pleasure; if entirely untranslatable, no wisdom. Nemerov stuns readers with puns to make them sense new connections. "One profits by the view," says the speaker in the title poem of *Guide to the Ruins* (*CP*, 51); he is himself a guide, but the generalized "profit" that one might suppose, if seeing the line by itself, belongs to a tourist whom he is lecturing, turns out to be something more specific. He is talking about his own career. A phrase in the opening stanza takes a similar turn when it is repeated at the end: "one sells the available thing, time / And again" becomes "One sells always time / Dissembled in heroic stone." Nemerov can work an entire poem around such a dubious title, as he does also in "Brainstorm," where an actual storm inspires a man in an upstairs room to thoughts of chaos and destruction, followed by an internalization of the storm:

He came to feel the crows walk on his head
As if he were the house, their crooked feet
Scratched, through the hair, his scalp. He might be dead
It seemed, and all the noises underneath
Be but the cooling of the sinews, veins,
Juices, and sodden sacks suddenly let go;
While in his ruins of wiring, his burst mains,
The rainy wind had been set free to blow
Until the green uprising and mob rule
That ran the world had taken over him,
Split him like seed, and set him in the school
Where any crutch can learn to be a limb.

Inside his head he heard the stormy crows.
                              (*CP*, 196–97)

The man has brought within himself first the house and, at last, the entire natural world as, lost in thought, he remains impervious to the realm that initially inspired his reveries. The storm without has fanned the horror within, as if Nemerov were self-consciously extending the opening motif of *The Prelude*: a "correspondent breeze" arises from within the passages of the mind to meet and surpass the gentle wind Wordsworth feels touching his face. Did the title "Brainstorm" come first, or did the poet find it in a brainstorm of his own as he was working through a poetic exploration? If so, he has alerted us to the relationship between sudden inspiration (the Eureka principle behind a "brainstorm") and the gradual derangement suffered by the man in the poem.

Nemerov's poems sometimes dramatize and explain their titles simultaneously. "Brainstorm" is one example. Another is "Thought" (*CP*, 392–93), itself both a thought and a definition of thought, which begins with a revitalized cliché that paradoxically disproves its own assertion, a kind of displaced syllogism of the "All Cretans are liars" sort:

> Thought is seldom itself
> And never itself alone.
> It is the mind turning
> To images. Maybe
> Idea is like the day,
> Being both everywhere
> And always in one place.

The solitary thought in the first stanza is grammatically isolated in a relatively bare setting; only the implicit personification rendered through the cliché (as in "he is seldom himself these days") sets up the subsequent move to images and similes. "Turning to" means, of course, both "turning attention to" and "turning into," so the mind and its animation are ready for a metamorphosis into the world it perceives (and half-creates, in Wordsworthian schemes). A second stanza describes a palette of natural harmony—leaves shaken by wind, grass bending in the wind and in shadow, minnow-waves mingling in shallows at the shore—and the last one continues the initial conjectures:

> And mind in some such way
> Passing across the world
> May make its differences
> At last unselfishly
> The casualties of cause:
>      It's likeness changes.

The abstractions have bracketed the empirical scene, mind and thought preparing one for the things of this world and becoming, in turn, affected by them. This bracketing extends to smaller levels of verbal nuance: "itself" replaced by "unselfishly," and "turning" by "passing." The conclusion affirms the transformations within change itself, to meet changing conditions, and the penultimate line, with its one dramatic pun ("casualties" as victims and accidents) and its quasi-visual rhyming of "casualties" and "cause," proves the inexact fit of all correspondences. The poem expresses clearly the nature of muddled, or at least frequently changing, perceptions.

The Janus-of-a-joke allows the poet to defy both logic and explanation. A pun condenses opposing or related ideas, marrying them in a single unit. Likeness is possible only where identity is not, as two later poems succinctly prove. "Being of Three Minds" aphoristically defines the nature of metaphor, allying it to the pun and to all likenesses that cross boundaries:

> I
> Between identity and difference
> Logicians say that likeness lies; it lies,
> They say, because it can do nothing else
> On a ground that's nothing but its boundaries,
> Distinguishing the different from the same
> By puffing out the nothing of a name.
>
> II
> What great magician could have cast the spell
> That broke the stump of Babel from the sky
> And raised Jerusalem the Golden high
> On mortgage money from the vaults of Hell?
>
> Some spellers say it was the little i
> That differences deify and defy.
>
> (*CP*, 416)

Among the other tricks of the poem is Nemerov's reminder of Hopkins's principle that words that sound alike mean alike. But this is no "mere" cleverness; rather, it is a fundamental truth with moral as well as logical and poetic ramifications. "Likeness" itself makes a partial rhyme with "lies," and "lies" partakes of prevarication and situation, so likeness, or metaphor, must consequently occupy a middle territory between the realms of discovery and invention. The "nothing" of a name (is Nemerov considering at some level Shakespeare's "noting"-"nothing" pun from *Much Ado*?) is a considerable something, since it divides and classifies where perhaps in nature itself one would see no identities at all.

And from the purely linguistic and logical considerations of the first stanza Nemerov moves to the historical and moral ones of the second, which poses a question about the relationship between the origin of language and linguistic differences (themselves, in families, variations on the theme of likeness and difference) and the spiritual relationship of humans to God. The concluding couplet not only resolves the question but also brings together the seemingly disparate subjects of the two stanzas. By relying on the two kinds of "spelling," and by repeating the "difference" of line 1 (along with a more delicate echo in "i" of the second word, "identity"), Nemerov makes his capping point, proving the existence of both difference (in sound, meaning, human intention, and achievement) and connection (between the two realms of the stanzas). Thus does wit create, as well as serve, its maker's wisdom.

As a kind of coda to Nemerov's ongoing *ars poetica*, which from the start of his career has lain not far beneath the surface of his nominal subjects, one might consider "The Metaphysical Automobile" (*CP*, 452), which shows again how poetry mediates between the dualities of logic and the chimeras of mere fancy. "It's abstract nouns, among the myths of mind, / Make most of the trouble," he begins, reminding readers that the fabled beasts of yore, unseen because unreal, have been replaced in this age by *isms* of one sort and another, and by the divisiveness of pronouns everywhere establishing warring factions, pitting "us" against "them." The second section investigates the neat clarity of logical dichotomies:

> You can't resolve a contradiction by
> Getting between the warring opposites.
> The idea of a car either has a dent
> In its left front fender or it downright don't,
> There's no third way. For on the roads of thought
> You're either nominalist or realist,
> The only question universals ask
> Is is you is or is you ain't my baby?
> And mild conceptualists, those innocent
> Bystanders, stand to get hit from either side.
> Accursed are the compromisers and
> The sorry citizens of buffer states,
> Nor fish nor flesh nor fowl nor good red herring,
> And spued out by the Lamb, the great I am.

But the clarity here reveals a falsehood; warring opposites can in fact be resolved, as Nemerov demonstrates in the concluding stanza. The roads of thought are, after all, a mere figure of speech, within which (as opposed to real roads) compromise *is* possible. The chimera and hippogriff, beasts that never were, exist on these imagined roads precisely because they were conceived by thought, and thought into conception.

Likewise, the "metaphysical" automobile of the title, vaguely hinted at by "the idea of a car" in the third line above (reminding one that the idea of a car is not the car itself), may allow for contradictions that the real car will not:

> In the eternal combustion engine, force
> Is from the contradicting opposites,
> And yet their warfare passes into play:
> The pistons know that up opposes down,
> Closed in their cylinders they cannot know
> Around, and would not be converted by
> The revelation of the wheel. So straight
> Flat roads of logic lie about a globe
> On which the shortest way between two points
> Happens to be a curve. And so do song
> And story, winding crank and widdershins,
> Still get there first, and poetry remains
> Eccentric and odd and riddling and right,
> Eternal return of the excluded middle.
>
> (452)

Nemerov's achievement has from the start of his career been his reminder that oddness and evenness, far from occupying the antithetical positions to which a logician might consign them, are in fact a pair of shaded complements. The eccentric, it appears, may be closer to the center, the riddling closer to revelation, than one otherwise might think, especially when an "eternal" engine has replaced a merely internal one. The middle position, excluded by philosophy from Aristotle onwards, returns in the realm of myth (no wonder that the last line alludes to all recent students of myth, from Nietzsche to Eliade) and, more significantly, in the oddness of language, everywhere quirky and everywhere right.

# THREE

# The Moral Imperative in Anthony Hecht, Allen Ginsberg, and Robert Pinsky

Twenty years ago, Susan Sontag suggested "Jewish moral seriousness and homosexual aestheticism and irony" as the primary forces in the modern sensibility.[1] Gay poets have no monopoly on irony, as the cases of Howard Nemerov, Richard Wilbur, Anthony Hecht and John Hollander, to cite a few, prove. Nemerov and James Merrill both inherited the mantle of W. H. Auden, although only Merrill shares Auden's sexual preference. Nor do American Jews have, ipso facto, a greater share of moral seriousness (consider Robert Bly, Amy Clampitt, Robert Hass, and Robert Lowell). And yet Sontag's theory has a curious validity for contemporary poetry. She has identified two strands, sometimes separate, sometimes intertwined, that stand out prominently in the contemporary fabric. In fact, at least as far as poetry goes, the three major forces in a collective "sensibility" might be the Jewish-moral, the gay-aesthetic, and the Southern-agrarian, the last represented in these pages by A. R. Ammons, but reaching backward to Robert Penn Warren and forward to Dave Smith and Charles Wright.

The view of and from the natural world (especially one a Southerner might propose) encourages descriptive more often than discursive strategies: this is why Ammons seems to stand a little to one side in this book. But all three temperaments—the Jewish, the homosexual, the Southern—share a peripheral status, which affords their representatives an eccentric or adversary relationship to the dominant culture. For this reason, didacticism becomes an understandable, if not always an inevitable, impulse. Any poet, especially one aware of a secondary position in his or her environment, would agree with Allen Ginsberg's observation, recalling both Shelley and Orwell, that "whoever controls the language, the images, controls the race."[2] Poets one generation away from immigrant status are most aware of the political power of language as an instrument of enfranchisement and assimilation.

This chapter concerns three poets who share a Jewish heritage and a New York background. Rather than thinking of a New York "school"

of Jewish poets, I suggest something of the richness of American poetry by looking at the work of poets who are Jewish, if only in a secular
sense. To Ginsberg, Hecht, and Pinsky, one might easily add Ben Be-
litt, Marvin Bell, Irving Feldman, Donald Finkel, Paul Goodman, Mar-
ilyn Hacker, Daniel Hoffman, Kenneth Koch, Howard Moss, Delmore
Schwartz, Louis Simpson, and Theodore Weiss, all poets who either
grew up close to New York or spent much of their lives there.[3] My
band of three stands both for the larger group and for different poetic
strategies that any "didactic" poet might employ: exhortation, exem-
plification, explanation, and parable. I overlook the obvious, considerable differences among the three in favor of the *rapprochement* and
matchmaking available within the pages of criticism rather than in life.
In his autobiography, Albert Einstein identified three "features of the
Jewish tradition that make me thank my stars I belong to it": "The
pursuit of knowledge for its own sake, an almost fanatical love of justice, and the desire for personal independence."[4] Without necessarily
limiting to Jews these three characteristics, I examine in these poets
the Arnoldian "moral seriousness" that Sontag, echoing Einstein's
terms, associates with their tradition. What exactly does it mean to talk
about ethical intensity in poetry?

All three poets are interested in moral problems, and all attempt
different, equally exemplary ways of bringing to poetry issues from
the ethical sphere. All have had academic careers, Ginsberg's perhaps
a little less conventional than the others', and Pinsky and Hecht have
written distinguished prose. Hecht may seem the least obvious candidate for my "didactic" badge, but his four scrupulously written volumes show how a naturally "lyric" poet opens his work to satire, narrative, and autobiography in order to encompass ethical concerns and
to provoke moral responses. Whereas Ginsberg, or in a different way
Robert Lowell, turns his attention to public events, and whereas Adrienne Rich defines and defends a body-centered politics, Hecht seems
at first a throwback to older, sterner paradigms: a colder moralist than
any other writer discussed in this book, he is today's preeminent poet
of evil. And yet because he resolutely stands by conventional forms in
a distrustful age that associates them with other kinds of convention-
ality, his poetry has a shock value at once chilling and reassuring. One
might do well to modify the famous response of Dr. Johnson to Milton: "we read Milton for instruction, retire harassed and overbur-
dened, and look elsewhere for recreation; we desert our master and
seek for companions." Masterful and companionable at once, Hecht
speaks of pain, evil, the horrors of history, as both observer and participant, imperious prophet and fellow sufferer.

From virtually the first page of *A Summoning of Stones* (1954) to the
last of *The Venetian Vespers* (1980), Hecht asks one continual question:
"What's become of Paradise?" ("La Condition Botanique," *SS*, 4), or
"What is our happiest, most cherished dream / Of paradise?" ("The
Venetian Vespers," *VV*, 62).[5] The question reflects neither Yeatsian
nostalgia for vanished orders nor regret for the loss of pastoral realms
and innocent, childlike pleasures; rather, it contains a deeper moral
dimension, often dismissed or ignored by pastoralists who also look
back regretfully but only sensuously. Hecht's province is the loss of
ethical innocence and the ontogeny of evil. For paradises are lost, in
his world, as a result of human sin, not error. The perennial religious
question, *unde malum*, has yielded to him, in thirty years of poetry, no
easy answers. Like Voltaire, whose "Poem Upon the Lisbon Disaster"
he adapts, Hecht has no sympathy for a foolish meliorism in a godless
universe where felt pain has neither explanation nor consolation:

> From Flawless Love ills can have no descent;
> Nor from elsewhere, since God's omnipotent:
> Yet they exist. Such paradox has checked
> And baffled the weak human intellect . . .
> I am all ignorance, like a Ph.D.)
>
> (*MSS*, 69–70)

Hecht has asked the same questions, stalking a moral center that always evades him. His questions, and those answers that are temporary
at best, place him more squarely in the camp of Hebrew doubters than
that of Christian apologists, and they also explain why a large number
of his speakers or characters have succumbed to insanity, perversion,
or moral enervation. These questions, persistently asked but unanswered, record what Brad Leithauser has labeled "a journey from
darkness into greater darkness."[6]

From the start, Hecht has gestured toward fable and exemplum, to
the forms but not the substance of easy moralizing. Individual titles
recount chapters in a philosophical quest: "The Place of Pain in the
Universe," "Discourse Concerning Temptation," "A Lesson from the
Master" (*SS*); "The Seven Deadly Sins" (with engravings by Leonard
Baskin), "The Man Who Married Magdalene," "Improvisations on Ae-
sop" (*HH*); "Black Boy in the Dark," " 'Dichtung und Wahrheit,' "
"Poem Upon the Lisbon Disaster" (*MSS*). Others with neutral titles
follow the same paths. "Samuel Sewall" (*SS*) is a moral lesson on the
subject of vanity, "A Poem for Julia" (*SS*), a contemplation of art and
sexuality, "Harangue" (*SS*), a meditation on the presumed value of the
human knowledge of death. "A Lot of Night Music" (*MSS*), a pro-

grammatic reflection on contemporary poetic schools, takes a wistful look at the genuine voice of the bard who reminds readers of "an Aesopic Age when all the beasts were moral / And taught their ways to men; / Some herbal dream, some chlorophyll sublime / In which Apollo's laurel / Blooms in a world made innocent again." In "The Ghost in the Martini" conscience speaks as a genie from a glass with beaded bubbles winking at the brim to a man in his cups about the foolishness of middle-aged adultery (one never learns who wins the argument). Everywhere in his work, Hecht recourses to moral horrors, the tragedies of history. Even in "House Sparrows" (*VV*), Biafra and Auschwitz merit a mention: perhaps random here, the references make sense to any reader aware of the obsessions within the whole body of the poetry.

Hecht is most at home in two kinds of poems, which he has made distinctly his own. I call the first "emblems" because they either resemble (like "The Seven Deadly Sins") their seventeenth-century predecessors or invite a quasi-allegorical interpretation. Longer and more horrifying are the case studies, in narrative or autobiographical detail, of depravity, instability, and sadism. These poems, beginning with "A Roman Holiday" (*SS*) and building to the longest of the monologues, "The Venetian Vespers," feature protagonists who seem both fully human and only partially alive because they all attest to Hecht's focus on obsession and aberration as gauges to character. These figures are unnamed, as if Hecht has preempted Browning's interest in abnormal psychology and raised his individuals, all breathing human passion, far above the particularities of space and time. And in all, the unstated lesson modifies the admission from the early "The Place of Pain in the Universe" (*SS*): "Observe there is no easy moral here." Hecht's didacticism, even in allegorical or emblematic expressions, turns away from facile standards and admonitions.

The early, familiar "The Gardens of the Villa d'Este" (*SS*, 35–39) pictures a scene, in an elaborate stanzaic pattern, that Nemerov or Wilbur, or any of the heirs of Yeats-by-way-of-Auden would have found congenial, but what looks here like a poem of the American in Europe admiring art and nature, a contemplation of ancient civilization, turns into something deeper and stranger. Not only do the gardens themselves inspire a contemplation and a decision from the observer, but the elaborateness of the poem's form and the elaboration within the elegant refinements of his speech also build toward an explicit "lesson" that the poem serves up at its ending. The poem treats a natural encounter as a didactic occasion, much in the way Wordsworth's "Nutting," for example, rehearses a spot of time in which youthful bravado and rapine instill a moral sensation in a young adventurer who, as an adult teller, passes on a feebler, poetically detachable lesson to his auditor. Here is Hecht's conclusion:

> Susan, it had been once
> My hope to see this place with you,
> See it as in the hour of thoughtless youth.
> For age mocks all diversity, its genesis,
> And whispers to the heart, "*Cor mio,* beyond all this
> Lies the unchangeable and abstract truth,"
> Claims of the grass, it is not true,
> And makes our youth its dunce.
>
> Therefore, some later day
> Recall these words, let them be read
> Between us, let them signify that here
> Are more than formulas, that age sees no more clearly
> For its poor eyesight, and philosophy grows surly,
> That falling water and the blood's career
> Lead down the garden path to bed
> And win us both to May.

Hecht possesses Wordsworth's didactic impulse, but trained as he is in the tactics and language of high modernism, submerges his lesson within an artfully refined context. It becomes clear by the poem's end, however, that he is returning to even older, more conservative vehicles for poetic preaching: the emblem, the apostrophe. Hecht's first volume is Yeatsian in diction but not in purpose: one can cull from its opening poem, "Double Sonnet" (*SS*, 3), concerning erotic conquest and failure, a posey of Yeatsian phrases: "cave," "lamplight," "striving," "a practice of the blood," "mastery and quiver," "sacred dolphins," "Pythagorean heavens." "The Gardens of the Villa d'Este" maintains the Yeatsian language ("cause to sing loud," "commend my music," "finer proportion," "artifice of an Hephaestus net"), but embeds it within an archness inherited from Auden and a final moral that places the poem within the tradition of the seventeenth-century Maying invitation. The speaker both learns and teaches, at first responding to landscape as though moving his eye from Baedeker to scene, and next invoking a muse for artistic-erotic success. Here is his opening:

> This is Italian. Here
> Is cause for the undiminished bounce
> Of sex, cause for the lark, the animal spirit
> To rise, aerated, but not beyond our reach, to spread

Friction upon the air, cause to sing loud for the bed
  Of jonquils, the linen bed, and established merit
    Of love, and grandly to pronounce
      Pleasure without peer.

    Goddess, be with me now;
    Commend my music to the woods.
  There is no garden to the practiced gaze
Half so erotic: here the sixteenth century thew
Rose to its last perfection, this being chiefly due
  To the provocative role the water plays.
    Tumble and jump, the fountains' moods
    Teach the world how.

                                    (*SS*, 35)

The language of the guidebook ("This is Italian," "the practiced gaze,"
"this being chiefly due") reaches a temporary climax in "teach the
world how," but is otherwise restrained by the pomp of an enlightened
hedonism.

Six stanzas detail the "finer proportions" within "the sum of inter-
secting limbs," the deft weaving of art and nature reflected in the "intricate mesh of trees," the statuary, and the movement of water, almost
humanized in their lively activity:

                          the giggling water drops
    Past haunches, over ledges, out of mouths, and stops
      In a still pool, but, by a plumber's ruse,
        Rises again to laugh and squirt
        At heaven, and is still

      Busy descending. White
      Ejaculations leap to teach
      How fertile are these nozzles.

                                    (36)

Within this paradise invented by human mastery, inspired by and including the erotic forces of nature that in their turn inspire the human
onlookers ("It was in such a place / that Mozart's Figaro contrived /
The totally expected") resides not "God's rational, wrist-watch universe," but insects that, like Marianne Moore's "real toads," prove that
humans may attempt but will always fail to control the elements:

      Actually, it is real
      The way the world is real: the horse
    Must turn against the wind, and the deer feed

Against the wind, and finally the garden must allow
For the recalcitrant; a style can teach us how
    To know the world in little where the weed
        Has license, where by dint of force
        D'Estes have set their seal.

(37)

What seemed intially all Yeatsian elegance turns out to be a comedy of
human ineptness poised against a background at once complementary
and subtly undermining. The garden passively submits to the presence of human lovers both because (like Wordsworth's "patient" hazel
bower in "Nutting") it has no choice and because it will remain after
the nocturnal pairs depart.

Finally, Hecht updates Herrick's "Delight in Disorder," deliberately
offering an ironic twentieth-century "lecture" on the relationship between order and chaos, art and nature, labor and natural growth:

Tomorrow, before dawn,
    Gardeners will come to resurrect
Downtrodden iris, dispose of broken glass,
Return the diamond earrings to the villa, but
As for the moss upon the statue's shoulder, not
    To defeat its great invasion, but to pass
        Over the liberal effect
        Caprice and cunning spawn.

For thus it was designed:
    Controlled disorder at the heart
Of everything, the paradox, the old
Oxymoronic itch to set the formal strictures
Within a natural context, where the tension lectures
    Us on our mortal state, and by controlled
        Disorder, labors to keep art
        From being too refined.

(38)

But to the conventional lessons of "controlled disorder" and "formal
strictures / Within a natural context," Hecht adds a thoroughly unexpected gloss in the final two stanzas (quoted earlier): the overt borrowing from "Tintern Abbey" ("the hour of thoughtless youth") contains
an implicit repetition of Yeats's "Young, we loved one another and
were ignorant" by which the speaker instructs his Susan in the fatuous
delusions of youth. The lesson, finally delivered in more than the formulas that have somewhat facilely preceded it, casts a bitter look at the
naturalistic consolations of Wordsworth (and the Yeats of "After Long

Silence"), preferring the pleasures (albeit temporary ones) of bed and May.

Despite its elegance, its delight in scenes and tropes of high wit and irony, "The Gardens of the Villa d'Este" betrays the two recurrent aspects of Hecht's temper: a fascination with sexual obsession and a tone of sadness, even in exuberance, that pervades the longer narratives as well as this emblematic poem. At the heart of his books lies an unspoken fear or terror, perhaps a result of Hecht's own service in World War II, all the more horrifying for being elegantly implied. At Christmas ("A Roman Holiday," *SS*), blood and expiation, guilt and civilization are interwoven but unavailing: "Blood is required, / And it shall fall." Even in the first volume, poems written by a man not yet thirty, the speaker never *seems* young; even lust (in "The Gardens of the Villa d'Este" or "As Plato Said") for all its centrality seems sophisticated, doomed, and tired. A stern puritanical voice suppresses the pastoral delights of the Cavaliers to which he often alludes.

*The Hard Hours* sounds at first more relaxed than *A Summoning of Stones*, but the *hard*ness continues the stoniness of the first volume. Even the lesson in the poem from which the volume derives its title teaches of our common lot, attending as well to specific individual horrors: "Adam, there will be / Many hard hours, / As an old poem says, / Hours of loneliness. / I cannot ease them for you; / They are our common lot" ("Adam," 31). The informality of the opening lines of the first poem gives way to scenes of greater hardship and cruelty. So, "A Hill" (2–3) begins offhandedly in the voice of a debonair skeptic who prepares us for, and simultaneously disavows, the surprises that follow: "In Italy, where this sort of thing can occur, / I had a vision once—though you understand / It was nothing at all like Dante's, or the visions of saints, / And perhaps not a vision at all." The figure of *occupatio*, the age-old rhetorical trick of having things two ways at once (of course we're now prepared to think of Dante and saints, to look for correspondences, even negative ones), opens to a morning scene in Rome when, for a moment, the speaker loses consciousness of his immediate environment, and a Wordsworthian spot of time returns him to a winter's scene, in childhood, on a hill where he heard

> What seemed the crack of a rifle. A hunter, I guessed;
> At least I was not alone. But just after that
> Came the soft and papery crash
> Of a great branch somewhere unseen falling to earth.
>
> And that was all, except for the cold and silence
> That promised to last forever, like the hill.

The understated horror perhaps owes something to comparable moments in Frost ("The Most of It," "An Old Man's Winter's Night"). One never learns what exactly happened there, nor of course can the adult decide why the scene should have held him in its grip both at the time and thereafter. Restored to his Italian setting (almost immediately, one infers), he is nevertheless haunted by what Wordsworth called "a dim and undetermined sense / Of unknown modes of being; o'er my thoughts / There hung a darkness, call it solitude, / Or blank desertion" (*The Prelude* 1.392–95).

Hecht's poetry, whether deliberately spine-tingling, as here, or more graphically lurid, is permeated by Wordsworthian "visionary dreariness." Frightened, temporarily dazed, the adult speaker of "A Hill" extends the effect of his vision both forward (to a "today" ten years after the Roman shock) and backward (to the aftermath in childhood of the original event):

> for more than a week
> I was scared by the plain bitterness of what I had seen.
> All this happened about ten years ago,
> And it hasn't troubled me since, but at last, today,
> I remembered that hill; it lies just to the left
> Of the road north of Poughkeepsie; and as a boy
> I stood before it for hours in wintertime.
>
> (3)

Such easy five-stressed lines, covering an unspecified depth of horror, set the stage for the more grimly sadistic poems that follow. Like Wordsworth, Hecht is bent upon the preservation of spots of time and upon a demonstration of the tricks and sleights of memory; his didactic program also involves nothing less than an exploration of the inherent evil in humans. He gives Wordsworth's themes but through characters who would be at home in Browning, and in the technique and language of modern America.

The exquisite, chilling "Behold the Lilies of the Field" (*HH*, 10–12) offers the reminiscence of a soldier-courtier upon a psychiatrist's couch. It is a study of a specific patient and of the horrible idea of patience—understood equally as waiting and as tragic endurance. Both lucid in its visualization and vague in its period (the speaker begins by referring to his mother on the telephone, before launching into his main story concerning the capture, torture, flaying, and stuffing of the Roman emperor Valerian), the poem charges the proverbial titular flowers with the double sadism of the modern doctor and the calm endurance of the ancient soldiers. The cure, based upon the beneficent techniques of modern Freudianism, may repeat and extend the original crime. The "doctor" speaks four times, always counseling relaxation, ease, patience (*"Lie back. Relax . . . ," "That's enough for now . . . ," "Look at the flowers"*). But patience is what the man has already learned; he unfolds his tale of capture by the enemy and then of being forced to witness the torture, healing, and final execution of his emperor ("and I was tied to a post and made to watch," "And we were made to watch," "And we were not allowed to close our eyes / Or to look away"). In a grotesque anticipation of the modern listener, the ancient doctor who first treated the flogged king and healed his back comes forward after the final sentencing to administer the slow flaying of the skin from the feet to the head. Patience is the allegorical lesson, taught and learned, at all levels, as the soldier at last reveals the pedagogic purpose behind the swinging of the newly stuffed Valerian in the wind:

> And young girls were brought there by their mothers
> To be told about the male anatomy.
> His death had taken hours.
> They were very patient.
> And with him passed away the honor of Rome.
>
> (12)

Hecht significantly expands upon the old story of Valerian's death. Gibbon does not mention the alternation of torture, healing, and final, exquisite torture; in fact, he readily dismisses the legend: "the tale is moral and pathetic, but the truth of it may very fairly be called in question. . . . It is at least certain that the only emperor of Rome who had ever fallen into the hands of the enemy languished away his life in hopeless captivity."[7] But for Hecht's purposes, the "moral and pathetic" possibilities are too great to resist.

Such sadism recurs in Hecht's volumes, most notably in the double scenes of torture, one from the English Renaissance, the other from World War II, in " 'More Light! More Light!' " (*HH*, 64–65), whose easy quatrains are complicated by a slight metrical uneasiness and the instablility of rhyme:

> No light, no light in the blue Polish eye.
> When he finished a riding boot packed down the earth.
> The Lüger hovered lightly in its glove.
> He was shot in the belly and in three hours bled to death.

In the uncertainty implicit in quatrains that casually expand from ten to as many as sixteen syllables while retaining the undertone of a pentameter line one can sense the uneasiness of a twentieth-century moralist with crimes for which he can discover neither an explanation nor a consolation. "The Deodand" (*VV*, 6–8), the most recent of the poems of cruelty, also shares in the subtlety of Hecht's method, his teaching (so to speak) about and away from a central text. It begins as a description of Renoir's "Parisians Dressed in Algerian Costume," and builds to a central proposition, from Santayana, about the *lessons* of history, specifically the "crude imperial pride" within the appropriation ("exploitation") "of the primitive," the "homages of romantic self-deception" emblemized by the make-believe in the oppressors' costuming:

> Have they no intimation, no recall
> Of the once queen who liked to play at milkmaid,
> And the fierce butcher-reckoning that followed
> Her innocent, unthinking masquerade?
> Those who will not be taught by history
> Have as their curse the office to repeat it,
> And for this little spiritual debauch
> . . . . . . . . . . . .
> Exactions shall be made, an expiation,
> A forfeiture.

Hence the poem's title, with its implicit allusion to Marvell's "Nymph Complaining," the only other poem I know of that employs the technical term for a forfeiture to expiate a crime.

As often in Hecht's moral world, the person forfeited, the deodand himself, may very well be an innocent, and the last stanza of the poem describes a French Legionnaire who, in the final months of the Algerian war, is captured, dressed grotesquely as a woman, and whose fingers are cut off by his captors, at whose hands he is literally forced to eat. Led on a leash from town to town, he sings special lyrics to a popular show tune:

> Donnez moi à manger de vos mains
> Car c'est pour vous que je fais ma petite danse;
> Car je suis Madeleine, la putain,
> Et je m'en vais le lendemain matin,
> Car je suis La Belle France.

The lesson is a simple one: cruelty begets cruelty, and the innocent suffer. But perhaps no one is innocent. The deliberate rhythmic fluctuations within conventional forms; or the way of beginning innocently with description and then tempering a visual object with a garish reminder of the social contexts and consequences of art; or the use

of paired scenes and uncertain time schemes—all these devices reflect
a fascination with the moral ambiguities that lie beneath apparent simplicities. Like any temperamental moralist, Hecht is attracted to easy
pictures, fables, emblems, but he realizes the inadequacy of all vehicles, the deception in all categories, and the questions implicit in all
answers. Drawn to acts of representation, he simultaneously resists be-
lieving in representational accuracies.

One usually, and incorrectly, associates technical facility with ease
and frequency of utterance, but Hecht has been, it seems, deliberately,
painstakingly slow in his output. The great questions of evil and God's
silent complicity have been asked in postwar poetry as well as prose,
although European and Russian poets rather than American poets
have had the firsthand experiences that typically provoke questions of
such an existential magnitude. Hecht's truest precursors, from whom
he seems to have derived inspiration as well as epigraphs, are Shakespeare and Melville, but it may be that what I have labelled the Jewish
moral imperative counts as more important than any strictly literary
influence. The last poem in his second volume, " 'It Out-Herods
Herod. Pray You, Avoid It.' " (*HH*, 67–68), describes the way children
invest a father with the roles of Santa Claus and God, while the father
knows that he could not have saved one life from the gas chambers.
The aftermath of Buchenwald, along with other scenes of torture, defilement, and the punishment of the innocents, appears again in the
volume's longest poem, "Rites and Ceremonies" (38–47), which asks in
true Jewish fashion all "the famous ancient questions." Not exclusively
an exemplum, like some of the shorter ones I've cited, this most morally charged of Hecht's poems constitutes both a theodicy and an updating of *The Waste Land*. Like Eliot (whom he cites in the title of his
second section, "The Fire Sermon," which contains the importuning
"O hear my prayer, / And let my cry come unto thee"), Hecht makes
a formal and a scenic medley of his poem, interspersing lyric—apostrophe and description—with longer-lined narratives and meditations.

At its thematic center the poem announces a didactic moral as an
epigram: "The contemplation of horror is not edifying, / Neither does
it strengthen the soul." This formal proposition, whether taken as a
dramatic utterance appropriate to its occasion or as a more generalized hypothesis about the inefficacy of moral deliberation, calls up a
question central to all of Hecht's work: does bearing witness to the
barbarities of history have any ethical power? Unless one takes as a
sardonic irony the apostrophe throughout the poem to a God who
does not answer and who may not hear, one must infer that the temporary doubt in the aphorism above is included in the obsessive con-

templation only as an eddy flowing backward against a prevailing current. Observation, in its double sense of taking notice and taking part, becomes the poet's major discursive strategy as he both describes events and performs the "rites and ceremonies" of the poem's title. He "observes," but he also questions.

Part 1 ("The Room") begins with a twenty-four line invocation to God, "author of all things," the furnisher and governor "*in whom* [line 18 shockingly announces] *we doubt*," and of whom the forty-two-year-old survivor asks, "Who was that child of whom they tell / . . . whose holy name all shall pronounce / Emmanuel?" The address ended, the poem opens with easier, longer lines to a narrative recollection of concentration camp atrocities, which begins with an image of a dead German soldier whose body greets the liberating armies. The speaker cannot forget, twenty years later, the camps or the complicity of the Catholic church (which only recently "has voted to 'deplore' " the horrors), and by the fifth stanza of the recollection the soldier-liberator has merged with the victims:

> Are the vents in the ceiling, Father, to let the spirit depart?
> We are crowded in here naked, female and male.
> An old man is saying a prayer. And now we start
> To panic, to claw at each other, to wail
> As the rubber-edged door closes on chance and choice.
> He is saying a prayer for all whom this room shall kill.
> *"I cried unto the Lord God with my voice,*
> *And He has heard me out His holy hill."*
>
> (39)

Not any human villain or even a machine but this "strange room / Without windows," as he describes it several lines earlier in his imagined entry into the death chamber, will kill the inhabitants thereof. Murder has been refined, perfected: no mechanism is visible, and consequently no blame is overtly fixed. The old-fashioned propriety of "*shall* kill" (emphasis mine), combined with what in retrospect will seem the naive suggestion that God has heard the victim's prayer, ends the section with horrible ironic force.

One rite finished, another begins. Section 2 ("The Fire Sermon") mirrors the first, now beginning with a narrative and concluding with a lyric apostrophe. The time has changed (the setting is medieval); the ceremony (a sacrifice of Jewish victims) has not. A European plague, which "struck among the Christians / As among other peoples," convinces the King of Tharsis to abort a journey to Avignon for the baptism of his people, and provokes in the speaker a central religious inquiry into the suffering of the innocent: "If it was a judgment, it struck home in the houses of penitence, / The meek and the faithful were in no wise spared." But, he grimly continues, "presently it was found to be / Not a judgment," in a voice filled with bitter awe at the efficiency of the machinery wrought by the "will of the people," and with the placid, toneless assurance of a tour guide showing visitors the cathedral at Strasbourg:

> The preparations were hasty
> But thorough, they were thorough.
> A visitor to that town today is directed to
> The Minster. The Facade, by Erwin von Steinbach,
> Is justly the most admired part of the edifice
> And presents a singularly happy union
> Of the style of Northern France
> With the perpendicular tendency
> Peculiar to German cathedrals.
>
> (41–42)

Here, witnessed by "Everyone who was not too sick," including "the students / Of the university which later gave Goethe / His degree of Doctor of Laws," "the Jews [were] assembled . . . Children and all, and tied together with rope." They were then burned, for their presumed poisoning of the wells that created the plague.

This toneless, almost random, section is followed by six stanzas of tightly ordered invocation and lament, a ritualized prayer that harks back to Eliot and the Ash Wednesday service:

> O that thou shouldst give dust a tongue
> To crie to thee,
> And then not heare it crying! Who is strong
> When the flame eats his knee?
> O hear my prayer,
>
> And let my cry come unto thee.
> Hide not thy face.
> Let there some child among us worthy be
> Here to receive thy grace
> And sheltering.
>
> (43)

This prayer is, at best, unanswered, perhaps unheard, and the third section ("The Dream") opens with the dull admissions about the uselessness of contemplating sorrow quoted above. Martyrdom, both the act of torture and its implied lessons about strength of character, "be-wilder[s] and shame[s] us" who lack the martyr's perfection.

After its flat opening lines, the section turns to a scene of Joachim Du Bellay in Rome at carnival, contemplating in elegantly rhymed five-line stanzas the Corso and the inebriating gestures preceding "the seemly austerities of Lent." With his standard strategy of juxtaposing different verse forms or different scenes that reflect upon, after they have contrasted with, one another, Hecht describes the running of the race through its "mile-long gorgeous course," with the populace lining the sides, ready to strike with "whips and sticks" first the asses, then camels and Barbary horses and whatever other beasts await their turn in the general folly of misrule. He asks a question that evokes Keats's in "Ode on a Grecian Urn" ("Who are these coming to the sacrifice?") but, by avoiding Keats's "sacrifice," he icily calls attention to his own. The speaker, seeing through Du Bellay's eyes, notices something new and offers his stoic worldly advice on how to confront human pain by subsuming it within the more general, and therefore less frightening, category of historical decline:

> The children shout. But who are these that stand
> And shuffle shyly at the starting line?
> Twenty young men, naked, except the band
> Around their loins, wait for the horn's command.
> Christ's Vicar chose them, and imposed his fine.
>
> Du Bellay, poet, take no thought of them,
> And yet they too are exiles, and have said
> Through many generations, long since dead,
> "*If I forget thee, O Jerusalem, . . .*"
> Still, others have been scourged and buffeted
>
> And worse. Think rather, if you must,
> Of Piranesian, elegiac woes,
> Rome's grand declensions, that all-but-speaking dust.
> Or think of the young gallants and their lust.
> Or wait for the next heat, the buffaloes.
>
> (44–45)[8]

In "woes / buffaloes" one can hear the moral imperatives behind Hecht's refined technique, the reduction of human misery through a virtually mock-heroic rhyme that enables Hecht the modernist to cast his colder eye upon the sentimental reflections of the French Renaissance; the "Think rather . . ." likewise mitigates suffering, transforming it into a compensatory elegy. The doubling of scenes to effect a moral recognition becomes a virtual hallmark of Hecht's style: in addition to the poems already discussed, I think of "The Cost" (*MSS*, 3–4), in which Trajan's Column and its sculpted figures, dead but immortal, are literally circled by a young Italian couple on a Vespa. The whole poem merges a Keatsian examination of art's relation to life with Yeats's obsession with the problems of youthful, bodily ignorance.

The final "ceremony" in "Rites and Ceremonies" is "Words for the Day of Atonement," where at last Hecht speaks in the language of the Old rather than the New Testament. Yet even here the opaque setting ("It is winter as I write," he says in the middle of the section, words designated for an autumn holiday) and references produce not so much a linear meditation as a weaving of prayer, litany, and questioning, in tones importuning, querulous, humble, sophistic, and hopeful. The speaker begins, confident in his worldly wisdom, noting that the evil prosper, the good suffer, but also that "the Lord of hosts had left unto us / A very small remnant" (45). Some, in fact, survive within a paradoxical "wilderness of comfort," and the poet proposes as a common moral imperative that to identify "to what purpose . . . Had best be our present concern." The section consists, however, of alternating questions and answers, worries and consolations, arranged so as to bewilder and ultimately to comfort us with all that a reasonable twentieth-century person might long for. To his question whether we shall find our Lear, "mad, poor and betrayed enough to find / Forgiveness for us," who learns that "none does offend," all he can offer is absence: "Listen, Listen. / But the voices are blown away."

Ultimately the appeal to God for forgiveness and mercy is an appeal to self-interest, his as well as ours:

> The soul is thine, and the body is thy creation:
> O have compassion on thy handiwork.
> The soul is thine, and the body is thine:
> O deal with us according to thy name.
> We come before thee relying on thy name;
> O deal with us according to thy name;
> For the sake of the glory of thy name;
> As the gracious and merciful God is thy name.
> O Lord, for thy name's sake we plead,
> Forgive us our sins, though they be very great.
>
> (46)

Hecht repeats the "famous ancient questions" of Job and the voice from the whirlwind, but in his hypnotic repetition ("thy name") he challenges God to redeem himself through human reliance upon him.

Since the entire poem has witnessed and combined various historical scenes of martyrdom, persecution, and inhumanity, the only moral or theological solution it can render at last is a plea for forgiveness of common sins, those perpetrated in ignorance as well as in full consciousness. The last hope is that some, after all, do survive, and upon them hinge human trust and salvation:

> Father, I also pray
> For those among us whom we know not, those
> Dearest to thy grace,
> The saved and saving remnant, the promised third,
> Who in a later day
> When we again are compassed about with foes,
> Shall be for us a nail in thy holy place
> There to abide according to thy word.
>
> Neither shall the flame
> Kindle upon them, nor the fire burn
> A hair of them, for they
> Shall be thy care when it shall come to pass,
> And calling on thy name
> In the hot kilns and ovens, they shall turn
> To thee as it is prophesied, and say,
> *"He shall come down like rain upon mown grass."*
>
> (47)

The old round begins again. A new generation will be consigned to the flames, and some will miraculously, like Shadrach, Mischach and Abednego, survive untinged. It is a small consolation, but apparently the only one of which Hecht's poetry is capable. Since there are no human "heroes" among his characters, and since his mind tends naturally to despair and tragedy, to the sinister and the sadistic, the only remaining solace for moral regeneration lies beyond the realm of human comprehension.

"Rites and Ceremonies" stands out in Hecht's work, both for its length and formal variety and for reaching an apparent dead end. The major long poems that follow it return to moral and psychological dilemmas, defined through either characterization or *ekphrasis*, but they refuse the theological consolation that this poem has entertained. Having once considered religious humility, Hecht chooses to revert to the more comfortable roles of satirist, Browningesque monologuist, or detached observer. The stance of moral questioner is more congenial than that of religious suppliant. Whether in the form of dramatic monologue ("Green: an Epistle," "Coming Home," whose speaker is John Clare, "Apprehensions" [all *MSS*], and finally "The Venetian Vespers"), or in medleys like "Rites and Ceremonies" and epistolary poems such as "Poem Upon the Lisbon Disaster," Hecht concerns himself with the relationships between abnormal psychology and moral status. Not for nothing does he allude to *Othello* more frequently than to other works: the intemperateness of sexual jealousy and evil's motiveless malignity tempt him to analysis and exploration. In an allegorically conceived work like "Green: an Epistle" (*MSS*, 13–17) the Roethkean epigraph ("This urge, wrestle, resurrection of dry sticks, / Cut stems struggling to put down feet, / What saint strained so much, / Rose on such lopped limbs to new life?") prepares one to expect a poem about rebirth within nature, but the creepy speaker delivers instead his dirty little secret about "resentment, malice" through the description of botanical evolution from single-celled plants into "sequoia forests of vindictiveness," turning under the carbon process "into diamonds of pure hate."

Formal pleasure—the speaker's and the author's—attends upon these explanations of evil. I think also of the slow-paced homoeroticism of "The Feast of St. Stephen" (*MSS*, 46–47), which moves from harmless locker-room pranks to an updating of the saint's martyrdom in some modern field. Time and space are unspecified, but the refinements of cruelty keep the poem specific enough to stand as a model of moral precision as well as emblemization. The poem gives only intimations of the martyrdom from which it turns away (as "The Ghost in the Martini" recounts the chase, not the actual bedding, of the young girl). Hecht's art is morally complete but narratively teasing. Perhaps this explains his preference for conservative structures and, within his formal arrangements, for pairings and dualisms of the sort already noted.

One last poem deserves attention as exemplary of Hecht's appreciation of polarities as the best way for instructing an audience in moral dilemmas. From its Goethean title onward, " 'Dichtung und Wahrheit' " (*MSS*, 9–11) arranges itself around the kinds of dichotomies that teachers always find useful as approaches to, if not always accurate renditions of, moral truths. It is an intricate system of pairings, composed of halves each of which is itself divided into separate images, emblems, or considerations. In the first part, visual emblems—the Discobolus and "the clumsy snapshot of / An infantry platoon"—provoke questions about the relationship of art to experience and personal, as well as historical, hindsight. The perfection of the athlete's "marble heave," captured in a physical medium *and* "in mid-career" is

juxtaposed with the amateur photo of "grubby and indifferent men, /
Lounging in bivuoac," and both "stop history in its tracks." The
speaker finds himself in this army photo from long ago and frames
three questions that move from the general to the specific, carefully
modulating his responses to the picture until his attention comes to
rest squarely upon himself.

First, the general aesthetic topic: how does the perfection of art address a mortal audience?:

> We who are all aswim in time,
>   We, "the inconsistent ones,"
> How can such fixture speak to us?

Both "chisel and lens" embalm us within "arrested flights," and by the
act of "brute translation" (in its double sense of transport to another
medium and interpretation *from* that medium) "we / Turn into Ben-
thamites," like the father of utilitarianism who is no more than a
stuffed mummy that future generations may observe at will. The
questioning becomes more personal and more highly charged with a
duplicitous language suggesting elegy and impatience:

> Those soldiers, like some senior class,
>   Were they prepared to *dye*
> In silver nitrate images
>   Behind the camera's eye?
>                     (9, my emphasis)

In the third stanza, Hecht turns completely away from the marble purity of Myron's sculpture and toward the photo:

> It needs a Faust to animate
>   The wan homunculus,
> Construe the stark, unchanging text,
>   Winkle the likes of us
> Out of a bleak geology
>   That art has put to rest,
> And by a sacred discipline
>   Give breath back to the past.
> How, for example, shall I read
>   The expression on my face
> Among that company of men
>   In that unlikely place?
>                     (9–10)

The delicate modulations in diction impel us from the stilled, impersonal construction ("It needs a Faust") through a playful, Audenesque

archaism ("Winkle the likes of us") to the final, personal, and abso-
lutely straightforward question that ends the section. Hecht duplicates
in his readers his own surprise at discovering the self as an objet
trouvé, a souvenir of the past that provokes both specific questions
(Who was I then? What was I feeling? Whatever happened to me?)
and more general ones about the reanimation and renovation that attend the experience, and then the interpreting, of art. Having "put to
rest" our past selves, art may restore us to them, and to a chaster understanding of the very process of all understanding. From such *Dichtung*, then, comes the hope of *Wahrheit*, from such questions, construed through taut paradoxical arrangements, the possibility of
answers.

The poem's second part expands into Hecht's characteristic "explanatory" mode: easy, unrhymed, five-stress lines, which contemplate
the relationship of inspiration and accomplishment, and thence of
world and word, text and commentary. Like the first part, the second
moves from an initial single figure (here Mozart has replaced the Discus Thrower) to a consideration of the pedagogue's "we": "We begin
with the supreme donnée," but mirroring the first section, this one
begins rather than ends with epistemological questions, now posed in
the comfortable assurance of declarative structures, whose certainty is
reduced by their provisional incompletion:

> Easy enough to claim, in the dawn of hindsight,
> That Mozart's music perfectly enacts
> Pastries and powdered wigs, an architecture
> Of white and gold rosettes, balanced parterres.
> More difficult to know how the spirit learns
> Its scales, or the exact dimensions of fear:
> The nameless man dressed head-to-foot in black,
> Come to commission a requiem in a hurry.

Posing as statements, these questions about the double relationship of
art to its age and to the growth of its creator are possible, I think, only
because they amplify the explicit questions from the preceding part of
the poem. They are disguised, but their very dress suggests a growth
in the assured knowledge to which the speaker directs us.

The same sort of pedagogic *faux-naiveté* is developed again toward
the end of this paragraph, where the natural teacher interposes his
rhetorical strategies to heighten the reader's responses:

> Just how such truth
> Gets itself stated in pralltrillers and mordents
> Not everyone can say. But the 'cellist,

Leaning over his labors, his eyes closed,
Is engaged in that study, blocking out, for the moment,
Audience, hall, and a great part of himself
In what, not wrongly, might be called research,
Or the most private kind of honesty.

From the gentle evasion of "not everyone can say," through the
equally gentle litotes and conditional verb (a teacher's tool, surely) of
"in what, not wrongly, might be called research," Hecht both defines
and exemplifies a strategic movement of isolation, concentration, and
momentary creative intensity that exposes the performing self, opening him and the audience of which he is unmindful, to Mozart's truths.
Thus, a *musicalische Dichtung* becomes *Wahrheit*, and thus, also, the formal movement of the poem duplicates a truth it contains. The articulation within the poem, like the communication of a professor on a
podium, constitutes a performative utterance.

The second section of the second part deserves quotation in full for
its expansive opening up from the solitary figures who preceded it to
a collective truth that both surrounds the paragraph and, by way of a
clever reformulation, reflects all the dualities within the enterprise:

We begin with the supreme donnée, the world,
Upon which every text is commentary,
And yet they play each other, the oak-leaf cured
In sodden ditches of autumn darkly confirms
Our words; and by the frailest trifles
(A doubt, a whisper, a handkerchief)
Venetian pearl and onyx are cast away.
It is, in the end, the solitary scholar
Who returns us to the freshness of the text,
Which returns us to the freshness of the world
In which we find ourselves, like replicas,
Dazzled by glittering dawns, upon a stage.
Pentelic balconies give on the east;
The clouds are scrolled, bellied in apricot,
Adrift in pools of Scandinavian blue.
Light crisps the terraces of dolomite.
Enter The Prologue, who at once declares,
"We begin with the supreme donnée, the word."

In the ancient trope of the *liber naturae*, a nod in the direction of Shelley's autumnal leaves, Hecht moves away from the visual and musical
arts upon which he concentrated earlier. Now his matter is entirely

literary: both the private act of reading and the public one of attending to a performance. With the least insistent allusiveness he evokes Shakespeare, Wordsworth ("the very world of all of us, wherein / We find our happiness or not at all"), Eliot (part 5 of *Ash Wednesday* for the "word"/"world" play) and Stevens's scholar of the single candle.

Hecht is not normally an allusive poet, so the referential density here calls a greater attention to itself than it might if written by a more assiduous borrower. His ploy is didactically mimetic: by doubling and redoubling, Hecht embeds others' words within his own, literally containing the truths of the opening and closing lines, themselves a virtually rhymed couplet that calls attention to the similarity of "world" and "word." Since a single phoneme is all that enforces the difference between world and word, we can hear both the absoluteness of nonidentity and the similitudes effected by the rhyme. What, the poem prompts us to ask, is text, and what is commentary? By appropriating Eliot, Shakespeare, Shelley, Stevens, and Wordsworth to himself, has Hecht commented upon their words with his own? Or does his revision (an echo or allusion is not, after all, a repetition but a reminder) constitute a new, original text?[9] We find Auden's distinction between primary and secondary worlds is updated and possibly undone when at the poem's end we return to two beginnings: that of the stanza and that of the Gospel of John, itself of course a commentary upon that still earlier text in Genesis that elaborates on the relation between word and world.[10] That it is a Prologue who enters to deliver what is also a conclusion repeats the earlier lesson that in the end the scholar returns to the freshness of the (perhaps earliest) world, itself now a glittering dawn but an enacted one. At the last, in the circularity of method, the snaking back within itself of a poem that has been based upon successive polarities, Hecht undoes the very doublings he has also successfully exhibited. As he ended the first part of the poem by holding before him a photograph that is in part a mirror, so he ends the whole with a doubling that also mirrors a point of origin. The "pentelic balconies" echo and reflect, with variation, the "Parian arm" of the Discus Thrower, making the poem an even greater system of correspondences and encirclings.

Hecht's methods as a poet-teacher distinguish him by degree from others often classified as formalists or wits, poets in the line of Auden reaching back to Ben Jonson. For one thing, he is seldom witty in the way Nemerov and Merrill are, for whom puns are irresistible even though never merely ornamental. For another, the persistently somber tone registered by glances or even hard stares at scenes of sadism and cruelty, and at the fundamental moral status of the universe, encourages us to think of him as one of the sages, though hardly ancient, of the nineteenth-century didactic tradition. And finally, though his volumes contain sparkling descriptive (what might be called "purely lyric") poems (in *MSS* alone, "An Autumnal Retreat," "Sestina d'Inverno," and "The Lull" stand out), it is those in which the didactic impulse speaks most clearly that one hears Hecht's most authentic, because strangest, voice, a worldly, inquisitive one, asking God to justify evil and seeking to instruct the reader in the collective moral ambiguities of the world and its human inhabitants.

Allen Ginsberg has been a thorny presence in American culture for thirty years. Reading the *Collected Poems*,[11] which is freighted with a good deal of annotation to its topical and personal references, one feels one is witnessing the history of an age as much as of an individual. No one since Whitman has taken upon himself such a close identification of self with society, detailing its history, landscape, and politics as well as his own place within or without. Journalism and poetry have never been joined so closely as in these pages. What one reads is not just the notes of an observer, alternately anguished, desperate, satiric, fantastic, hectoring, tender, elegiac, and funny, but the mirror of American life in the atomic age. Ginsberg has had as little trouble getting headlines into his poetry, indeed sometimes making his poetry *out of* headlines, newsflashes, captions, even cartoon figures, as he has had in getting his name into the headlines.

But this most visible, most "public" of poets is also the most marginal. As a Jew and a homosexual, he shares a double distinction according to Susan Sontag's formulaic appraisal of our collective sensibility. Helen Vendler has already called him quadruply an outsider, given his political sympathies and his psychiatric experiences in addition to his sexual and religious eccentricities.[12] And yet, reading Ginsberg's work, the quantity of which exceeds its quality (rather like that of Byron, another figure of exuberant excess), one gets a picture of what America was like during a crucial period of its history. Reading Ginsberg is like sitting at a microfilm machine quickly going through forty years' worth of the news, only it is more moving, comic, and instructive. Allen Ginsberg, the dharma clown on the soapbox, a borscht belt comedian masquerading as Uncle Sam, turns out to be both the observant, paranoid outsider and the mythic voice of America itself:

> I have mystical visions and cosmic vibrations.
> America I still haven't told you what you did to Uncle Max
>    after he came over from Russia.

I'm addressing you.
Are you going to let your emotional life be run by Time
  Magazine?
I'm obsessed by Time Magazine.
I read it every week.
Its cover stares at me every time I slink past the corner
  candystore.
I read it in the basement of the Berkeley Public Library.
It's always telling me about responsibility. Businessmen are
  serious. Movie producers are serious. Everybody's serious but
  me.
It occurs to me that I am America.
I am talking to myself again.

("America," *CP*, 146–47)

In this 1956 poem one hears the blending of outsider and insider,
paranoia and fist shaking, pathos and high comedy, social commentary and personal confession, that leads at last to a populist fervor:

America this is quite serious.
America this is the impression I get from looking in the
  television set.
America is this correct?
I'd better get right down to the job.
It's true I don't want to join the Army or turn lathes in
  precision parts factories, I'm nearsighted and psychopathic
  anyway.
America I'm putting my queer shoulder to the wheel.

(148)

Looking at himself and his country, Allen Ginsberg finds that they are
sometimes antagonists, sometimes mirror images.

From *Howl* onward Ginsberg's poetry has developed techniques for
teaching that include a full measure of jokes and harangues. Like any
good teacher, he has been willing to make a fool of himself in order
to get his audience's attention and then to encourage them to learn
and profit from his example. For all the bulk of Ginsberg's poetry, it
is hardly ponderous. As a didactic performer, he has preferred confrontation to explanation, hammering to subtlety, repetition to variation. Where Hecht exemplifies, and Pinsky expatiates, Ginsberg exclaims: unlike his sometime rival and Columbia chum John Hollander,
he uses more exclamation points than question marks. His punctuation, like his grammar, gives one clues to the effectiveness and effects

of the poetry: staccato in rhythm, often verbless, it blurts, stabs, or chants, depending on the speaker's variable moods. Forceful, not subtle, immediate rather than meditative, the poetry itself suggests one reason for its author's popularity: it is a performance, even in its appearance on the page.

Vendler identifies Ginsberg's three characteristic flaws as a too-topical journalism, sexual bathos, and a simpleminded populism. I propose as the positive counters to these flaws the very things that constitute his uniqueness as a poet-teacher: an attention to the mundane reality of the public sphere (i.e., his poetry conceived in its totality as *Planet News*); a willingness to display the self, in its pathetic or lurid vulnerability, in order to awaken in his audience a sensitivity to the attractions and deceptions of the flesh; and a Whitmanesque identification of the singer with the subjects, scenes, and audience of his song. In Ginsberg one sees the man who suffered and was there; one joins him in that suffering, in those places. To change the frame of reference slightly: no one since Louis xiv has dared to say, as Ginsberg virtually does above, "l'état, c'est moi." The imperial self wears motley here; self-glorification comes through the Chaplinesque art of self-exposure. From his own worst fears (solitude, failure in love, political persecution) the performer on his tightrope makes of his vulnerability an offensive strategy to challenge his readers' complacencies.

In many ways, those aspects of Ginsberg that have put him so much in the public eye go against his poetic, or temperamental, grain. The ecological poet, the political poet, the public, performing, clowning poet came late and afterwards vied in Ginsberg's less flamboyant moments with an inner, elegiac voice. In 746 pages of Ginsberg's *Collected Poems*, the first authentic political questions appear on pages 64 and 65 ("A Poem on America," "After Dead Souls"), after an apprenticeship devoted to songs, both Blakean and loony, and to imitations of Dante and Marlowe (printed on pages 749–56 of the appendix). *Howl*, the seminal work, but not that of a young poet, begins on page 123; it has been prepared for a little in tone and subject, but its method, a sympathetic teacher's guide to the underworld, is something new. Even "Siesta in Xbalba" (97–110), the first long poem and a breakthrough in form and subject, is still largely personal until the end, which adumbrates the cultural differences between Mexico and the United States.

Ginsberg constantly depends on twin sources of power, public and private (as in "At Apollinaire's Grave," 180), and his strictly personal meditations make up the bulk, but also the best part, of his oeuvre. Looking back on the subject of his famous visionary moment—reading

Blake in East Harlem in 1948 ("Psalm IV," 238)—he provides not only a reminiscence of his ever-receding source of primal energy but also a tacit explanation of all subsequent attempts to regain a power that suffers the Wordsworthian fate of fading into the common day. So much of the poetry from *The Fall of America* (1973) onward laments loss—of sexual potency, of friends, of prophetic zeal—that one might easily think of Ginsberg as primarily a poet in the elegiac tradition of all the English Romantics *except* Blake. In his fifties, throughout most of *Plutonium Ode* (1982), he finds his poetic subjects largely in deprivation: "Don't Grow Old" (*CP*, 710), a recollection of his father; "Maybe Love" (723), the pathos of gay old age; "Reflections on Lake Louise" (733), as he worries about the afternoon of sudden death ("If I had a heart attack on the path around the lake would I be ready to face my mother?").

As an elegist and as a purely descriptive poet, in parts of *The Fall of America*, Ginsberg merits comparison with Lowell, Warren, and Ammons. What earns him a place in a study of didacticism is his constant development and manipulation of the tricks of the teacher's trade, which he uses more shamelessly than any of his contemporaries. Sometimes he's a Jewish mother, giving unsought for advice ("Who to Be Kind to," *CP*, 359); sometimes a stand-up comic, trying a shtick ("This Form of Life Needs Sex," *CP*, 284), in his case the perpetually pathetic comedy of a vow to enjoy heterosexuality even when his heart's not in it ("You can fuck a statue but you can't have children"); sometimes a mock-preacher:

> O brothers of the Laurel
> Is the world real?
> Is the Laurel
> a joke or a crown of thorns?—
>
> Fast, pass
> up the ass
> Down I go
> Cometh Woe
> ("I Beg You Come Back & Be Cheerful," *CP*, 236)

The main source of his teacherly power is a simultaneous identification with America—his subject and his audience—and a sense of alienation from it. Thus, on the one hand, the Whitmanesque exuberance of "America," quoted above, and his strong claim, "I will haunt these States" (*CP*, 460), and, on the other, the familiarity with the abyss, sometimes comic—"What do I have to lose if America fails? / My body?

My neck? My personality?"—and sometimes rueful—"too late for laments / too late for warning— / I'm a stranger alone in my my country again" (445).

In the *Phaedrus* Plato first proposed the erotic energy of pedagogy. A good teacher loves his students and is willing to punish or criticize them, as a parent would, for their own good. At the same time that he is becoming a Yeatsian smiling public man, an embodiment of wisdom, the teacher is gradually cut off from the age and sexual potency of his students. This discrepancy explains the double attitude of Ginsberg to his audience. It also begins to explain the particular combination of educational methods, some of which he shares with other poets discussed in this book, that he uses in his combined harangue, assault, and admonition of that audience. For Ginsberg, prophecy takes the place of statement, and the voice of one crying in the wilderness is, above all, a voice. One can place Ginsberg at one end of a linguistic spectrum the other end of which John Ashbery occupies: Ginsberg's poetry is all *voice*—that is, it is capable of being *heard*, even when read from the page, as the words of a real, fully emotional speaker. Ashbery's, on the other hand (this partly explains his absence from these pages: even though so much of his poetry seems mock-didactic, discursive in the sense of wandering, one can never readily identify a speaker) is *lisible*, but never audible. The teacher has disappeared behind the screen of the page, from which he never truly emerges. Ginsberg's is a poetry of presence: one is instructed by a human teacher rather than, as in Ashbery's work, the equivalent of a teaching machine in a laboratory.

Ginsberg possesses two gifts undeniably useful to poets and teachers: a large vocabulary, which extends through technical matters in many areas, and an attention to a wide range of subjects (history, politics, chemistry, physics, psychology, religion). His is more often a poetry of specificity than of generalization. He neither makes aphorisms, quotable nuggets of wisdom of the sort that Auden or Nemerov might leave one with, nor speculates on larger abstractions, like Ammons or Merrill in his trilogy. "The Ignu" (*CP*, 203), an uncharacteristic poem, stands out in his work as a strange attempt to define something. The specificity of his poetry explains its learnedness, its annotatability, and its reliance on lists as a formal, and didactic, principle.

Sometimes the list dramatizes the seemingly aleatory nature of our world. The poem strings together random objets trouvés in which one sees evidence of the richness or banality of civilization. "Junk Mail" (*CP*, 657) proceeds formulaically from "I received in mail," and builds to a catalogue of political, social, charitable requests for money from all over (*Monthly Review*, American Friends Service Committee, the sons of Julius and Ethel Rosenberg, United Farm Workers of America, the NYU Gay Peoples Union, *Energy and Evolution Quarterly*), all, according to the precise dating of his collected poems, "opened midnight, New York, September 4, 1976." The printed garbage of our civilization collectively reflects the manifold richness and dilemmas of our society. Amid the chaotic specificity, a personal note seems to intrude toward the center: "Give Poets & Writers' CODA to a friend      subscribe United Nations Childrens' Fund      severe malnutrition      Starvation faces 400 to 500 million children poorer countries. Dwarfism / disease blindness mental retardation stunted growth crop failures drought flood      exhausted wheat rice reserves skyrocketing fuel costs      fertilizer shortages      Desperately need your help." Something whackily comic arises from the pathos here: the famous single-breath lines, sped up for articulation, inundate us, just as we are overwhelmed by the junk mail we daily receive, ignore, and discard. Ginsberg's poetic method calls attention with cool factuality to the greatest international disasters, combined with those normal human appeals made out of self-interest or venality: the buildup, as in the lines above, leads to a sigh or a giggle of relief. A second climax comes, appropriately, at the end, signalling the not-so-random development of this list: "Dear Citizen of the World: First days explosion bomb radioactivity starve Ozone layer? Isn't it time we did some thing? / 1) Send cooperators ten addresses w/ zip codes 2) Mail friends endorsement 3) Write your Congressman President Newspaper editor & Presidential Candidate. / As a final move, the World Authority would destroy all Nuclear Weapons." From an innocent, apparently random accumulation of requests, Ginsberg builds to a premonition, or admonition, of nuclear holocaust and its possible aversion.

So, too, what appears to be an improvised set of variations, a rap poem, so to speak, "Hadda Be Playing on the Jukebox" (*CP*, 635), begins with a neutral formula and expands to a denunciation of organized crime and its connections to national politics, then to an incantation about American involvement in foreign affairs ("Hadda be Capitalism the Vortex of this rage") to a final vision of international mayhem:

> Hadda be rich, hadda be powerful, hadda hire technology from
>   Harvard
> Hadda murder in Indonesia 500,000
> Hadda murder in Indochina 2,000,000
> Hadda murder in Czechoslovakia

> Hadda murder in Chile
> Hadda murder in Russia
> Hadda murder in America

There is method in Ginsberg's seemingly mad technique, whether he wishes to build a performance outward in ever larger circles of denunciation and political protest, as here, or to force one to experience the plenty of the universe through its iteration, as in "Graffiti 12th Cubicle Men's Room Syracuse Airport" (*CP*, 535), which includes want ads for sex, political pronunciamentos, opinions addressed to no one in particular (and therefore to everyone), the formula for LSD, and so forth. Not even Whitman catalogued America's richness by examining the sites of its elimination.

The principal stylistic effect of Ginsberg's populism is the inclusion of large quantities of detail in his poetry. His language is the most specific of any contemporary poet's in topicality, numbers of proper names, and references to current affairs. Yet his nonfactual diction is often so unfocused that one has the discomforting experience of reading names of people one recognizes in verbal situations that are totally banal. This is the only *Collected Poems* with a guide to the characters at the back, but even in a book that constantly proclaims its own topicality it is disheartening to come upon such journalese as in this passage:

> toward dusk ate marshmallows at the News Stand and drank
>   huge cold grape soda eyeing:
> this afternoon's *Journal* headline FBI IN HARLEM, what kind of
>   Nasty old Epic
> Afternoons I imagine!
>
> (347)

Ginsberg has always chosen what John Ashbery, in *Three Poems*, solemnly considers one alternative—"put[ting] it all down"—rather than leaving it all out. Such is the time-honored way in the American melting pot for all the ingredients the cook comes by. A neutral term for this tendency is all-inclusiveness. A positive one is generosity, and a negative one would be indiscriminateness. (Ginsberg shares the dilemma with Frank O'Hara and A. R. Ammons.) Just reading the list of magazines acknowledged at the end of the *Collected Poems* is an experience in Americanism. Going quite literally from A to Z (*Adventures in Poetry* to *Zero*), the places where Ginsberg's poems first appeared run the gamut from the established (the *New York Times*, the *New Yorker, Paris Review, Partisan Review*) to the ephemeral (*Bugger, Kuksu,*

*Yugen*). He has never, it seems, deprived any magazine of his bounty. One can tell whether such largesse constitutes a genuinely democratic poetics or results instead from laziness only with reference to individual texts, but in two adjacent poems, "Man's glory" and "Fragment: The Names II" (*CP*, 260–61), one experiences a clear visual and auditory testimony to the power of the list as both a catalogue of place names invoked religiously and an exercise in Ginsberg's ongoing collective elegy, which began with the first line of *Howl*, for friends dead or ruined.

There are two significant stylistic patterns in this cataloguing. Given the natural materialism of any list, it is no wonder that Ginsberg's poetry seems primarily an exercise in objects, nouns rather than verbs. The only subject that seems to inspire him to more than newsflashes or headlines is sex, and the very rhythm of buildup to orgasm is caught by the intensity and variation of repeated formulas slowly transformed ("Please master can I touch your cheek . . . ," 494). But for the most part the march of history is documented, frame by frame, item by item, and reduced by a technique of headline-writing to the status of newsflashes:

> N B C B S U P A P I N S L I F E
> > Time Mutual presents
> > > World's Largest Camp Comedy:
> > > > Magic In Vietnam—
> > reality turned inside out
> > > changing its sex in the Mass Media
> > > for 30 days, TV den and bedroom farce
> > Flashing pictures Senate Foreign Relations Committee room
> > > Generals faces flashing on and off screen
> > > > > > mouthing language
> > > State Secretary speaking nothing but language
> > > McNamara declining to speak public language
> > > > The President talking language,
> > > > > Senators reinterpreting language
> > > > General Taylor *Limited Objectives*
> > > > > > *Owls* from Pennsylvania
> > > > > Clark's Face *Open Ended*
> > > > > > Dove's *Apocalypse*
> > > > > > Morse's hairy ears
> > > > > > ("Wichita Vortex Sutra," *CP*, 401–2)

The ongoing, swirling syntax of passages like this works by accumulation and extension. It points to the second important aspect of Ginsberg's style: the way it tends, as Charles Molesworth has suggested, to the paratactic rather than the hypotactic.[13] His "non-subjugating syntax" has political analogies, of course, as Molesworth's phrase implies: to register everything equally is to do justice to both the random barrage of daily news that we all receive and the sense that our minds make of it. One law for the lion and the ox, said Blake, is oppression: Ginsberg wants to acknowledge the separate laws of individual creatures but also to control them by his own iteration.

In addition to reading Ginsberg's political radicalism into his poetic technique one can see his method as a rhetorical and didactic one. Sameness of iteration gives consistency and therefore potency to articulation. Teachers traditionally give examples of hypotheses as they assert ideas deductively. The nonordering of events in Ginsberg's vast diaries is only an apparent chaos: in reality his discrete items bombard singly and cumulatively with the subliminal force of headlines or the formulas of a soapbox orator who circles back to main points, always attacking from a slightly different point on a circumference. Thus the importance of the poem as an agglomerated performance, as he remarked in his *Paris Review* interview: "the poem *discovered* in the mind and in the process of writing it out on the page as notes, transcriptions."[14] The phrasing attests to a double allegiance, one to the mind as the repository of poetic truth, the other to the action of composing as the process of creation. The first suggests a quasi-Platonic notion of anamnesis, discovering something one wasn't formerly aware of knowing, in this case through the discipline of receptivity; the second values the process of writing, even if hallucinated, automatic, or random, as the means of preparing for a final truth that always lies beyond the poem's end. In authentically Jewish fashion, Ginsberg believes that poetic finality, like the messiah, is always *yet to come*. The forward-looking nature of his politics and his poetics is recorded by an apposite syntax of seemingly infinite sameness, but one that eschews both subordination and temporality in favor of a similar form for individual perceptions, and remarks that suggest simultaneity even as they move relentlessly onward.

"I propose that things in common are much more important than distinctions," Ginsberg responded to a student's question at a Berkeley seminar.[15] His haunting repetitions in lists, clauses without verbs, and chanted observations certainly support this belief. At the same time, his concern for the rich multiplicity of American life forces him to attend to its particularities, not its unity:

> I propounded a final question, and
>       heard a series of final answers.

What is God? for instance, asks the answer?
  And whatever else can the replier reply but reply?
Whatever the nature of mind, that
  the nature of *both* question and answer.

     & yet one wants to live
    in a *single* universe
        Does one?

Must it be one?
  Why, as with the Jews
  must the God be One?
   O what does
  the concept ONE mean?
   IT'S MAD!

   GOD IS ONE!

   IS X

   IS MEANINGLESS—

    ADONOI—

   IS A JOKE—

    THE HEBREWS ARE

   WRONG—(CRIST & BUDDA

   ATTEST, also wrongly!)

—What is One but Formation
    of mind?
  arbitrary madness! 6000 years
Spreading out in all directions simultaneously—
       ("Aether," *CP*, 249–50)

Whether he gives his primary allegiance to oneness or multeity (especially in his more desperate moods, e.g., "thinking America is a chaos," *CP*, 235), Ginsberg relies on his catalogues as the sole suitable mode for poetic instruction.

The daily news and the loony listings ("I prophesy . . . I prophesy . . . I prophesy," he exclaims in "Television Was a Baby Crawling Toward That Deathchamber," *CP*, 272) that Ginsberg has hurled at his audience for more than thirty years have turned out to be wonderfully accurate in their reflecting, reporting, and predicting of political reality. The unspecific, blanket condemnation in "War Profit Litany" reminds us that the military-industrial complex has always protected its own self-interests. Part of the charm of Ginsberg's egregious teaching technique is an unabashed hubris, which, as I've suggested, uses hyperbole to call attention to the deep truths of his social and political visions. Hear the voice of *this* Blakean bard, who present, past, and future sees:

> I want to be known as the most brilliant man in America
> Introduced to Gyalwa Karmapa heir of the Whispered
>    Transmission Crazy Wisdom Practice Lineage
> as the secret young wise man who visited him and winked
>    anonymously decade ago in Gangtok
> Prepared the way for Dharma in America without mentioning
>    Dharma—scribbled laughter
> Who saw Blake and abandoned God
> To whom the Messianic Fink sent messages darkest hour
>    sleeping on steel sheets "somewhere in the Federal Prison
>    system" Weathermen got no Moscow Gold
> who went backstage to Cecil Taylor serious chat chord structure
>    & Time in a nightclub
> who fucked a rose-lipped rock star in a tiny bedroom slum
>    watched by a statue of Vajrasattva—
> and overthrew the CIA with a silent thought—
>
> ("Ego Confession," *CP*, 623)

This "extraordinary ego . . . unafraid of its own self's spectre" wants "to be the spectacle of Poesy triumphant over trickery of the world. / . . . whose common sense astonished gaga Gurus and rich Artistes— / who called the Justice department and threaten'd to Blow the Whistle." Ginsberg's whimsy leads to the other source of his didactic power. For all his mystical leanings, experiments in consciousness, and otherworldly visions, Ginsberg is a thoroughly secular poet, one for whom the world is real. The greatest poverty, said Stevens, is not to live in the physical world. Ginsberg's materialism gives readers his voluminous lists, his headlines, his paratactic, sometimes verbless, incantations, and it also gives them his various *voices*, always distinctly his own.

Like James Merrill, whose experiments with tone have led him to otherworldly visitors (or them to him), Ginsberg ranges through different voices in a joint effort to create his own multiple self and to serve his performer's instinct to keep an audience awake. Fluctuations in tone are possible only in poets consciously in control of the principle of voice: the dramatic performances for which Ginsberg has become celebrated come naturally out of the drama invested within the multiple personae of the poems. His homage to Kenneth Koch, "Homework," shows his mastery of the language of television commercials, his global ecology, and his political energy:

> If I were doing my Laundry I'd wash my dirty Iran
> I'd throw in my United States, and pour on the Ivory Soap,
>    scrub up Africa, put all the birds and elephants back in the
>    jungle,
> I'd wash the Amazon river and clean the oily Carib & Gulf of
>    Mexico,
> Rub that smog off the North Pole, wipe up all the pipelines in
>    Alaska,
> Rub a dub dub for Rocky Flats and Los Alamos, Flush that
>    sparkly Cesium out of Love Canal
> Rinse down the Acid Rain over the Parthenon & Sphinx, Drain
>    the Sludge out of the Mediterranean basin & make it azure
>    again,
> Put some blueing back into the sky over the Rhine, bleach the
>    little Clouds so snow return white as snow,
> Cleanse the Hudson Thames & Neckar, Drain the Suds out of
>    Lake Erie
> Then I'd throw big Asia in one giant Load & wash out the
>    blood & Agent Orange,
> Dump the whole mess of Russia and China in the wringer,
>    squeeze out the tattletail Gray of U.S. Central American police
>    state,
> & put the planet in the drier & let it sit 20 minutes or an Aeon
>    till it came out clean.
>
>                                                         (*CP*, 731)

The poem displays a playful insouciance in its central conceit (one of the few poems in which Ginsberg maintains such a consistency), a canny reinvigoration of childish cliché ("so snow return white as snow"), some seemingly accidental rhetorical devices (the zeugma in "blood & Agent Orange" and "let it sit 20 minutes or an Aeon," the asyndeton that gathers rivers into a single corporate entity ["Hudson Thames & Neckar"]), and the naive hopefulness of its political faith. Few poets (Blake, of course; Whitman sometimes) can create a successful song of innocence, but the political naiveté of "Homework" is produced by a cagey fox who knows how to trick his prey. Although a full catalogue of Ginsberg's masks or tones would require almost as many pages as his own work, I'd like to make a brief survey of the field, pointing out the pedagogic vigor behind the poetic voices.

In poems with titles like "Ego Confession" (*CP*, 623), "Manifesto" ("Let me say beginning I don't believe in Soul," *CP*, 617), "This Is About Death" (35), "I Beg You Come Back & Be Cheerful" (235), "Understand That This Is a Dream" (303), "A Vow" (460), "After Thoughts" (536), "What I'd Like to Do" (602), Ginsberg announces personal credos with straightforward immediacy. The poetry seems to hold nothing back. In his best poems, like "My Sad Self" (201), the visionary catalogue becomes a lesson, the private becomes public, owing to the deft handling of both topicality and tonal inflection (not for nothing does this poem pay homage to Frank O'Hara). For all his historical goofiness, Ginsberg is often, movingly, a melancholic. The poem begins with a formulaic statement as old as Shakespeare's sonnets ("When . . . then"), but the vertical movement of the first stanza promises the poet's mortality rather than his salvation:

> Sometimes when my eyes are red
> I go up on top of the RCA Building
>             and gaze at my world, Manhattan—
>                     my buildings, streets I've done feats in,
>                         lofts, beds, coldwater flats
> —on Fifth Ave below which I also bear in mind,
>                     its ant cars, little yellow taxis, men
>                         walking the size of specks of wool—
>         Panorama of the bridges, sunrise over Brooklyn machine,
>                     sun go down over New Jersey where I was born
>                         & Paterson where I played with ants—
> my later loves on 15th Street,
>                 my greater loves of Lower East Side,
>                     my once fabulous amours in the Bronx
>                             faraway—
>         paths crossing in these hidden streets,
>                 my history summed up, my absences
>                     and ecstasies in Harlem—
>             —sun shining down on all I own
>                 in one eyeblink to the horizon
>                 in my last eternity—
>                             matter is water.
>
>                                         (201)

This is a poetry of statement, which registers emotions through the nuance of a heroic vocabulary ("streets I've done feats in," "my later loves . . . my greater loves," "absences and ecstasies") that leads to a thought reminiscent of Keats's embittered self-epitaph ("Here lies one whose name was writ in water").

Thence begin the solitary musings of the walker in the city, "staring into all man's / plateglass, faces," looking for reflection and original response, tamely going home to dinner, experiencing tears but no desire, "confused by the spectacle around me." The liquid movement of meaningless activity ("Man, woman, streaming over the pavements") conduces to a vision of a personal and final end:

> And all these streets leading
> so crosswise, honking, lengthily,
> by avenues
> stalked by high buildings or crusted into slums
> thru such halting traffic
> screaming cars and engines
> so painfully to this
> countryside, this graveyard
> this stillness
> on deathbed or mountain
> once seen
> never regained or desired
> in the mind to come
> where all Manhattan that I've seen must disappear.
> (202)

This is the elegiac, quiet Ginsberg, still imitating the rhythms of Williams and sounding the depths of a personal sorrow that he makes universal by releasing it from individuality (the RCA building, "all the details of *my* world") to the generality of unspecified sadness: "this countryside, this graveyard, this stillness" becomes "deathbed or mountain" without articles, and a metonymy for any person's past experiences in time or space.

Even when sedate, Ginsberg usually sounds more volatile than he does in "My Sad Self," but this melancholy contemplation dramatizes his mastery of minute calibrations in tone, allowing him to refer to ordinary events as heroic, romantic, banal, and expansive, by turn. One can find similar fluctuations—louder, more public ones—in those poems to be delivered from the symbolic podium upon which Ginsberg as teacher-preacher so often mounts. "What I'd Like to Do" (*CP*, 602), for example, takes the simple form of a series of wishes and resolutions, randomly arranged and including the topoi of retirement from the world, poetic composition, logical paradoxes ("step in same river twice"), and sexual activity interspersed with sexual abnegation, but it ends with a lyrical softness unpredicted by any previous tone or the poem's containing form:

> Chant into electric microphones, pacify Rock, enrich
> skull emptiness with vocal salami taxicabs, magnetize nervous
>     systems,
> destroy Empire State's dead Life Time smog,
> Masturbate in peace, haunt ancient cities for boys, practice
>     years of chastity, save Jewels for God my own ruddy body,
>     hairy delicate antennae
> Vegetable, eat carrots, fork cabbage, spoon peas, fry potatoes,
>     boil beets, ox forgiven, pig forgotten, hot dogs banished from
>     celestial realms cloud-roofed over Kitkitdizze's green spring
>     weeds—milk, angel-Milk
> Read Dostoyevsky's Brothers Karamazov I laid down half-
>     finished a dozen times decades ago
> Compose last choirs of Innocence & Experience, set music to
>     tongues of Rossetti Mss. orchestrate Jerusalem's quatrains—
> War's over, soft mat wood floor, flower vase on inkstand, blue
>     oaks gazing in the window.

From the mundane (finishing a great book one has always resolved to get through) to the heroic, from the surreal ("vocal salami taxicabs") to the self-improving, the resolutions end in the calm finality of stasis: objects arranged as for a still-life, and no verbs, no selfhood. "Effort and expectation and desire," Wordsworth's phrase for our being's heart and home, is relinquished in favor of the passivity of mere being, as the scene and the dreaming speaker settle squarely *into* this world but pass for the moment beyond it as well. Out of Ginsberg's whackiness there emerge moments of such transcendence, announced as here by the absence of tone, of volition, and of passion.

In heightening his tone by paradoxically eliminating it, Ginsberg here reminds us of his debt to Williams, to American imagism, and to the orientalism he shares with Gary Snyder. These lines provide an unusual quiet moment in Ginsberg's otherwise noisy poetry. Reading him is like riding a roller coaster—always moving, and moving rapidly at that. The man crowned May King in Prague has also written some of the major elegies of the past thirty years; public performance and private regret are the two sides of Ginsberg's poetic ritual. Likewise, paranoia and aggressive silliness go hand in hand; as in a drugged haze he first imagines "police clog the streets with their anxiety" and then his own explosive response:

Tear gas! Dynamite! Mustaches!
I'll grow a beard and carry lovely
        bombs,
I will destroy the world, slip in between
          the cracks of death
      And change the Universe—Ha!
I have the secret, I carry
        Subversive salami in
           my ragged briefcase
"Garlic, Poverty, a will to Heaven,"
    a strange dream in my meat:
("I Beg You Come Back & Be Cheerful," *CP*, 235–36)

The radical as burlesque comic, the lunatic who speaks truth: Ginsberg assumes whatever momentary mask will keep his audience's attention, and his own antic disposition hammers home mad claims that contain nuggets of wisdom:

Here I am—Old Betty Boop whoopsing behind the skull-
    microphone wondering what Idiot soap opera horror show we
    broadcast by Mistake—full of communists and frankenstein
    cops and
mature capitalists running the State Department and the
    Daily News Editorial hypnotizing millions of legional-eyed
    detectives to commit mass murder on the Invisible
which is only a bunch of women weeping hidden behind
    newspapers in the Andes, conspired against by Standard Oil,
which is a big fat fairy monopolizing all Being that has form'd it
    self to Oil,
and nothing gets in its way so it grabs different oils in all poor
    mystic aboriginal Principalities too weak to
Screech out over the radio that Standard Oil is a bunch of
    spying Businessmen intent on building one Standard Oil in
    the whole universe like an egotistical cancer
and yell on Television to England to watch out for United
    Fruits they got Central America by the balls
nobody but them can talk San Salvador, they run big
    Guatemala puppet armies, gas Dictators, they're the Crown of
    Thorns
upon the Consciousness of poor Christ-indian Central America,
    and the Pharisees are US Congress & Publicans is the
    American People

who have driven righteous bearded faithful pink new Castro
1961 is he mad? who knows—Hope for him, he stay true
& his wormy 45-year dying peasants teach Death's beauty sugar
beyond politics, build iron children schools
for alphabet molecule stars, that mystic history & giggling
revolution henceforth no toothless martrys be memorized by
some pubescent Juan who'll smoke my marihuana—
Turn the Teacher on!

> ("Television Was a Baby Crawling Toward That
> Deathchamber," *CP*, 274–75)

The repetitiveness within and among his poems proves Ginsberg's willingness to forego originality in favor of the reiteration of important lessons. It may well be that a native American naiveté, a hopefulness inherited from Thoreau and at least one aspect of Emerson, has inspired a greater degree of what I have labeled didacticism among American poets than among those of other nations. The Shelleyan mantle of legislation sits more comfortably on American than on British shoulders; combined with a sense of daily renewal and rebirth, this prophesying instinct keeps Ginsberg confident and public throughout a career and in spite of a disposition that might otherwise tend in the direction of the elegiac and the introspective. At the end of "The Change: *Kyoto-Tokyo Express*," a litany of hellish visions and Boschian political vignettes, Ginsberg commits himself to return and rebirth. In such imaging resides endless potential:

> From this single
> birth reborn that I am
> to be so—
>
> My own Identity now nameless
> neither man nor dragon or
> God
>
> but the dreaming Me full
> of physical rays' tender
> red moons in my belly &
> Stars in my eyes circling
>
> And the Sun the Sun the
> Sun my visible father
> making my body visible
> thru my eyes!
>
> (330)

This ending of *Planet News* (1963) prepares Ginsberg for a return to America (after *King of May* in 1965, the subsequent volumes that begin with *The Fall of America* [1973] are primarily local). Despite his travels and his experiments with foreign philosophies, religions, and medicines, Ginsberg remains a distinctly homegrown product. For all the explicit topicality of his poetry, its references to public issues and personalities, it remains an unorganized work, never building to a philosophical system or to anything more than momentary statements of faith. Ginsberg does not tell stories or use parables, like Hecht or John Hollander, because he has little sense of what they might stand *for*. Richly imagistic, the poetry is almost bereft of metaphor: "Things are symbols of themselves" he boldly announces on the title page. As a teacher, Ginsberg does not explain, and turns aside from the ardors of expatiation because he lacks the linear, discursive tendency that explanation demands. Nor does the Aristotelian frame of narrative suit a speaker who finds beginnings and endings equally problematic.

Instead, in Ginsberg are acts of circling and of repetition—statement, harangue, kvetching, comic self-exposure, proclamation—that assault, implore, berate, excite, surprise, confuse, tease, amuse, and charm in a dizzying kaleidoscope of tones. As a teacher Ginsberg is a prophet of a post-McLuhan age who knows how to barrage readers with multiple images, whole armies of them. No other poet has so richly, if bizarrely, inherited Whitman's seigneurial copiousness.

The voice of moral outrage with which Ginsberg has been long associated, and which comes one might say by right to a twentieth-century Jeremiah, is heard nowhere more stridently and authentically than in "Howl," the seminal poem, the controversy over which virtually assured its notorious success. It is more clearly structured than anything else in Ginsberg: the brilliant, and longest, first part that derives from the opening proposition ("I saw the best minds of my generation destroyed by madness"), then a series of relative clauses meant to picture, through aggregation, those "angelheaded hipsters . . . who" fill its pages; the second and third parts, shorter and apostrophic, addressed to Moloch as the symbolic representation of nightmare, machinery, and deadly mechanization, and then to Carl Solomon, the human prisoner incarcerated, as the speaker's double, in the Rockland asylum; the appended "Footnote to Howl," a series of exclaimed "Holy! Holy! Holy!"s as benediction and antidote to all that has gone before.

"Howl" (126–33) diagnoses a condition first by defining it. What did the best minds of his generation do? They . . . "bared their brains to Heaven under the El . . . passed through universities with radiant cool eyes . . . studied Plotinus Poe St. John of the Cross telepathy and bop kabbalah . . . threw their watches off the roof to cast their ballot for Eternity . . . " and so on. Next "Howl" explains its cause: "What sphinx of cement and aluminum bashed open their skulls and ate up their brains and imagination? / Moloch! Solitude! Filth! Ugliness! Ashcans and unobtainable dollars!" For all its obvious debt to Blake, Williams, and Whitman (one may construe the whole first section as Ginsberg's catalogue equivalent to "I hear American singing"), "Howl" is an Ovidian fable both in its overall scheme of providing an etiology of a current state of affairs and in its incidental, smaller details that often look like surrealistic metamorphoses ("who faded out in vast sordid movies, were shifted in dreams, woke on a sudden Manhattan, and picked themselves up out of basements").

A walker in the city, Ginsberg everywhere *marks*, as Blake does in London, the conditions of madness, poverty and deprivation, and their mental causes as well as effects: "Moloch whose name is the Mind!" Looking like a diagnosis of a problem by a witness, the poem turns out to be a sympathetic insider's view as well. Ginsberg, as perennial "beat" outsider, is very much *of* the landscape he surveys, and his acts of sympathetic identification with Carl Solomon fill the entire third section ("I'm with you in Rockland where . . ."); they also begin with the title and dedication, which ask to be read as a verbal command: "Howl for Carl Solomon," administered and then obeyed by the single speaker who proceeds with his observations in response to his own imperative. From observation to sympathy is one kind of didactic movement. Adrienne Rich remarks that unless the teacher is in love with the mind of the student he is practicing rape.[16] Ginsberg allows eroticism to blossom in "Howl" through such empathy ("ah Carl, while you are not safe I am not safe, and now you're really in the total animal soup of time"), especially in the endings to the three sections, which break through the stylistic and emotional boundaries that the opening incantations have defined.

The first section interrupts its chronicling by addressing Carl Solomon in the impassioned, sympathetic remark quoted above, and winds to an end by equating the daring of artistic innovation with the sacrifice of Christ: breaking through a syntax that has remained fairly consistent ("who . . . ," etc.), the speaker now sacrifices himself, his subject, and his poem, on the rood of American civilization. Ginsberg has called the end of the section "an homage to art but also in specific terms an homage to Cezanne's method." [17] His effort "to recreate the syntax and measure of poor human prose and stand before you speechless and intelligent and shaking with shame" at last deifies him, "the madman bum and angel beat in Time," and he

> rose reincarnate in the ghostly clothes of jazz in the goldhorn
> shadow of the band and blew the suffering of America's
> naked mind for love into an eli eli lamma lamma sabacthani
> saxophone cry that shivered the cities down to the last radio
> with the absolute heart of the poem of life butchered out of
> their own bodies good to eat a thousand years.
>
> (131)

From such desperate annihilation, of self and of society, comes the hope of redemption, proffered here through the Christian allusion and the half-zany radio jingle quality ("good to eat") of the final image. The change in tone and syntax at the conclusion also dramatically corresponds to the multiplicity of identity (Ginsberg as Carl Solomon, the victim as the savior, the Jew as Christ, the prisoner as saint) that Ginsberg has made a distinctive theme.

As the first section transgresses its own syntax at the end, reaching a momentary climax, so do the second and third parts. The exclamations to a Moloch who embodies the poverty, oppressiveness, and industrial wastes of modern life give way to a release from the oppression of the very apostrophes as Ginsberg envisions an apocalyptic escape from Moloch's juggernaut. What seems like the destruction of the American dream turns out to be the cause of its realization:

> Visions! omens! hallucinations! miracles! ecstasies! gone down
> the American river!
> Dreams! adorations! illuminations! religions! the whole
> boatload of sensitive bullshit!
> Breakthroughs! over the river! flips and crucifixions! gone
> down the flood! Highs! Epiphanies! Despairs! Ten years'
> animal screams and suicides! Minds! New loves! Mad
> generation! down on the rocks of Time!
> Real holy laughter in the river! They saw it all! the wild eyes!
> the holy yells! They bade farewell! They jumped off the roof!
> to solitude! waving! carrying flowers! Down to the river! into
> the street!
>
> (132)

The verse enacts the movement from confinement to release by replacing the apostrophic responses to the horrifying opening question ("What sphinx of cement and aluminum bashed open their skulls? . . . Moloch!") with new exclamations of mad visionary fulfillment. The pattern of syntactic transformation becomes, in other words, a didactic model for the psychological and social changes the revolutionary speaker urges upon his readers.

Excluding the "Footnote to Howl," written (or at least dated) before the completion of the entire poem and containing a litany of praise that incorporates the heterogeneous and heterodox reality of Ginsberg's world, one may hear in the end of the poem's third section its true climax, one that confirms the pattern of repetition followed by the sudden undermining of syntax and tone in the earlier parts. Having identified with Carl Solomon ("I'm with you in Rockland") seventeen times, Ginsberg begins his release from confinement in the antepenultimate line with an antic response to his country:

> I'm with you in Rockland
>> where we hug and kiss the United States under our
>> bedsheets the United States that coughs all night and
>> won't let us sleep

(133)

Overwhelming the enemy, subduing him in a comic assault, the two prisoners can now release themselves from their mental, almost Blakean, imprisonment:

> I'm with you in Rockland
>> where we wake up electrifed out of the coma by our
>> own souls' airplanes roaring over the roof they've come
>> to drop angelic bombs the hospital illuminates
>> itself    imaginary walls collapse    O skinny legions
>> run outside    O starry-spangled shock of mercy the
>> eternal war is here    O victory forget your underwear
>> we're free

The climax submits itself to a final revision, however, and is succeeded by a sad statement of separation, as Ginsberg's elegiac temperament overwhelms his hopeful, revolutionary zeal and restores him (and readers) to a painful awakening:

> I'm with you in Rockland
>> in my dreams you walk dripping from a sea-journey on
>> the highway across America in tears to the door of my
>> cottage in the Western night

(133)

In this anticlimactic dream one sees Ginsberg's true acknowledgement of a plight that is both separate and shared. One also sees the twin

halves of his poetic personality—the ecstatic and the elegiac—that together have served him from his first utterances to his latest. Our fun-
niest poetic teacher may also be our saddest.

In chapter 18 of the *Biographia Literaria* Coleridge borrows William
Browne's epithet for his Elizabethan contemporary Samuel Daniel—
"well-languaged"—and applies it to Wordsworth, whom, several chapters later, he praises for the "weight and sanity of the thoughts and
sentiments [won] from the poet's own meditative observation." Like
Daniel, says Coleridge, Wordsworth writes in "that style which, as the
neutral ground of prose and verse, is common to both."[18] The *neutral-
ity* of a poetic language that seems to hide rather than to flaunt its
figurations might be the apt choice for a poet more interested in
weight and sanity, in meditation and moral observation, than in the
"memorabilia of the mystic spouts" that Stevens claims "the fops of
fancy in their poems leave" ("Le Monocle de Mon Oncle"). Robert Pinsky belongs among those whose language, while obeying the idiomatic
rules of their own age, is intelligible beyond the fashions of a given
time. Like others in the line of the poet-critic, Pinsky has been interested equally in the creation and the analysis of poetry. His two critical
books complement his three volumes of verse in style and moral purpose: each half of his output illuminates the other. In both the poetry
and the criticism there abides a unity, of which the principal ingredients are ethical ambition, sanity, a sense of humor overlaying an elegiac ground, and above all, something to say. The criticism is intelligent but not pedantic; the poetry is lucid and meditative but not
prosaic. Although he seldom writes epigrams, Pinsky often writes ep-
igrammatically and, like Landor (the subject of his first, Wintersian
book), he has "a special sense of what an occasion is." Part of his artistic
credo, again like Landor's, "is the attractive serenity acquired by fact,
even the most passionate fact, as it moves into oblivious time."[19]

Among Pinsky's three volumes of poetry, the first two are more cen-
trally located in the tradition of Jewish ethical seriousness than the
third, which tests new strategies of presenting elegy in short, lyric
structures (although the title poem, "History of My Heart," maintains
Pinsky's ongoing effort to think in larger, in this case narrative, terms).
*Sadness and Happiness* (1975) and *An Explanation of America* (1979) reveal the ethical nature of Pinsky's meditations, his inheritance of a Horatian sanity that, unlike that of Auden and Nemerov, looks soberly at
personal and civic realities but without the reassuring defenses of verbal wit.[20]

The title poem in *Sadness and Happiness* epitomizes Pinsky's instincts for generalization based on specific evidence, for the lure of abstraction, and for the intellectual's compulsion to move outward from a personal center to larger peripheries. His tone, like Nemerov's, owes something to the secular skepticism of Montaigne, which encourages him first to make, and then to qualify, the abstractions that are a professor's goal, temptation and undoing. Although one may speak of "sadness" and "happiness" as opposites, he says, there exist predominantly gray middle states of desire, and the lines between categories always blur under close scrutiny. In spite of efforts to measure the opposing qualities, they become, in memory, surprisingly indistinguishable: "the strangely / happy fondling" of past failures, or the speaker's realization of "how happy I would be, or else / decently sad, with no past."

Almost as a corollary to his focus on what Pope labelled "the isthmus of a middle state" of our human condition, Pinsky has devised a "middle" style for his thirteen-part poem. A sinuous syntax elaborates and encompasses his mental meanderings and definitions. These sentences maintain the illusion of fluent, meditative speed, while they keep the poem close (as do the short lines) to the tightness of Landor and Ben Jonson. Here, for example, are the closing quatrains:

> It is intolerable
> to think of my daughters, too, dust—
> *el polvo*—or you whose invented game,
> Sadness and Happiness, soothes them
>
> to sleep: can you tell me one sad
> thing that happened today, Can you think
> of one happy thing to tell me that
> happened to you today, organizing
>
> life—not you too dust like the poets,
> dancers, athletes, their dear skills
> and the alleged glittering gaiety of
> Art which, in my crabwise scribbling hand,
>
> no less than Earth the change of all
> changes breedeth, art and life
> both inconstant mothers, in whose
> fixed cold bosoms we lie fixed,
>
> desperate to devise anything, any
> sadness or happiness, only
> to escape the clasped coffinworm
> truth of eternal art or marmoreal

infinite nature, twin stiff
destined measures both manifested
by my shoes, coated with dust or dew which no
earthly measure will survive.

(SH, 27–28)

Although he ventures into other forms—lyric reminiscences, quasi-dream poems—Pinsky does best with the long meditation that gives him ample space to savor the play of his mind. The section above deals with the subject of "measurement" in four-stress lines that form a single sentence. Meter allows the poet to measure, define, and contain his subject, but it may come perilously close to the "destined measures" of eternal art and infinite nature, both of which are deadly. He therefore tries to control his material and to keep it open to an enlivening randomness. Measure is like any dichotomy: a poetic foot that demands stressed and unstressed syllables resembles a game with which to put children asleep. Categories like "sadness" and "happiness" exist in theory but not in life; likewise, all polarized opposites, even in sound effects, must be tempered by an adult understanding that death will obliterate all. Even a simple phrase like "dust or dew" yokes together two opposing terms, rendering their opposition unnecessary and irrelevant by the very fact of alliteration and by the explicit realization that no "earthly measure will survive them." Poetic discursiveness encourages the "middle style," *sermoni propiora* as Horace defined it, and Pinsky's professorial allusiveness (Stevens and Donne speak softly through the lines above) nudges him into capacious, leisurely forms in order first to present, and next to protect himself against, the desperation that he recognizes as one's earthly plight.

The "Essay on Psychiatrists" is the triumph of *Sadness and Happiness*, a poem that happily unites theme and form. Surveying the field of his title, and attempting to say something new about this thoroughly modern professional figure, Pinsky confesses, first of all, that he has never sought the wisdom of a psychiatrist. (Whether his poem benefits from an outsider's objectivity or suffers from the lack of a participant's experience is another interesting question.) The poem ranges from a contemplation of *The Bacchae* (is Pentheus or Dionysus the true psychiatrist in the play?), through descriptions of the comic strip figure Rex Morgan, M.D., through Landor's Imaginary Conversation between Sidney and Fulke Greville, and to memories of Yvor Winters. Pinsky concludes sadly that he has "failed / To discover what essential statement could be made / About psychiatrists that would not apply / To all human beings, or what statement / About all human beings would not apply / Equally to psychiatrists." They are just like the rest of us, he proposes, in his lucid final lines:

> Even in their prosperity which is perhaps
> Like their contingency merely more vivid than that
> Of lutanists, opticians, poets—all into
>
> Truth, into music, into yearning, suffering,
> Into elegant machines and luxuries, with caroling
> And kisses, with soft rich cloth and polished
>
> Substances, with cash, tennis and fine electronics,
> Liberty of lush and reverend places—goods
> And money in their contingency and spiritual
>
> Grace evoke the way we are all psychiatrists,
> All fumbling at so many millions of miles
> Per minute and so many dollars per hour
>
> Through the exploding or collapsing spaces
> Between stars, saying what we can.
>
> *(SH, 73–74)*

Both diction and syntax here combine the populism of Whitman with hints of Wallace Stevens's heightened elegance: the colloquialism of "into . . . [this and that]" and the ordinariness of "goods and money" (not to mention "tennis and fine electronics") abut the more elevated "liberty of lush and reverend places," "contingency and spiritual grace" and the high bourgeois, if not positively archaic, "lutanists," "caroling," and "elegant machines." Goods and money combine spirituality with the contingencies of secular life: what more American strain could one imagine in a poem, whose lists both equate and distinguish constituent elements.

The problem of psychiatrists, "saying what we can," is everyone else's, especially (no surprise) that of poets, who, according to *The Situation of Poetry* (1976), have "a need to find language for presenting the role of a conscious soul in an unconscious world."[21] It is appropriate to the generalizations made here about Jewish ethical seriousness that Pinsky emphasizes the conscious soul, the captain of individual moral choice, rather than the repressed, unconscious self that psychoanalysis attempts to resurrect, as the condition for creative mental health.[22] His remarks on "discursiveness," defined alternatively as wandering and explanation, go a long way toward explaining how Pinsky's own poetry came to be the way it is: rambling, like A. R. Ammons's, which he likes, as well as compressed, like J. V. Cunningham's, which he also admires. Yearning for the physical world, he says, "reminds us of our solitude . . . of the contingency and randomness of the world the senses know"; this echoes his notion, in "Essay on Psychiatrists," that although the senses can know only discrete particulars, one cries out for larger, abstract categories with which to make sense of the world. Although "sadness" and happiness" may ultimately collapse as antithetical terms beneath scrutiny, they are needed as scaffolding for building an understanding of those individual feelings one tries to define.

Pinsky's strongest poem, *An Explanation of America*, is also his longest. Framed by a preparatory lyric ("Lair") that suggests, inter alia, the imagery of parturition, and an epilogue ("Memorial") in the form of an elegiac lament, the poem is an exemplary professorial performance: addressed to the poet's daughter, it attempts to instruct her about the past, in the present, for the future. Like Robert Lowell, Pinsky is concerned with public life and history and the individual citizen's place in them, but his characteristic tone is less agonized and tense, more subdued than Lowell's. And where Lowell's Rome is Juvenal's, Pinsky selects the earlier empire, that of Augustus and Horace, for his historical analogy to America. His poem affirms the basic line of English verse, in its five-beat, largely iambic rhythms, and a native American dialectic, most clearly adduced in its tri-partite structure inherited from Stevens's *Notes Toward a Supreme Fiction*. Instead of Stevens's "It Must Be Abstract," "It Must Give Pleasure," and "It Must Change," Pinsky gives readers "Its Many Fragments," "Its Great Emptiness," and "Its Many Possibilities" to explain the "idea" of these states. He proves that explanation has its own eloquence, and pedagogy its distinctive rhythms.

Whitman called America the greatest poem of all, a statement absorbed and revised by poets as diverse as Pinsky, Ammons, and Ginsberg, all of whom make of their native land a subject as well as a metaphor. The first third of Pinsky's poem treats the same paradox that Ammons so often deals with: permanence and change, and the question of whether one can ever make a home in motion, in a land where everyone is on the move. Pinsky borrows the old definition of a nation as "the same people living in the same place," but since America is always changing and fragmented, with all things lessened and made precious with time, the nation is also "different people living in different places." Even places, paradoxically, move. Pinsky's large theme, how to make a place, a nation, or a dream useful, repeats Thomas Jefferson's proposition that "the earth belongs in usufruct to the living." (One may also be reminded of the note sounded in Pope's "Epistle to Burlington," especially when Pope remembers that "Rome was glorious, not profuse, / And pompous buildings once were things of use.") Again, like Ammons, Pinsky finds his primary problem to be one of definition. Although the professor needs categories and boundaries to render his explanation to his daughter, he also realizes the impoverishment or the downright falsity of all definitions. As he movingly asks in the third section:

> A boundary is a limit. How can I
> Describe for you the boundaries of this place
> Where we were born: where Possibility spreads
> And multiplies and exhausts itself in growing,
> And opens yawning to swallow itself again?
> What pictures are there for that limitless grace
> Unrealized, those horizons ever dissolving?
>
> (*EA*, 42)

To echo Gertrude Stein, there is no "there" there when one tries to pin down the subject, especially when it is as large and uncontainable as the country itself. The "compulsive explainer" as Pinsky defines himself (6), who often feels the need "to make some smart, professorish crack," is as uneasy with explanations as he is with the very idea of countries:

> Because as all things have their explanations,
> True or false, all can come to seem domestic.
> The brick mills of New England on their rivers
> Are *brooding, classic*; the Iron Horse is quaint,
> Steel oildrums, musical; and the ugly suburban
> "Villas" of London, Victorian Levittowns,
> Have come to be civilized and urbane.
> . . . . . . . . . . . .
> For *place*, itself, is always a kind of motion,
> A part of it artificial and preserved,
> And a part born in a blur of loss and change—
> All places in motion from where we thought they were,
> Boston before it was Irish or Italian,
> Harlem and Long Branch before we ever knew
> That they were beautiful, and when they were:
> Our nation, mellowing to another country
> Of different people living in different places.
>
> (18–19)

Precisely because he is naturally skeptical of the very generalizations to which he is drawn, Pinsky uses as his basic technique for organizing the long poem the "interweaving" of various strands—of ideas, references, images, motifs—that Adrienne Rich also employs in her recent longer works. Such turns and returns allow the poem to accumulate its meanings through repetition and variation rather than through the simpler working out of a linear argument. Like America, Pinsky's explanation of it moves and stays the same simultaneously. From an initial concentration on individual parts ("fragments" is his term) through the frustrations attendant upon the realization of emptiness, both internal and topographical, he builds his hopes, for land, poem, and daughter, into the final section of "possibilities," knowing too much to make stronger assertions.

An elegist as well as a seer, Pinsky reminds readers that one's aspirations for oneself always differ from those for one's children. Like Brutus, we are committed to struggle; the Horatian dream of self-sufficiency on a Sabine farm must be reserved for the next generation. But America's boundlessness encourages millenial hopes and impulses, thereby defeating dreams of Horatian sufficiency. The "contingency" that Pinsky discusses in "Essay on Psychiatrists" proves too European a concept for him in his attempt to project his daughter into a future of boundless possibilities within a land where emptiness and infinity make a twinned pair.

This charting of the development of the "idea" of America from a beginning in infinite particulars, through a fall into emptiness, to the promise of "everlasting possibility"—seems like an appropriation, mutatis mutandis, of Harold Bloom's application of Lurianic schemes of cosmic catastrophe to the scope of literary history.[23] Even Pinsky's reliance on others' voices, through allusion or translation, parallels the political and historical course of America, always absorbing and converting its immigrants into citizens. In lines generally bereft of rhetorical flourishes and full of straight speaking, Pinsky has modernized past poets—Horace (one of whose epistles he translates), the English Romantics, Whitman, and Stevens. It is an absorbing democratic performance, the poem becoming a melting pot of others' voices within the tones of Pinsky's meditations. Indeed, the homage to the past, instead of distracting from the contemplation of the present, reminds a contemporary audience that Pinsky's own historical sense, like that of the America he describes, alternates between anticipation and nostalgia (another reason for the paired lyrics that surround the long title poem). Like children ("ornaments to our sentimental past, / They bind us to the future"), the joint creative enterprise of memory and expectation winds down the paths of personal and historical time. Consciousness, that great Romantic burden, is power, as Pinsky asserts when he equates the strangeness of the wide American spaces (Ad-

rienne Rich deals with similar landscapes in her recent poetry) with
the emptiness of a man trying to write a poem about the loneliness he
shares with "the contagious blankness of a quiet plain":

> In the dark proof he finds in his poem, the man
> Might come to think of himself as the very prairie,
> The sod itself, not lonely, and immune to death.
>
> None of this happens precisely as I try
> To imagine that it does, in the empty plains,
> And yet it happens in the imagination
> Of part of the country: not in any place
> More than another, on the map, but rather
> Like a place, where you and I have never been
> And need to try to imagine—place like a prairie
> Where immigrants, in the obliterating strangeness,
> Thirst for the wide contagion of the shadow
> Or prairie—where you and I, with our other ways,
> More like the cities or the hills or trees,
> Less like the clear blank spaces with their potential,
> Are like strangers in a place we must imagine.
>
> (*EA*, 23–24)

The man resembles Stevens's Snow Man, becoming a part of the wintry landscape that his mind mirrors; the poet and his daughter repeat
the adventure of all American immigrants confronting the vastness of
the continent; the living people hear the past speak to them, as Whitman does in "A Passage to India": "The Past—the dark unfathom'd
retrospect! / The teeming gulf—the sleepers and the shadows! / The
past—the infinite greatness of the past!" The excerpt quoted above
shows how naturally Pinsky combines grandeur of vision with intimacy
of tone and execution. The ecstasy of infinite aspiration never releases
the poem from its stated intentions of explaining, with patience and
love, an "idea" to a real audience who comes to figure as a character
in its creation. The professor is delivering a lecture that is authoritative without seeming authoritarian because the poet develops a potentially epic subject with great tenderness, defining and then defending
his own brand of patriotism as he prepares the next generation for
the historical and imaginative enterprise of understanding its country.

The implicit forward-lookingness of all Jewish thought, which I
have discussed as a corollary to my analysis of Allen Ginsberg's syntax
and which may also offer a partial explanation of Anthony Hecht's unwillingness to propose final causes, finds its place in Pinsky's longest
work in the form of a bequest to the daughter who is both the audi-

ence for the poem and the repository of the poet's hopes for a better
life. Being at home in a place that is essentially foreign demands an
act of imagination comparable to the one required of a poet attempting an act of explanation. For this reason, the poem ends with a Janus-
like look in two directions. Its penultimate section, entitled "Mysteries
of the Future," is a prolonged meditation on death and one's choices
of legacies ("It's fearful to leave anything behind, / To choose or make
some one thing to survive / Into the future . . ."). America, Pinsky believes, uses nostalgia and progress as the twin national gestures that
might forestall being enveloped by the nightmare of time. What one
really needs (and what his poem attempts to nurture) is a historical as
well as a geographical sense of place and time. The section appropriately concludes with an epitaph, that of an eighteenth-century African
slave, a man born free but confined in the land of liberty to the tyr-
anny of slavery. The epitaph incorporates motifs from Pinsky's historical ruminations on the relationship of freedom and finality, a relationship that one might say defines his own credo, which comes right
before:

> To speak words few enough to fit a stone,
> And frame them as if speaking from the past
> Into the void or mystery of the future,
> Demands that we be naked, free, and final.
>
> (55)

These lines embody the lapidary qualities that Pinsky so admires in
the poetry of Landor; they also stand for his own estimate of his technique and goal, as poet and historian, to speak on behalf of the past
and with hopes for the future, within the reality of the present.

Just as Auden refused to end "New Year Letter" on a note of religious climax, focusing instead on the real human being whom he addressed as an embodiment of moral and spiritual values, so Pinsky also
chooses to end by returning to his daughter, now three years older
than she was when he began the poem. In "Epilogue: Endings" he
recounts the girl's participation as Mamillius in a college production
of *The Winter's Tale*, an appropriately romantic text concerning the nature of death, hope, rebirth, and legacies. Happy endings, in spite of
deaths, *can* occur, in art and perhaps also therefore in life; those
Shakespearean pastoral daydreams, "holding Truth up against the
rules of Romance," may give birth to some impossible happy ending
for us.

The "us" means both poet and daughter, and the country of which
they are a part. Finality opens to new beginnings, even for the landscape:

> Nothing can seem more final than the mountains,
> Where Empires seem to grow and fade like moss—
> But even mountains have come to need protection,
> By special laws and organized committees,
> From our ingenuities, optimism, needs.
> The passion to make new beginnings can shatter
> The highest solitude, or living rock . . .
>
> (EA, 58)

Since the country extends over "several zones of time and climate," even climate, like landscape, will outlive human demands and movements. "Where nothing will stand still / Nothing can end," Pinsky realizes, thereby replacing the epitaphic sentiments of the previous section with the confident American reliance on new beginnings, for the land and for its inhabitants. Just as James Merrill pictures the cosmos as an expanded version of the human psyche in which nothing is ever lost, so Pinsky conjures an image of a divine ecological harmony that builds a nation out of infinite parts into a whole with no seeming beginning or destiny:

> Nothing was lost—
> Or rather, nothing seemed to begin or end
> In ways they could remember. The Founders made
> A Union mystic yet rational, and sudden,
> As if suckled by the very wolf of Rome . . .
> Indentured paupers and criminals grew rich
> Trading tobacco . . .
>
> (60)

The historical vision within the epilogue is framed by the actual depiction of the daughter as Mamillius. Following the lines above, part of the long section that describes a romantic vision of America's growth, politically and economically as well as visually, Pinsky returns to his daughter, now on stage and receiving the audience's applause. The cast is smiling and holding hands,

> as if the Tale
> Had not been sad at all, or was all a dream,
> And winter was elsewhere, howling on mountains
> Unthinkably old and huge and far away—
> At the opposite edge of our whole country,
> So large, and strangely broken, and unforeseen.
>
> (61)

Pinsky's audience knows, as well as he does, the double truth implicit in his conclusion: winter is both elsewhere and always with us in an America that contains multitudes, of weather and people.

Robert Pinsky occupies a middle position, appropriate to someone who manifests the "well-languaged" middle style, between Anthony Hecht and Allen Ginsberg. Like Hecht, he prefers a pentameter line, his inheritance from an essentially conservative prosodic tradition, and like Ginsberg he focuses his attention squarely upon a contemporary American scene, attending to its place in history and his own in it. Neither hectoring from a soapbox, like Ginsberg, nor seeming to explore the depths of characters imagined in confessional monologues or narratives, like Hecht, Pinsky compels us to consider—sanely and at leisure—the civic role of the poet within the citizenry of which he counts himself a member. Less than twenty years younger than Hecht and Ginsberg, Pinsky is from another generation, the one that came of age after World War II. He represents the assimilation of the immigrant Jewish experience into the secular mainstream of American life. Without relinquishing any of the moral force that we think of as a part of the Jewish heritage, he expatiates upon the moral dilemmas of this age with the assurance of someone whose sanity and social status allow him the benefit of a position that might be labeled central rather than peripheral.

# FOUR

# Myths of Concretion, Myths of Abstraction: The Case of A. R. Ammons

After the publication of *The Excursion*, Coleridge wrote a letter to Wordsworth laying out his hopes and fears about the relationship between poetry and philosophy, and, more important, about Wordsworth's presumed capacity to write the first genuinely philosophical poem. Sensing the affinities between his friend and collaborator and a distant Roman who is our first major didactic poet, Coleridge makes a rigid distinction that he then proceeds to dismember:

> whatever in Lucretius is Poetry is not philosophical, whatever is philosophical is not Poetry: and in the very Pride of confident Hope I looked forward to the Recluse, as the *first* and *only* true Phil. Poem in existence. Of course, I expected the Colors, Music, imaginative Life, and Passion of *Poetry*; but the matter and arrangement of *Philosophy*—not doubting from the advantages of the Subject that the Totality of a System was not only capable of being harmonized with, but even calculated to aid, the unity (Beginning, Middle, and End) of a *Poem*.[1]

Coleridge was, of course, to be disappointed in his hope, but in his distinction between philosophy and poetry he established the grounds for the prejudice in favor of the short lyric that defined most Romantic and post-Romantic tastes from Edgar Allan Poe through Cleanth Brooks. Ironically, he set up at the same time an alternative hope for modern poetry: the ability to encompass grander worlds, meanings, and abstractions than the tiny lyric will permit. Poetry's reach has always exceeded its grasp, and one measure of the poetry of the past two centuries is the variety of means it uses to bridge the gap between the two. One might call the "passion of Poetry" and "the matter and arrangement of philosophy" the Coleridgean equivalent of Horace's *delectare* and *prodesse*, especially since both critics suggest the hopeful possibility for a marriage between the two, the creation of a tertium quid.

The will to epic and the impulse to lecture apparently go hand in hand: when poets think big they also think philosophically, and length of utterance usually comes with seriousness and depth of purpose. To put the matter somewhat differently, when poets wish to write a long poem (rather than a medley of the sort favored by essentially lyric poets like Tennyson, Berryman, and Robert Lowell), they have two avenues open to them: they can write either a narrative, following the traditional path of epic, or a philosophical, meditative work, tracking the path of post-Renaissance poets. To explain the world poets either tell a story or make an examination. The way of narrative and of etiology are older but the way of analysis may be more congenial to contemporary explicators, who distrust history as a possible guide to truth. Didactic poets, by definition, wish to explain things. A more recent appreciation of Lucretius reminds us of that Roman's modernity and also of his usefulness as a model for a didacticism that takes science, a normally "untenable" area for poetic thought, as its major subject: "Poetry is not poetical for being short-winded or incidental, but, on the contrary, for being comprehensive and having range." Thus, Santayana on Lucretius's appropriation of what the philosopher-critic calls "the workshop and busy depths of nature, where a prodigious mechanism is continually supporting our life."[2]

As an explainer, A. R. Ammons is without peer. He constantly tells where he is going, taking retrospective glances when necessary at where he has been. He surveys his terrain, a landscape composed partly of the world around him and partly within the confines of his meditating mind. Even the physical universe includes both what can be seen with the naked eye and what is either cosmic or subatomic. And the entire process includes, as well, the relationship of word to line to page that we come to know as the poem that we read and upon which he is commenting even in the process of composing it. World, mind, their inscriptions within each other, and the consequent inscription made by the creative intelligence imposing itself upon its material: such is the perpetual arena in which Ammons stakes his claims, makes his discoveries, and teaches his lessons. It is, moreover, an arena in which science provides both a source of metaphor, figuration for our emotional and mental lives, and also a subject matter: Ammons shares Auden's and Nemerov's interest in scientific discovery and James Merrill's impulse to present "poems of science," explanations of worldly reality whose primary subject matter is biochemical, ecological, and geological.

Among the poets discussed in this book Ammons stands out not by virtue of his subject matter or of his technique (a poetry that Helen Vendler with some exaggeration calls bereft of adjectives and the pres-

ence of human figures),[3] but because he seems, from the very beginning, to have known himself and his interests. His poetry neither develops nor changes, formally or technically, in any significant ways.[4]
Reading through thirty years' worth of poetry one can see a quantita-
tive distinction between the longer poems and the short lyrics, but
aside from this (and the quirks of punctuation that have come to define Ammons's streaming longer efforts), little else separates the nominally simple and easy lyrics from the meandering, expansive ruminations. Ammons tells us over and over that his main theme, perhaps his
sole one, is the relation of the one and the many, and this old pre-
Socratic dichotomy, along with variants (inside versus outside, up versus down, center versus periphery, freedom-verging-on-entropy versus stability-turning-into-imprisonment), is his obsession. To these
older concerns he brings a modernist's self-consciousness about the
role and nature of language, how it fits into the various ways of con-
ceiving the world and how it also creates those very ways.

   "Motion" succinctly presents Ammons's creed about the relationship
between language and poetry. Words, he says, are "tags, labels"; language, arbitrary by its nature, is

>       the
>    method of
>    distinguishing,
>    defining, limiting:
>    poems
>    are fingers, methods,
>    nets,
>    not what is or
>    was:[5]

Ammons shares the didactic habits of repetition and listing with Allen
Ginsberg and Adrienne Rich; acts of definition are characteristic of all
the poets considered in this book. What separates Ammons, in addition to the seemingly lazy charm of the short lines, arbitrarily divided,
broken by his colons, is the insistent depiction of language at work
attempting to explain itself: no other poet gives such self-consciously
measured degrees of figuration in his work. The metonymic "tags, labels" and then "methods" and "nets" as means of defining poetry (Ammons relies heavily on the "$x$ is $y$" formula for both simple and abstract
acts of clarification) are deliberately different from the prosaic gerunds, which may still remind us of certain figurative associations, primarily through their etymologies (to define is to limit, after all). And
both metonyms and gerunds seem less figurative than the more gen-

uinely metaphoric "fingers," which punningly resonates when we consider its own relation to the Greek dactyl (i.e., finger) as a way of measuring or defining a block of verse.

Ammons continues by describing the music (rather than the meaning or substance) of poetry by professing a theory of pure meaninglessness through a negative formulation: poetry "traps no / realities, takes / no game" (although one may recall that by such logic poetry *is* a game); at last, in an old-fashioned simile, he tells what poetry is *like*:

> but
> by the motion of
> its motion
> resembles
> what, moving, is—
> the wind
> underleaf white against
> the tree.
>
> (*CP*, 147)

The last three lines stand out like an imagist poem or a pseudo-haiku, a piece of pure description to which the poem has progressed after several steps of moving away from "what is" to what the motion of poetry's motion resembles. Resemblance, not identity, is all one can get, however; even the "motion of its motion" ambivalently moves one both closer to (in the direction of a Platonic idea) and farther away from (as the motion of the motion is an echoic, subsidiary force, not a primary one) the nature of the true subject. The most characteristic touch comes in the phrase "what, moving, is," which brings mere being into a collision with motion and simultaneously defines being as the product of motion ("whatever is *is* by virtue of perpetual motion") and asks readers to hear, by an aural removal of commas, the participle become a gerund, and so the entire phrase become a deeper act of definition within the larger, surrounding ones: "what is the nature of moving?" he seems to be asking, as throughout his work questions and conundrums often wear the grammatical guise of statements.

The tension between participle and gerund noted above opens up a dimension of conflict throughout Ammons's work. Like Lucretius, who describes a world in which stasis and movement provide the poles for understanding, Ammons seems perpetually torn between a sense of fidelity to the onrushing change of atomic and cosmic nature and a wishful, almost nostalgic, belief that poetry, or language itself, can furnish suitable acts of definition. In the early, lovely "Gravelly Run" (*CP*, 55), he begins by pretending he could become like Wordsworth's

Lucy, herself "rolled round in earth's diurnal course, / With rocks and stones and trees":

> I don't know somehow it seems sufficient
> to see and hear whatever coming and going is,
> losing the self to the victory
>     of stones and trees,
> of bending sandpit lakes, crescent
> round groves of dwarf pine:

"Whatever coming and going is" reverses normal syntactic expectations and allows us to hear a phrase doing double duty: Ammons wants to know whatever is coming and going in the sway of natural circumstance, but he also wants to know the nature of "coming and going," that peculiar, doubled abstraction the understanding of which might also ensure a self-understanding. Beneath the charm of Ammons's naturalistic poems lurks an impulse toward abstraction, in phrasing and in substance.

Ammons's poetry, again like Lucretius's, has as its two characteristic, excessive flaws the dullness of prosaicism and the airiness of abstraction. He is well aware of both, and both are the necessary risks of a scientific, discursive poet. He acknowledges his dilemma just as he begins to settle into smug contentment with the blocked and well-defined stanzaic units he has made for himself:

> how handsome the stanzas are
> beginning to look, open to the total acceptance, fracturing into
> delight, tugging down the broad sweep, thrashing it into
> particulars (within boundaries): diversity, however—as of
>
> the concrete—is not ever-pleasing: I've seen fair mounds
> of fine-stone at one end or the other of highway construction
> many times and been chiefly interested in the "hill": but
> abstraction is the bogey-boo of those incapable of it, while,
>
> merrily, every abstractor brings the concrete up fine: one,
> anyway, as Emerson says, does well what one settles down to:
> it's impossible anyone should know anything about the concrete
> who's never risen above it, above the myth of concretion
>
> in the first place:
>
>                          ("Extremes and Modulations," CP, 329)

Concrete furnishes the concrete example of "the concrete" upon which all abstractions, the hills that develop from fair mounds and then flatten out into roadbeds, are built; Ammons nods soberly toward the very "myth of concretion" that he has constructed and then rises above it, passing it by. The fun, as Robert Frost knew, is in how you say the thing.

Along with Merrill, Nemerov, and Auden, Ammons has realized the famous prophecy from the preface to the 1800 *Lyrical Ballads*, in which Wordsworth looks forward to the day when Science "shall be ready to put on, as it were, a form of flesh and blood," and "the Poet will lend his divine spirit to aid the transfiguration, and will become the Being thus produced, as a dear and genuine inmate of the household of man."[6] Ammons shares with Nemerov a concern with intricate ecological and mental dependencies and with philosophical debates between unity and multeity, or nominalism and realism. The fragile strength of webs and nets glimmers through the lines of both: there is a similar breezy alternation between colloquial speech (the kind that a real "flesh and blood" person might use) and exact scientific nomenclature. Both poets have a knack for self-irony that modifies the heaviness of the prophetic mantle they occasionally wear. Ammons even pays implicit homage to Nemerov's blue swallows, those birds whose tails are dipped into an invisible ink, which we attempt to read:

> O calligraphers, blue swallows, filigree the world
> with figure, bring the reductions, the snakes unwinding,
> the loops, tendrils, attachments, turn in necessity's precision,
> give us the highwire of the essential, the slippery concisions
>
> of tense attentions! go to look for the ocean currents and
> though they are always flowing there they are, right in place, if
> with seasonal leans and sways:
>
> ("Extremes and Modulations," *CP*, 334)

At least two habits separate the sophisticated city boy who turned to nature late and the countrified scientist, both of which are evinced by the homage above. The shape of Ammons's poems on the page, their visible presence riddled with colons that stand as marks of equation and subordination, connection and separation, is unlike the well-wrought wares of Nemerov.[7] More significant is Ammons's view of the world, borrowed from Emerson but more horrifying, a Lucretian vision of potential chaos sufficient to wither and overwhelm man's dreams and his very place. Ammons fears inundation from nature and language (compare "a word too much repeated falls out of being" with Nemerov's "Man's greatest intellectual pleasure is to repeat himself").

Ammons's encyclopedic lists, like Whitman's catalogues but often without their ringing enthusiasm, expose the dangers of openness. As in *Tape for the Turn of the Year*, Ammons's greatest failing is the tedium of indiscriminateness. Like John Ashbery and Allen Ginsberg, Ammons wants to get everything in: "I'll have to say everything / to take on the roundness and withdrawal of the deep dark: / less than total is a bucketful of radiant toys" ("Cut the Grass," *CP*, 288). Reading Ammons, one often wishes to tell him to get on with it, to avoid the simple detail ("ants ran over the whitish greenish reddish / plants"), the philosophical repetition ("the precise and necessary worked out of the random, reproducible, the handiwork redeemed from chance"), and the enthusiastic banality ("The wonderful workings of the world: wonderful, / wonderful"). But these are the price and correlative of the magical visions:

> earth brings to grief
> much in an hour that sang, leaped, swirled,
> yet keeps a round
> > quiet turning,
> beyond loss or gain,
> beyond concern for the separate reach.
> > > ("Saliences," *CP*, 155)

The simple monosyllables open up at "quiet turning," a little phrase whose ambiguity (is "quiet" a noun, "turning" a participle, or does the adjectival "quiet" modify the gerund "turning"?) assures at least a minor consolation in a world that ignores our individual fates. Even the delicately delivered half-rhymes ("brings," "grief," "leaped," "reach") that sound the common fate of human aspiration are poised within a framework of the alliterative *r*'s throughout the lines, which steady and mollify our existential fears.

Like Nemerov in his more fearful moments, Ammons is generally an antipastoral poet. For all his fascination with the details of the natural world, and despite his precise attempts to capture its dappled, Hopkinsesque grandeur, Ammons often seems alone and uncomfortable out of doors. In God's house there may be many mansions, but Ammons usually picks one without apparent walls. "I chose the wind to be delivered to": his desire to be part of a general Emersonian unity is countered by inevitable feelings of loss, as in "Gravelly Run," which denies animism and insists with Blake that there is no natural religion. Although the "cedars' gothic-clustered / spires could make / green religion in winter bones," one is not at home in this wintry scape. The mitigations of *could* are too soon made solid. Ammons marches to the verge of natural contentment and containment, and then backs away:

no use to make any philosophies here:
    I see no
god in the holly, hear no song from
the snowbroken weeds: Hegel is not the winter
yellow in the pines: the sunlight has never
heard of trees: surrendered self among
    unwelcoming forms: stranger,
hoist your burdens, get on down the road.

(CP, 56)

The typical Ammons landscape, whether a south Jersey shoreline or
an Ithaca mountain lake, is bare, wintry, or unappealing in conventional ways: gravel, gullies, roils, mud, and dunes attract him most. In
them he is most, because least, at home.

    This potential for a Lucretian alienation amid the fragmentary at-
omistic world produces the singular hallmark of Ammons's poetic diction—its polysyllabic and abstract words laced with jaunty colloquial-
isms. Lucretius, too, was comfortable with the arcane, the archaic, and
the manufactured many-sided word. A line like Ammons's "multifila-
mentous chains knobbed with possibility" joins abstraction to physical-
ity, and the tongue-twisting appeal of long words is cemented by a
single Germanic monosyllable. The balance between polysyllabic per-
versity and commonness corresponds to the tension within the external world, which is threatened by "discontinuities" and "disoriented
chains," "motions building and tearing down," entropy tearing at order. Potential terror threatens the mind everywhere:

    after these motions, these vectors,
orders moving in and out of orders, collisions
    of order, dispersions, the grasp weakens,

    the mind whirls, short of the unifying
reach, short of the heat
    to carry that forging:
    after the visions of these losses, the spent
seer, delivered to wastage, risen
    into ribs, consigns knowledge to
    approximation, order to the vehicle
of change, and fumbles blind in blunt innocence
    toward divine, terrible love.

("Prodigal," CP, 77)

The divine love, Ammons's approximation of Dante's love that moves
the sun and the other stars, is terrible precisely because he so seldom

apprehends it except through an occasional direct reference, as above, or through other "approximations" of knowledge and poetic assurance.

One of Ammons's recurrent themes is "the possibility of rule as the sum of rulelessness" ("Corsons Inlet"), but *only* the possibility. If Ammons had not existed his advocate Harold Bloom would have had to invent him as a contemporary model who swerves away from Shelley, Emerson, and Whitman by siphoning them through the instruments of Lucretius, his true precursor. Ammons combines the visionary chaos in Lucretius's atomic particles with the visionary, microcosmic auguries of Blake (who hated the atomism of Newton and Democritus). Blakean energy erupts in Ammons's exclamations—"errors of vision, errors of self-defense! / errors of wisdom, errors of desire!" ("Jungle Knot"); Blakean contentment in his reflective quietude—"the talk of giants, of ocean, moon, sun, of everything, / spoken in a dampened grain of sand" ("Expressions of Sea Level"). Like Nemerov on trees, Ammons on spiderwebs traces the imagery of philosophical possibility in the world ("Identity"): there can be neither total genetic coding, eliminating differences and possibilities for how a single spider builds its web, nor total freedom, destroying the patterns in the webs of a single species. The truth resides somewhere between the two. Even as Lucretius perceives harmony as a balance between the destructiveness of Mars and the creativity of *Venus genetrix*, with an accompanying balance in his hexameters between long, convoluted paragraphs and pithy epigrams, concise summaries, so does Ammons chart chaos and order with comparably varied language and by the alternation of longer poems with shorter ones.

The relentless account making in Ammons's ecological ledger is usually leavened by his wit; in this, at least, he is full of surprises. No one else but Emerson, but without the same touch, talks to mountains, and to no other living poet do mountains talk back. No one else would so wryly entitle a poem "If Anything Will Level With You, Water Will" (the title alone gives a new meaning to that other title, cited above, "Expressions of Sea Level"), and certainly no one else as prone to large, meandering forms has so keen an instinct for the miniature:

> The reeds give
> way to the
>
> wind and give
> the wind away

("Small Song," CP, 222)

Whittling away at, or riffling, his peripheries, and accumulating, shoveling, or amassing detail in the hope of either distilling an essence or accounting for everything, Ammons always arrives at "the bumfuzzlement—the impoverished diamond" in finding an arc line, inside which there is nothing and outside which there is also nothing. The amplitude of his language, its fluctuations between the abstract and the colloquial, demonstrates both that nature is inevitably alienating, since it will not accommodate itself to the categories of human longing, and that every walk is a new walk, a new linguistic and perceptual beginning. Vision is beyond him and so he settles for clear seeing. Unity is provisional; the odd assortment of linguistic shards corresponds to the discrete, radiant objects of fear and desire that surround him.

Ammons's longer poems (almost anything more than two pages qualifies as "long") provide object lessons in poetic organization—his own odd ways of effecting the transitions or turns that Wordsworth said constituted the major odal qualities of "Tintern Abbey"—and, more important, testify to his rightful place among today's pedagogically minded poets. At the start of this chapter I suggested that one cause of the genesis and the ongoing popularity of the philosophical-meditative poem since *The Prelude* has been the displacement of narrative and the machinery associated with epic by the self-conscious monologue of a mind contemplating the world (or "the dialogue of the mind with itself," in Matthew Arnold's famous phrase). Ammons's first book-length poem, *Tape for the Turn of the Year* (1965), begins with a timid discussion of its own possible subjects and, like *The Prelude*, glances at classical epic with a nostalgic sigh before pressing on to more immediate concerns:

> I wish I had a great
> story to tell: the
> words then
> could be quiet, as I'm
> trying to make them now—
> immersed in the play
> of events: but
> I can't tell a great
> story: if I were
> Odysseus, I couldn't
> survive
> pulling away from
> Lestrygonia, 11 of

12 ships lost
with 11 crews:
        (*TTY*, 8–9)

Ammons gives two new twists to the standard trope of unreadiness or the unwillingness to follow conventional epic tales. First, he implies a qualitative difference between the "quiet" unself-conscious words of Homer and the noisier prattle of the modern poet wrestling vociferously with his own ineptitudes. And second, he equates his inability to tell Odysseus's story with his failure to be anything like the epic hero himself. Not only is he not Homer but, more important, he is not the Prince of Ithaka nor was meant to be. Ammons is canny enough to realize that his own poetry has, in fact, an Odyssean theme—the effort of a modern man to discover a cosmic home for himself—but he also knows that "it doesn't unwind / into sequence: it stands / still / and stirs / in itself like / boiling water / or hole of maggots." (There is a further Homeric note in that during the composition of the poem he is awaiting a letter from Ithaca, New York, with an invitation to teach at Cornell.) The centripetal reaching for home, an acceptance of and by the universe, is rendered anew by the literal twistings of this poem, composing itself by unrolling and recoiling: the poet places an adding machine tape into his typewriter and, as it unwinds from a wastebasket on the floor, he records upon it the sequence of days from 6 December to 10 January. "Unwinding and unwound, it / coils again on / the floor / into the unity of its conflicts." The wry philosopher gives a new meaning to the organicist's dream of the wedding of form and content: his poem literally twists as it metaphorically tropes upon its epic and meditative predecessors.

Whereas Wordsworth, or a contemporary like Robert Lowell, memorializes the past by revisiting and revising it, Ammons preserves the present moment by adhering to the random tentativeness of experience. *Tape* carries the diary to a foolishly logical inevitability, but in so doing it replaces narrative, epic or romantic, with a grab bag of vignettes and, increasingly as Ammons discovers his true metier, with minilectures on the nature of things. Both the form and the content share an organizing principle:

        if
structure without life is
meaningless, so is
        life without structure:
we're going to make a
dense, tangled trellis so

> lovely & complicated that
> every kind of variety will
> find a place in it or on
> it:
>
> (44–45)

So, in addition to commenting on the weather and other changing details of life in southern New Jersey, the poem remarks the process of its own composition. It is provisional (a term Ammons himself applies to his work) in both senses of that term: it seems temporary and of the moment, but it also provides the sustenance necessary for survival. In the small lines forced upon him by the size of his paper, Ammons discovers rapidity and richness:

> safe in these cages, I
> sing joys
> that never were
>         in any thorough jungle:
>
> but bctimes & at times
> let me out of here:
> I will penetrate into the
> void
> & bring back
> nothingness
> to surround all these
>         shapes with!
>
> closing in
>         without closing:
>         running through
> without filling:
> opening out
>         with walls:
>
> (63–64)

The itemized responses to the world's details produce a double effect: a positive accumulation of things, and a negative, icy sense of the isolation of meaningless facts, Ammons's rendition of Pascal's silent eternal spaces:

> so many people
> with bodies only:
>         so many bldgs with
>         mere addresses:

> buses, subways, cabs,
> somebody everywhere:
>
> fragments: faces never to
> be seen again: isolations:
>
> poets, peeks of need,
>         loose cold
>         majesties,
> sizing heights, cut off
> from the common
> stabilizing ground of their
> admirers:
>
> (129–30)

Lost in the city (he is recalling a visit to New York to attend a reception for Mrs. William Carlos Williams), Ammons contemplates the anonymity of contemporary life, a theme that recurs throughout this Odyssean poem in counterpoint to the details of a life with wife, hearth, and home. Approaching the end of his poem, Ammons yearns for a surcease to weariness and frustration. He has bludgeoned the reader, he says, "with every form of emptiness," as the tape and time are running out as well as running through.

Ultimately the poem is a list of its own making. The poet reconciles himself with what he has got and given: "I wrote about these / days / the way life gave them." Ideally, however, he would

> be like a short poem:
> that's a fine way
> to be: a poem at a
> time: but all day
> life itself is bending,
> weaving, changing,
> adapting, failing,
>         succeeding:
>
> (204)

Taking his leave, Ammons thanks us with a reminder of his bequests: he has given us, he says, "my emptiness," with no revelation (what Virginia Woolf used to call the "cotton wool" of ordinary life).[8] From start to finish it has been a long journey:

> I've given
> you my
> emptiness: it may

not be unlike
        your emptiness:
        in voyages, there
        are wide reaches
        of water
        with no islands:

I've given you the
interstices: the
        space between
        electrons:
        I've given you
        the dull days
when turning & turning
revealed nothing:
I've given you the
sky,
uninterrupted by moon,
bird, or cloud:
        I've given
you long
uninteresting walks
so you could experience
vacancy:

old castles, carnivals,
ditchbanks,
        bridges, ponds,
                steel mills,
                cities: so many
interesting tours:

the roll has lifted
from the floor &
our journey is done:
thank you
for coming: thank
you for coming along:

the sun's bright:
the wind rocks the
        naked trees:
        so long:

                (204–5)

Bequests, summations, the legacy of accomplishment—the poem lists things and blanknesses, the interesting and the uninteresting together, and the road remains open although the poem is closed, cluttered and curled, on the floor.

*Tape* is a nervously experimental poem. Ammons is at a literal and figurative turning point: waiting for his job letter from Cornell; concerned as he reaches the male climacteric with the possibility of sexual failure; frustrated with all kinds of "cagings." The short lines correspond to a relatively short attention span, and to an emotional giddiness as he seesaws between childish wonder at the workings of the universe and insomniac fears of annihilation. He acknowledges his plight as Odysseus's in a parenthetical aside: "(if you were / sitting on a / distant strand, / longing for home, / you'd have to / conjure up things to / occupy the time, / too)" (136), but by the end of the poem he comes to rely on the salvation of art as the only possible relief from his anxiety. The salvation is unsurprising. Ammons is philosophically old-fashioned, in spite of both his concern with contemporary scientific discoveries and his seemingly cranky stylistic novelty. His crackpot antisocial gruffness, his cracker-barrel stances, his "good ole boy" southern diction (when he feels like reverting to it) conceal but barely a true conservative. Like most genuine eccentrics, Ammons is ordinary, and the lessons he preaches are the perennial favorites.

This is especially true when one considers his poetics, a subject to which he gives more than passing attention in *Tape* and in his other long poems. He is an unabashed, Coleridgean organicist ("unity & diversity: how / to have both: must: / it's Coleridge's / definition of a poem" [185]), and a worshipper at the modernist shrine of art: "poetry has / one subject, impermanence, / which it presents / with as much permanence as possible" (145). But language claims us and deceives us, disappointing where we most demand its complicity. In the universe, boundaries push to the edge of entropy, and the making of boundaries deadens or at least inhibits freedom; Ammons asks for an endless proliferation of centers. Likewise, "definition is death: / the final box: / hermetic seal" (171). Ammons's self-fulfilling and self-cancelling statement demands our simultaneous assent and refusal. It is a performative utterance, with colons taking on the job of equalizing the surrounding elements, the coffin itself hemmed in by the opening proposition and the concluding label; but since "definition" is by definition deadly, our impulse is to spurn even as we accept it. Who would choose to murder to dissect? Moreover, the definition is a logical impossibility, given Ammons's other stated and implicit judgments about the nature of language and its relation to reality: "there's unity, / but objects don't / describe it: / nor do words" (167). Where does this leave us?

It leaves us with the naturalist-bard's constant effort to press his mind against an external reality of which he is a part but from which he receives ample resistance. Ammons loves to make statements, to perform acts of definition, which provoke the semi-assent that we can vouchsafe only to poetic truths. "Poetry" (he says) "has no use, except / this entertaining play: / passion is / vulgar when not swept up / into the cool control / of syllables" (178–79). In a theory about the sway and genesis of poetry that comes half out of Shelley's "Defence" and half out of other statements of romantic primitivism, Ammons insists that language contains a fire, constantly renewable through the joint acts of concentration and inspiration. Not for nothing is the poem in part a lengthy address to a muse, who is herself a Lucretian *Venus genetrix* figure to the poet obsessed with the specifics as well as the general nature of all sexual behavior, beginning with his own. The old bard, Ammons boldly declares, depended only "on mead & word" (177) for his creations. For "mead" read external stimulus, for "word" read the conscious manipulation of his inherited language, capturing an isolated perception, relating it to others, transfiguring all into some unity, however transient, by the capture of "word & / image in surprise."

It is no novelty to think of poems as made things, although it seems somehow inconsistent with the apparent randomness of much of Ammons's work to revert to neoclassical rhetorical doctrine. (In *Sphere* he actually confesses that "I'm sick of good poems, all those little rondures / splendidly brought off, painted gourds on a shelf" [72]). Nevertheless, Ammons's conservatism inhabits his pages: "poetry is art & is / artificial: but it / realizes reality's / potentials" (177). The aphorism literally opens up (and opens one to) the linguistic truths it contains: *art*ificiality derives from art, just as *real*ity demands *real*ization. The "cool control of syllables" creates the poem's meaning through the resonant harmonies of its music. In *Tape* more than in the other long poems, these harmonies are varied and playful, owing largely to the visible presence of the poem as a continuous short-lined and swiftly moving congress. Ammons's obsessive horror of boundaries appears here playfully in his ability to "honor a going thing" (his opening command in his most Hopkinsesque poem, "Mechanism" [*CP*, 77–79]).

There is an additional twist to the causes and effects of Ammons's verbal shapings. In the visible fashioning of his poems one can literally *see* his playfulness, of course, but also his determination to produce a poetry that resembles (in this if in nothing else) that of e. e. cummings.

Current literary wisdom holds that all literature gives prominence to the *lisible*, because language is inscriptive. No priority is granted to voice, transcendent reality, or "world" because language itself creates, commands, and precedes the meanings that it inscribes, submerging its "referents" more and more deeply into a scribal palimpsest. I do not wish to tackle, let alone refute, Derridean orthodoxies, any more than I would choose (as might seem appropriate to poets like Ammons and Nemerov) to open an older linguistic can of worms, the debate between realist and nominalist theories of language. Still, it seems legitimate to credit Ammons with having created a poetry, like that of William Carlos Williams, that is genuinely unhearable. Any spoken rendition, as by a poet at a public reading, limits the possible insinuations of the poem, in the way any performance of a dramatic text must choose among opposing emotional or intellectual possibilities within it. And it also falsifies the effect and meaning inscribed by the appearance of lines snaking across and down a page. Even the matter of Ammons's famous punctuation forces one to consider his poems as "more inscribed" than, say, those of Nemerov, or Ginsberg, or James Merrill (the sacred books virtually demand to be read aloud in order to distinguish among the considerable cast of human characters—who are of course themselves distinguished through the means of literary characters on the page, but this is another story).

Looking at the last page or so of *Tape*, quoted earlier, one can see that Ammons' poetry works visually, in spite of all his claims for bardic music and syllabic sounds. He gives "sky" as he says he gives it, untouched by the literal objects that succeed it. Its presentation on the page reminds one that what he has in fact offered is "sky" rather than sky; he thus proves the accuracy of poststructuralist definitions of language's representational capacity. He gives "interstices" on pages where what is inscribed is embedded within white vacancies. He gives "uninteresting walks," but then literally surrounds the objects of his interest ("old castles" etc.) with a re-appraisal ("so many interesting tours"). One might ask as well whether that list is meant to constitute the experience of vacancy that the colon before it seems to promise (the colon as an act of equalizing the two items it separates) or, to the contrary, the substance of "interesting tours" that it precedes. What lineation and punctuation suggest in this case (and I take this example as a model for what Ammons does on virtually every page) is the way the mind in the act of proposing, and the reader in the act of viewing, the inscribed data, can reinterpret the substance of experience. The mere listing of places, in other words, effects a reevaluation: what initially seemed uninteresting becomes, through the intervention of several colons, a magical mystery tour.

Even closure is both resolved and questioned, in part by the punctuation, in part by the repetitions in diction. Poet and poem complete their journeys simultaneously, the paper literally levitating and symbolically disappearing, at least from the writer's blindered view of his typewriter. In a poem that has dealt frankly with sexuality, one can't help hearing in "thank you / for coming" a suggestion of climactic release (especially because the poet addresses himself in swift succession, sometimes at the same time, to reader, muse, and poem), a grateful sigh to both the adding machine tape and the indulgent reader for their patience. And in the amplified repetition of a polite formula ("thank / you for coming along") one hears a reminder of the length of the poem (and of the "long / uninteresting walks" it and we have made) and a preparation for the terminal cliché that promises both a farewell and a weary sigh (as if Ammons is saying "it's been so long" since . . . we might imagine what). "So long, it's been good to know you," "vaya con dios"—Ammons allows readers to supply whatever handy truth leaps to mind. One summons a cliché, almost by definition, to render an arbitrary ending when nothing more seemly or powerful is available. Here the ending has been both arbitrary and foregone: the poem will stop when the raw material, the blank paper, is run through. But like this trite farewell (which will ring hollow to any reader of Ammons's most anthologized piece, "Corsons Inlet," the great contemporary "pedestrian" poem, ending with a summary tautology, "tomorrow a new walk is a new walk"), the final inscribed mark is neither a period nor an open-ended blank, but the favored colon, which promises and denies everything and therefore nothing.

A voice could never do justice to the multiple sounds implicit in that colon: the slightly raised pitch that suggests reluctance; the flatter, conclusive sound a period might enforce; a monotone for two monosyllables that calls all tone, like all hypotheses and all philosophy, in doubt. By giving form to his own sexual, intellectual, and poetic anxieties, *Tape* confirms Ammons in his resolve and his capacity to write longer poems. Increasingly, in "Essay on Poetics" and *Sphere*, Ammons employs his conceptual machinery in the service of his interest in literature itself: for all his fascination with external nature, visible or not, Ammons has turned himself into a member of an imaginary philosophy department, lecturing his students not only on natural causes but also on aesthetics. Typically the two concerns coincide. Ammons gives a short run-through in "Summer Session" (much as a summer course miniaturizes and condenses materials from lengthier terms), a document of what he observes in the world of Ithaca, in and out of the classroom, and of what he must do to and for the undergraduates in his writing class. Planting and sowing; reading and writing; production and excrement: Ammons makes his usual pairings:

> in my yard's more wordage than I
> can read:
> the jaybird gives a shit:
> the earthworm hoe-split bleeds
> against a damp black clump:
>
> the problem is
> how
> to keep shape and flow:
>
> (CP, 248)

He accepts with generous irony the whole process of distilling or instilling knowledge, a process comparable to and at the same time vying against more basic hormonal urges:

> here are the 18-year-old
> seedbeds & the
> 19-year-old fertilizers:
> they have come for a summer session:
> knowledge is to be my insemination:
> I grant it to them as one grants flesh
> the large white needle:
> what shall I tell those who are
> nervous,
> too tender for needles, the
> splitting of iridescent tendons:
> oh I tell them nothing can realize
> them, nothing ruin them
> like the poundage of pure self:
> with my trivia
> I'll dispense dignity, a sense of office,
> formality they can define themselves against:
> the head is my sphere:
> I'll look significant as I deal with
> mere wires of light, ghosts of
> cells, working there.
>
> (CP, 260)

Like the physician in Lucretius, coating his bitter pill with honey, or like any other temperamentally didactic poet, Ammons *signifies* by looking significant, investing himself with pedagogic authority even though he realizes that the students naturally resist his lessons, which are, at best, only clever rehashings of clichés. Teaching "creative" writing, a fate of many contemporary poets, is a pleasant, harmless enough way of earning the necessary time to write one's own poetry: it also encourages Ammons to consider the organic nature of his own material. When referring to teaching, we naturally endow the verb with a double object, one direct and the other indirect: one teaches students, one teaches poetry. What Ammons increasingly considers is the how and why of teaching poems *to* students; in other words, a primary concern as he develops it in "Essay on Poetics" and *Sphere* is the nature and use of poetry, and its place in education.

His hypothesis comes literally as a conclusion to his various investigations: "the poem / is the symbolical representation of the ideal organization" (*CP*, 315). Ammons has said this before, but in "Essay on Poetics" (*CP*, 296–317) he arrives at his end after a meditative ramble through other notions borrowed and revised from romantic commonplaces. He acknowledges at the start a perceptual bias: "the way I think is / I think what I see: the designs are there: I use / words to draw them out—also because I can't / draw at all: I don't think: I see" (298). I take this as a thinly disguised version of Wordsworth's confession at the start of "Tintern Abbey": "I cannot paint what then I was," and a reliance upon the basic techniques of Lockean observation that the Romantic nature lyric confirmed for English poetry. As it happens, however, Ammons's homage to empiricism also contains the punning germ of his pedagogic concerns: "draw [i.e., lead] them out" is etymologically what educators do to their students.

He begins with a speculation about lyric as the mode that processes information, becoming a synthesis of bits, and as a shape that seems most to aspire to roundness ("all saliences bend to the same angle of / curve and curve becomes curve, one curve, the whole curve" [296]). As a model of assimilated wholeness, the lyric also permits "another wholeness, / another lyric, the same in structure" and Ammons is off and running with a contemplation of the "one/many" mechanism that everywhere enthralls him. An imaginary landscape with cows, copses, paths, and the possibilities of knowledge inferable through inscriptions of weather (a sort of "Tintern Abbey" of the mind) pulls him up short when he considers how the "blades of reason," stopping upon any word or any element in this imagined landscape, will destroy the whole picture:

> for language heightens by dismissing reality,
>
> the sheet of ice a salience controlling, like a symbol,
> level of abstraction, that has a hold on reality and suppresses
> it, though formed from it and supported by it:
>
> (298)

What Wordsworth, referring to the relation of mind and nature, terms in *The Prelude* an "ennobling interchange . . . of action from without and from within," Ammons here symbolizes through the image of an ice sheet pressing down against a medium resistant and supportive. Later he makes the same point, differently: "the reality under / words (and images) is too multiple for rational assessment and / that language moves by sailing over" (301). He updates Wallace Stevens's configuration of reality and imagination as interdependent, equal rivals, by picturing reality as that in which we find and admire infinite "centers." We wish, however, to inhabit the limits, peripheries, or high suasions that these centers infinitely lead us toward. We have the earth; we aspire to the place "where phenomena / lose their drift to the honey of eternity" (300). Such transcendent escape is as impossible linguistically as it is religiously.

The blades of reason will destroy an icy reality, that is, when we attempt to "define" by cutting through, by dividing, by clarifying through making boundaries. The way of analysis, as Ammons always allows, has its particular charms and failures; to these he adds the other way of "definition," the acceptance of "the multiplicity of synthesis," by seeing steadily and whole: "the grandest / clustering of aggregrates permits the finest definition" (302). Poetry works exactly in both ways together: "to heighten the crisis and pleasure of the reconciliation" it considers the etymology of "tree" (which comes from "true"), and it also considers the very elm in the backyard, the growth, shape, and progress of which Ammons then describes for several pages, reminding us of both Wordsworth's "single tree" in the Intimations ode, the one representing the many, and Yeats's chestnut tree, a whole greater than the aggregation of its constituent parts. Truth, Ammons decides, is a high assimilation of specific details and also a reduction, or distillation, of data into and by means of symbols. The point is to keep the mind open to variety:

> "no ideas but in
>
> things" can be read into alternatives—"no things but in ideas,"
> "no ideas but in ideas," and "no things but in things": one thing

always to keep in mind is that there are a number of
   possibilities:

whatever sways forward implies a backward sway and the mind
   must
either go all the way around and come back or it must be
   prepared
to fall back and deal with the lost sway

(308)

Having established the resilient openness of his mind, and having also
exemplified his principles through references to external nature, in
fact to his own backyard, Ammons is now ready for another appropriation, the poem's central definition-through-symbolizing. He pictures poetry as a landscape in a lengthy, charming fantasy that mingles
details from Shelley's "Mont Blanc" with his own perverse undermining of the classically sanctioned generic ladder.

   Ammons assembles a geography of poetic genres from the top
down: "I would call the lyric high and hard," he announces, reminding us of his opening depiction of lyrics as atomic particles—hard,
firm, lucid and, within the boundaries of form, reproducible. Like
Shelley gazing at his Alpine landscape (and using it as a figure for his
own "separate phantasy," wedding mind and matter), Ammons begins
at the summit and declines. The poet who would historically ascend
from eclogue to georgic to epic finds himself faced with a different
perspective. One glances at the top, and

then there is the rush,

   rattle, and flash of brooks, pyrotechnics that turn water white:
   poetry is magical there, full of verbal surprise and dashed
   astonishment: then, farther down, the broad dealing, the
      smooth

   fullness of the slow, wide river: there starts the show of genius
   .   .   .   .   .   .   .   .   .   .   .   .   .   .   .   .   .   .   .   .
genius, and

   the greatest poetry, is the sea, settled, contained

(309)

From the "snowline melt of individual crystalline drops" to the brook,
the river, and the "orientationless, but perfectly contained" ocean,
Ammons's visionary eye moves like Shelley's scanning the Alpine
scene from the inaccessible heights to the viewless ocean. The differ-

ence is that Ammons's application is a purely literary one: each of the genres (there seem to be four, of which only lyric is labeled) has its distinctive "uses and special joys." The content, Ammons assures us, updating Thales' cosmology, is a constant: water.

As water to the landscape, so (one infers) is language to poetry: the element of composition, always moving, always containable: "the verbal moves, depends there, or sinks into unfocused / irreality: ah, but when the mind is brought to silence, the / non-verbal, and the still, it's whole again to see how motion goes" (310). A poem, like a landscape, can be known and traveled around in: one can measure the motion of physical nature or of language and afterward, having reduced it to stillness, one can see it entirely. No poet has so neatly and correctly applied the Heisenberg laws of measurement, aligning them with Shelley's earlier effort to discover reality in the interacting processes of mind and nature. This application leads Ammons to one of his characteristically plain yet paradoxical definitions: "poems are arresting in two ways: they attract attention with / glistery astonishment and they hold it: stasis: they gather and / stay: the progression is from sound and motion to silence and / rest" (310).

Ammons is not producing a new theory of poetry but rather a startlingly old-fashioned (and therefore almost new) justification for teaching it. A poem is both part of our natural order and *like* part of the natural order: "poems, of human make, are / body images, organisms of this human organism." His figurations seem at times conventionally metaphorical (lyrics are like atoms, or hard, clear crystals), but at other times startlingly literal (the actual progress of a poem is from sound to silence). Working out of Coleridgean organicism and applying the sexual language for poetry that becomes common coin within his poems, Ammons returns to the most conventional defense for poetry: pleasure. He insists that the normal way of discussing poems—through history, meaning, and influence—is a pedantic evasion of the sexual processes that describe a poem's thrust and drive and the sexual pleasure ("superior amusement," he mockingly phrases it with his own parentheses) readers derive—actually? analogically?—from poems:

> organisms, I can tell you, build up under the thrust to
>
> joy and nothing else can lift them out of the miry circumstance:
> and poems are pure joy, however divisionally they sway with
>   grief:
> the way to joy is integration's delivery of the complete lode:
>
> (313)

Poems present themselves as symbols of integration, harmony, and the relationship between "high levels of oneness and the / numerous subordinations and divisions of diversity" (315). Ammons's conclusion, delivered with firm, even rhythms that seem virtually prosaic and that follow two excerpts from biology texts about the cooperative nature of matter within all ecosystems, asserts the helpfulness of poems in strengthening the mind, allowing it to organize its own energy and letting "the controlled / flows occur" (an example, here, of literal influencing) within the perceiving subject.

Ammons strikes, at last, a civic note, one that has no real source, I think, in either his Romantic or his native American forebears. Poetry produces patriotism:

> I used to wonder
> why, when they are so little met and understood, poems are
>   taught
> in schools: they are taught because they are convenient
>   examples
>
> of the supreme functioning of one and many in an organization
>   of
> cooperation and subordination: young minds, if they are to
>   "take
> their place in society" need to learn patience—that oneness is
>
> not useful when easily derived, that manyness is not truthful
>   when
> thinly selective—assent, that the part can, while insisting on
> its own identity, contribute to the whole, that the whole can
>
> sustain and give meaning to the part: and when these things
> are beautifully—that is, well—done, pleasure is a bonus
> truth-functioning allows: that is why art is valuable:
>
> (315)

And so from analogies with biology and geology, from the observation of domestic detail and the invention of a figurative landscape, Ammons lands squarely not just in his own backyard (he has composed the poem, he says, to help him get through a snowstorm) but in his own nation. The transcendental and organic dimensions of poetry have beeen seen before—they are cultural commonplaces by now— but Ammons's political version of natural harmony, although it derives from a Lucretian image of a cosmos in which politicized if not fully human particles engage in mutual combat and support, has a surprising lesson to teach all Americans living in an active common-wealth.

Like trees, children suffer and profit from both nature (their ge-netic code) and nurture (the effects of environment, individual cir-cumstance, and choice) to produce their distinctive destinies. What children, unlike the trees they might observe, can learn is patience, a lesson necessary for individual and political health. Patience, a reader of Ammons would surely argue, is also the virtue necessary for read-ing his poems, especially the long, meandering ones that circle around and back to favored spots, ideas, or metaphors, repeating, amplifying, proving, testing, including the smallest banalities of life and diction within the confines provided by a text. But at the same time, those banalities, along with deeper and more "salient" passages, create that very text that confines and (to speak as Ammons might) liberates them to flow so easily. Ammons has distinctly, if unintentionally, united the civic-mindedness of Allen Ginsberg or of the more measured, Hora-tian Robert Pinsky, with the all-inclusiveness of Frank O'Hara and his "I do this, I do that" poems. His worst sin, like O'Hara's and Gins-berg's, is non-exclusion, but every so often the apparent wandering points to the rhyming potential, actual or implicit, of words and the things they represent (a trait learned from Hopkins and shared with the English poet Charles Tomlinson): "I've been at this / poem or prose-poem or versification or diversification for three / or four days," he says at one point in "Extremes and Modulations," and even the very pairings invite us to hear or see "prose-poem" as both the opposite of "poem" and its result, coming as it does syntactically out of a prior state. Likewise, "diversification" is merely an extension of "versifica-tion" (a 1975 volume is entitled *Diversifications*; having made his pun in an earlier context, Ammons went on to profit from it), the same thing but longer and more varied, adding a syllable but rendering a rhyme, proving that poetry allows us to see more vividly than anything else the collusion of the one and the many.

*Sphere*, Ammons's 1974 Lucretian epic, embodies all the mental and stylistic habits of the poems discussed here, and might provoke the same kind of response that *The Excursion* did in Coleridge. Beginning with a nod in the direction of *De Rerum Natura*, the poem makes a simple statement: "The sexual basis of all things rare is really appar-ent." Its main subject, however, turns out not to be sexuality but the way sexual language allows us to understand the "intermingling of parts," a version of the standard one-many dilemma. Although his principles of organization are different from James Merrill's, Am-mons takes as his major concern an idea that is central to *The Changing*

*Light of Sandover* as well: shapeliness, centers, and boundaries are all versions of limited visions. When trying to encounter "the highest god," one is thwarted; indeed, one may never meet this "essence out of essence, motion without motion," which exists only peripherally, although one can catch occasional glimmers of it. The real subject of *Sphere* (as well as its shape) is Ammons's attempts to catch those fleeting glimpses—just as Merrill's, in the sacred books, is the effort to hear the sacred voices, channeled through a hokey medium.

The biological apparatus in *Sphere* allows Ammons to continue his earlier interest in education, specifically the role of poetry in education, throughout this various poem. In the fifteenth and sixteenth sections he develops an elaborate analogy (another reminder of his debt to the Shelley of "Mont Blanc") between our minds and anthologies of words ("good sayings") that are the genes, and poems and stories that are the chromosomes: "gene pool, word hoard." Critic and teacher examine and foster the relationship between the capacious anthology and possible additions, always checking to see whether the "new thing" might find an attachment in and with the anthology, an energy source that would flow between it and the store already accumulated. If not, "it dies, withered away from the configuration of the people: / but if it lives, critic and teacher show it to the / young, unfold its meaning, fix its roots and extend its reach" (17).The teacher now becomes a husbandman. Ammons cannot resist the delicious duplicity of "roots" to relate a literary scholar's activity to a gardener's. With the poet and critic, the teacher performs a function at once natural and civil:

> the anthology is the moving, changing definition of the
> imaginative life of the people, the repository and source,
> genetic: the critic and teacher protect and reveal the source
>
> and watch over the freedom of becomings there: the artist
> stands freely into advancings: critic and teacher choose, shape,
> and transmit: all three need the widest opening to chance
>
> and possibility, so perceptions that might grow into currents
> of mind can find their way: all three are complete men,
> centralists and peripheralists who, making, move and stay:
>
> (17–18)

Although the distinction between critic and teacher is arbitrary and never explained, it fits into Ammons's aesthetic and pedagogic schemes to imagine a triumvirate of guardians for his updated version of Yeats's "book of the people" who will encourage its growth and spread its currents: a trio who inhabit comfortably both the centers (where stability, coding, and knowledge reside) and the peripheries (the outlands, the saliences, the spaces of widest uncertainty) of the imagined garden within the literary, genetic, or cosmic sphere. The balance between one and many, or center and arc, is neatly epitomized in the last line above with its dramatic enacting of a definition through the syntax and sounds of its language: "move and stay" are possible only by virtue of "making," a word that literally combines them through rhyme—as if Ammons wants to press upon readers the way *making* combines the consonant of "moving" with the long vowel of "staying" and thus resolves the apparent paradox of the phrase.

Such resolution of oppositions is the consistent scheme as well as the subject of *Sphere*. As always, Ammons is tempted by the clarities of definitions, whether those of others or of his own making, but always backs away from them, understanding their limiting and potentially dangerous effects. As teacher and poet himself, he must both move and stay; one demonstration is the organization of the poem into 155 twelve-line stanzaic units, ongoing but never fully stopped or resolved until the concluding period. An obsession with division and openness is, I think, another, far from fortuitous, inheritance from Wordsworth and Lucretius, two didactic forebears. Observing a wintry landscape, Ammons makes of the image of pheasants walking out of snow thickets into and between a "white paling fence" an occasion to contemplate a favorite problem:

> it's hard to draw a line, the careful,
> arrogant, arbitrary imposition, the divider that blocks off
> and sets apart, the arising of difference and distinction:
>
> the discrete a bolus of slowed flux, a locus of depressed
> reaction rates, a boned and fibered replication: slowed
> but not stopped (heightened within its slows):
>
> (24)

Such joint mingling and separation derives, within the Romantic tradition, from the opening landscape in "Tintern Abbey," in which Wordsworth paints a picture of a landscape plotted and divided by "hedgerows," which he then modifies by denying them ("hardly hedgerows, / Little lines of sportive wood run wild"), and in which "one green hue" colors details that are otherwise separate. In other words, the unity and multeity of a visible scene give philosophical poets ample inspiration to make comparable divisions and unifications while recollecting their own lives. Elizabeth Bishop makes the same sort of gesture in "At the Fishhouses," her updating of "Tintern Abbey," but we can see the differences between her more reticent poetic temperament (one less prone to the kind of didacticism treated in these pages) and a more aggresssively discursive one by comparing Ammons's continual leaping into a scene for philosophical applications and Bishop's reluctance to do more than imply her conclusions. That Wordsworth himself may have inherited his wish to picture a landscape both unified and distinctive from Lucretius, as well as from the more immediate precedents of eighteenth-century locodescriptive verse, only increases the possibility for establishing bonds among the three poets. In fact, in *A Guide through the District of the Lakes*, Wordsworth commends a passage in Lucretius as evidence that poetry captures better than nature itself the beauty of vines and olive trees; it is a passage that might remind us, once we have made the necessary arboreal adjustments, of the opening lines of "Tintern Abbey": "a grey-green belt of olives might run between the vineyards to mark the boundaries, stretching forth over hills and valleys and plains; just as now you see the whole place mapped out with various charms, laid out and intersected with sweet fruit-trees, and fenced around with fruitful shrubs" (*De Rerum Natura*, 5.1370–78).

It may be "hard to draw a line," but that is what teachers, whether poets or critics, love and have to do. All definition is a form of closure, and since "closure ends all shows, the plain strict and the frowsy / brilliant" (#42), one can understand the risk involved in any attempt, and a poet's reluctance to commit himself. But, proceeding *pedetemptim*, "step by step" (Lucretius's self-evaluation), Ammons everywhere complements his reluctance to dash to peripheries with his sometimes resigned, sometimes daring, realization that he must, even if like a pedestrian, hazard his definitions: "we might as well make as much distinction / here as we can." To keep possibility open, his turnings often include a variation on a dialectic habit, inherited from Romanticism's appropriation of Socratic dialogue. In stanzas 54–55, one sees in miniature Ammons's technique, here applied to a common fixation:

> how to make the essential fashionable is the
> problem without promoting boredom for there is little variation
> day to day in the essential and, worse, when the fashionable
>
> hangs on it loses the quality of the fashionable: of course
> we are sure that the fashionable relates only peripherally
> to the essential so that it is nearly certain that to be
>
> fashionable is not to be essential: there is the aspect,
> though, of change that it is constant so that always to be
> fashionable is to participate in the lasting: problems

problems: the essential without specification is boring
and specification without the essential is: both ways out
leaves us divided but so does neither way: unless—and here

is the whole possibility—both essential and fashionable can
be surrounded in a specified radial essential, which is difficult:

(34–35)

Having built an intellectual structure, which identifies two logical possibilities (call them *A* and *B*), Ammons neatly summarizes and synthe-
sizes the opposing elements (since change is constant, "to be fashionable is to participate in the lasting"). Such dialectic maneuvering, as
always in Ammons, resolves nothing in itself, but occasions still further
reflective possibilities. He resumes his stance, taking two possibilities
(now *A* stands for the boredom of "the essential without specification"
and *B* for the boredom of "specification without the essential," phrases
whose very resemblance suggests a possible exit from logical difficulties), and somewhat more gently arriving at a new solution—admittedly a "difficult" one—that both "essential" and "fashionable" be included in a tertium quid, which he inelegantly labels the "specified
radial essential."

Ammons inherited his dilemma from the American and British Romantics: it has a double edge, linguistic and religious. When attempting to allow a single item or image to stand for an entire class, one is
overinvesting its boundaries. This is the sin (Ammons does not say
this, but it is clear) of synecdoche and metonymy. This is, however
understandably, asking the item to "do" a lot of work. But if one
moves beyond the level of paradigm to that of larger classes, then
"matter is a mere seed / afloat in radiance," and the individual is lost.
This is the sin of universal predication. Just as one item standing for
all loses its individual charge and falls beneath its own weight, so an
abstraction that ignores boundaries immerses particulars within the
total radiance. The religious application of the problem deals of
course with the identity of the Most High, whatever one chooses to
call it, which both comprehends and obliterates distinct particularities,
the atomies of existence. Here is where poems come in: all movement
themselves, they also move us, to a conclusion of silence (from sound)
and stasis (from their joint activity with us): "the purpose of the motion of a poem is to bring the focused, / awakened mind to no-motion"
(40).

Poets, then, like the poems they have created, push out diversely
into linguistic and experiential realms, assimilating greater degrees of
the unexpected into their expectations, and adjusting their expecta-

tions to shadings of tone and meaning. Ammons's image, borrowed jointly from Shelley and Wordsworth, returns to the poet a quasi-natural function in his pedagogic efforts:

> if raindrops are words, the poet is the cloud whose
> gathering and withholding overspills generously and unmissed
> from a great keeping: (depression, low pressure area): the
>
> false poet is a white wisp that tries to wrest itself into
> a storm: but the true storm moseys on with easy destructions
> like afterthoughts: how else but by greatness can the huge
>
> presence exist between the gifty showers, twists and blow-outs:
>
> (43)

And on he goes, detailing the short nonsense poem he has just composed en route from Northfield, everywhere spreading his own largesse, a poetic consciousness working from a center and relocating that center as his forces gather and spill themselves beneficently onto the page. A separate study might describe the ramifying, associative structures throughout Ammons's work, the most thoroughgoing example in contemporary poetry of the way an older empiricism (of Locke and Wordsworth) has been joined, via William James's "stream of consciousness," to the different kind of associationism that might be called Freudian. Suffice it here to say that the poem develops within itself a rhythm that allows passages of abstract definition to be followed by others of specific detail, ideas giving over to daily life, definitions to enactments, theory to application. Although Ammons says at one point that "the work of the staying mind is to burn up or dissolve the day's / images" (53), he also proves that the mind never stays anywhere for long. "Nothing shaped stays and shapelessness is dwellingless" (58), so where can one dwell? Everywhere and nowhere at once. Ammons *thinks* about travel, like Wallace Stevens, another famous stay-at-home, and unlike Elizabeth Bishop, who both questions it and participates in it, but for him the act of focusing the mind suffices, because what really interests him is the relation between theory, or rigid abstraction, and practical affairs. Since he acknowledges a basic temperamental difference between himself and his obvious American epic forebear ("I am not a whit manic / to roam the globe"), he ends up often sounding like a less precious Stevens, substituting for Stevens's opulence the rich linguistic arcana of science itself. "Can we make a home of motion" (76) is his large question, but since he refuses question marks, it is also a statement. We can.

One reason that we can is Ammons's serious, and virtually literal, acceptance of Whitman's famous pronouncement that "the United States themselves are essentially the greatest poem." Ammons explores the philosophical and poetic applications of this metaphor. Since a poem by definition is the clearest example of the one-many problem, incorporating literally (i.e., visibly) multiple parts and saliences within the formal limits imposed by shape and page, it follows that one can be both at home and traveling in poetry (cf. Keats's "On First Looking into Chapman's Homer," Dickinson's "There is no frigate like a book"), *and*, by virtue of an American birthright, that one can apply the principles of poetic organization to a political entity:

> I can't understand my readers:
> they complain of my abstractions as if the United States of
>   America
> were a form of vanity: they ask why I'm so big on the
>
> one:many problem, they never saw one: my readers: what do
>   they
> expect from a man born and raised in a country whose motto is
>   E
> *pluribus unum*: I'm just, like Whitman, trying to keep things
>
> half straight about my country: . . .
> .   .   .   .   .   .   .   .   .   .   .   .   .   .
>                    my country: can't cease from its
> sizzling rufflings to move into my "motions" and "stayings":
>
> when I identify my self, my work, and my country, you may
> think I've finally got the grandeurs: but to test the center
> you have to go all the way both ways: from the littlest
>
> to the biggest: I didn't mean to talk about my poem but
> to tell others how to be poets . . .

> (65–66)

And he continues his lessons with a "How-To-Write-A-Poem": as in learning to ride a horse or a bicycle, one's got to fall off a few times and learn the balance between forces before ultimately sailing right along. The jaunty, confident side of Ammons's temper, the obverse of the dark, brooding, fearful side, comes out in these playful renditions of advice giving: mind—his own, that of his readers, and the greater Emersonian oversoul (when he is in a mood to credit that one)—resembles the U.S., and both resemble a (or *the*) poem, the one under construction before one's eyes. Everyone can be a poet in a democracy, especially one that counts itself a melting pot. The unabashedly Ro-

mantic conception of mind and of poetry as congregations of conflict-
ing and harmonizing forces preoccupies Ammons on virtually every
page. He shares, however, the political application of this figuration
with Ginsberg and Whitman, and surprisingly with Robert Pinsky,
whose *An Explanation of America* begins with the identical premise that
one may lay the nation open to the grandest possible *explication de texte*.

The conclusion of the poem (roughly its last twenty-three sections)
vigorously repeats and readjusts the moods, tones, and messages of
the whole: the hopeful and the despairing, the confident and the
weary, the abstract and the fastidious sides of Ammons' personality
have one final moment in which to express themselves. He starts this
stretto of the piece with a question that affirms his debts to both American populism and Wallace Stevens: "what are my hopes: / it's hard to
tell what an abstract poet wants" (69). He is abstract insofar as he is
concerned with abstractions and because by this point he has identified
himself with *the* American poet as a composite of all the single ones: *e
pluribus poetis unus.* His answers to his own self-questioning summarize
his natural, ecological, and cosmic concerns:

> my hopes
>
> are for a context in which the rosy can keep its edges out of
> frost: my hopes are for a broad sanction that gives range
> to life, for the shining image of nothingness within which
>
> schools of images can swim contained and askelter: my hopes
> are that the knots of misery, depression, and disease can
> unwind into abundant resurgences:
>
> (69)

Such attention contains its own undoing, or at least its requisite dangers. Praying too much, one might forget to shop for dinner, Ammons
thinks; likewise, "if the abstract poem goes out and never / comes back,
weaves the highest plume of mind beyond us," it acquires a bitter,
deathly spirit: "we have so many ways to go wrong / and so often go
wrong" Ammons confesses, that abstraction, turning to airiness, calls
us *from* the things of this world (rather than, in Richard Wilbur's famous phrase about love, calling us *to* them), creates our gods and enables us to "float in plenitude rather than in / starved definition."[9] As
Merrill does in the sacred books, Ammons imagines order and chaos
a twinned configuration, like the visible and the invisible, the coherent
and the incoherent. The question remains: to which will he pledge his
primary allegiance?

Physical facts and his own occasional darker moods tend him toward the periphery, the outer darkness where light is finally defeated; Ammons's dreams of reenacting a Dantean journey through the stars are thwarted by entropy and his own desert spaces; science and autobiography conspire:

> I have dreamed of a stroll-through, the
> stars in a close-woven, showering bedazzlement, though
> diamond- or ruby-cool, in which I contemplated the universe
>
> at length: apparently, now, such dreams, foolish anyway,
> must be abandoned and the long, empty, freezing gulfs of
> darkness must take their place: come to think of it, though,
>
> I'm not unfamiliar with such gulfs, even from childhood, when
> the younger brother sickened and then moved no more: and
> ahead lies a gulf light even from slow stars can never penetrate,
>
> a dimension so endless not even the universal scale suits it:
> the wise advice, don't get beyond yourself into foolish
>   largeness,
> when at my step is a largeness the universe lies within:
>
> (72–73)

On the one hand he turns aside from the well-made poems, those that take no risks and prefer the potential deadness of small completions to the spaciousness of astronomical assimilations; on the other, he understands that pioneering journeys to the periphery end in a complementary deadness, a dispersal rather than a petrifaction. What is a poet to do? Ammons goes over in his mind the details of another habitual day, and significantly ends his poem with a double gesture: a lecture, a piece of advice to an importuning student ("another youth anxious for fame and sorry he doesn't / have it") and a vast, suicidal release that responds to the gesture of Shelley at the end of "Adonais," a precursive poem (though without the epic and scientific apparatus of *Sphere*) that also ends with a minilecture on the proper way to achieve immortality.

Death is the one event for which no preparation is possible, no repetition likely. (It is the opposite of the way one sexual experience prepares one for the next.) Nowhere does Ammons paint a bleaker picture of the vanity of human wishes and the little profit that worldly experience can bring:

> who knows
> whether in the middle years, after the flashing passions
> seem less like fountains and more like pools of spent flood

metal, one may not keep on partly because of that black sucker
at the end, mysterious and shiny: my skull, my own skull
(and yours) is to be enclosed—earpits, eye sockets, dangled-
   open

mouth—with soil, is to lie alone without comfort through
centuries and centuries, face (if any) up, as if anticipating
the return of the dream that will be only the arrival of

the nova: how sluggish consciousness, when in death
the nova is a wink away!

(74–75)

By such grim standards, the epic adventures of Whitman will serve not
a jot: Ammons would agree with Horace that "caelum, non animum,
mutant qui trans mare currunt" ("those who fly across the sea change
their skies, not their souls"). Ammons prefers for himself a Horatian
sufficiency: "I dream of a clean-wood / shack, a sunny pine trunk, a
pond, and an independent income: / if light warms a piney hill, it does
nothing better at the / farthest sweep of known space." Or so speaks
one side of his mind. Suddenly, however, and subtly, he begins a new
tack, specifically a nautical one. "We move and see but see mostly the
swim of / motion" he announces in stanza 146 (75). Such language
accords with his own flux and the images for it, but as he contemplates
motion within the swim of time, he begins to consider the human attempt to balance opposing forces (one is always forced to go below and
check one's metaphorical ballast) and he does so with an increasingly
clarified image from sailing:

   a wind may come up subtle or sudden and persist and you may

   have to go down and change the ballast, only to find when the
   wind does cease that uprightness in an imbalance is imbalance:
   (76)

And once again the opposing forces of the universe place us in their
midst, buoyantly supporting us, both as individuals and as a collective
mass; "we are alone in a sea," he asserts in one of his most beautiful
and daring stanzas, that

   shows itself nowhere in a falling surf but if it does not
   go on forever folds back into a further motion of itself:
   the plenitude of nothingness! planets seeds in a coronal

   weaving so scant the fabric is the cloth of nakedness:
   Pluto our very distant friend skims a gulf so fine and far
   millions and thousands of millions of years mean little to—

> how far lost we are, if saving is anywhere else: but light,
> from any distance or point we've met it, shines with a similar
> summation, margin affirmational, so we can see edges to the

> black roils in the central radiances, galaxies colliding in
> million-year meetings, others sprung loose into spiral
> unwindings: fire, cold space, black concentration:
>
> (77)

From "the plenitude of nothingness" and "the cloth of nakedness" Ammons receives energizing excitement rather than immobilizing fears. Adjusting his own intellectual and emotional balance to a cosmic and marine harmony of the tidal sways in which he locates his poetry, he brings the poem to its end, the sphere of its own motion having been amply clarified by an earlier image: "this poem is an elongated cylinder / designed to probe feeling, recognition, and realization, / to plunder the whoozies of the world sensationally and cause / to come to bear what is and may be" (75).

The effort to consolidate polar opposites finds an analogue in Ammons's political aspirations, as both an application and a variant of his Lucretian vision. Steering a middle course between "differences" and "the common tide of feelings," he hopes for the "specific congruence of form and / matter" in the creation of

> a united, capable poem, a united, capable mind, a united
>   capable
> nation, and a united nations! capable, flexible, yielding,
> accommodating, seeking the good of all in the good of each:
>
> (79)

Ammons's political slogans, his Fourth of July exclamations, are less original than his coupling of scientific language to his central metaphoric purposes, but they are no less a part of his didactic program, just as Whitman's rancorous mumblings are the inevitable result and also the cause of his democratic vistas. His ending, which is also the new beginning to which "Corsons Inlet" had testified at its conclusion, embodies what he had earlier called his "magnum hokum" in a uniquely American image, which itself metamorphoses out of and then back into the spiritual bark with which Shelley alights to follow the beckoning light of Keats at the end of "Adonais":

> to float the orb or suggest the orb is floating: and, with the
> mind thereto attached, to float free: the orb floats, a bluegreen
> wonder: so to touch the structures as to free them into rafts

that reveal the tide: many rafts to ride and the tides make a
place to go: let's go and regard the structures, the six-starred
easter-lily, the beans feeling up the stakes: we're gliding: we

*are* gliding: ask the astronomer, if you don't believe it: but
motion as a summary of time and space is gliding us: for a
  while,
we may ride such forces: then, we must get off: but now this

beats any amusement park by the shore: our Ferris wheel, what
  a
wheel: our roller coaster, what mathematics of stoop and climb:
  sew
my name on my cap: we're clear: we're ourselves: we're sailing.

                                                    (79)

The stanza floats between the vagueness of infinitive phrases, which
seem to extend from the preceding stanzas without truly clarifying
them (but which may actually be, retrospectively, infinitives of result:
"in order to float the orb . . . let's go and regard the structures") and
the assurances of present tense declaration ("we're gliding . . . we're
sailing"). Likewise, the globe of the preceding stanza ("a united
nations") turns into the floating orb of this one, which itself then metamorphoses into the floating but less spheroid rafts that he sets adrift.
    Ammons' childlike wonder ("we *are* gliding") finds a temporary jus-
tification in external authority ("ask the astronomer if you don't believe it"), but since everything in this stanza seems provisional, one
tone or image quickly supplanting another, we cannot be surprised
that the kid in him takes over for a moment as it would in any adult
reliving childhood pleasures and fears in an amusement park. The
stanza undergoes so many metamorphoses that the dizzying movements of the Ferris wheel ride have their stylistic implications for our
own experience. The orb, for example, seems initially to be the product of our moving it, but it then floats freely, "with the / mind thereto
attached." Just as soon as rafts have become land structures, lilies, or
bean poles, Ammons returns us to wavy gliding motions, as if preparing us metaphorically with a proof of his succeeding hypotheses that
motion summarizes space and time together, thereby enabling such
deft transferences, and that space is gliding us, rather in the way that
the mind, at the start of the stanza, was implicitly floating the imagined
orb. But as soon as he acknowledges that motion glides us, he reverses
if only for a moment his grammatical and cosmological priorities by
suggesting that "we may ride such forces." The final roller coaster ride

embodies all of the jumpy peripateias that this stanza, the poem in miniature, has been making. The "this" of the penultimate tercet reminds us that what we are riding at last is a mental roller coaster not in any littoral (or literal) amusement park but in a Coney Island of the mind. The final setting out exists only because the poet has subsumed his image, at last, within the clear dimensions of an imagined, internalized geography. It is appropriate that the poem comes to its one and only full stop on an assertion of perpetual motion. Even the choice of the progressive present tense ("we're sailing") uplifts us from temporality into a virtually infinite condition just at the moment when we might long for stillness. The period—itself an inscribed sphere—leaves us in full, giddy possession of Ammons's circularities. In his ending he demonstrates his earlier question/assertion: he *has* made a home of motion.

# FIVE

# "Driving to the Limits of the City of Words": The Poetry of Adrienne Rich

Polemic has its own natural claims to recognition in any discussion of didacticism, but it is neither for her political programs nor for her visionary anger that Adrienne Rich most warrants attention. Rather, it is her intelligent, insistent exploration of the grounds and possibilities of language itself that earns her a place in this book. She has seldom received the *literary* criticism she most deserves; understandably, her defenders usually take a feminist line, discussing and approving her poetry mostly in terms of its political content or in relation to her prose explorations, and her hostile critics simply adjust their sights in the same way but with an aim to destroy rather than to praise. Considerably less has been said about Rich as a poet; in their anxious desire to have their say about radical politics, lesbianism, female hysteria, patriarchal structures (the list could be extended), most critics have ignored the real innovations and the intelligent accommodation in Rich's poetry to linguistic concerns.[1] For her, diving into the wreck of civilization or consciousness always means moving into some untrodden region of her mind (Keats's description of his poetic program in the "Ode to Psyche") and exploring language itself.

This chapter's title comes from "Images for Godard," Rich's 1970 homage to the most political of film directors. The poem's opening images derive from Wittgenstein's speculation about the inevitably organic and constructed, one might say the civilized and urban, force of language as a defining, limiting place: "Our language can be seen as an ancient city: a maze of little streets and squares, of old and new houses with additions from various periods; and this surrounded by a multitude of new boroughs with straight regular streets and uniform houses."[2] Exploring the city of language, any poet risks entrapment within it because it offers itself as both maze and salvation; the poet must discover a map for the city that is inevitably identical to it. The inadequacy of language to experience is a subject shared by a majority of the poets I have labeled didactic, but Rich goes even further, emphasizing language's political horrors and its falseness. In an increas-

ingly bourgeois society, language consists of translations and fibs, lists
of things desperately strung together to make a necklace of shabby
desires. And, although "every existence speaks a language of its own"³
Rich wishes to discover in language a map not only for herself but also
for the larger community—often a community of women, sometimes
one that includes both sexes—of which she is a part. The adequacy of
language versus its inadequacy and the attempt to assert commonality
in the face of the knowledge of individuality are her constant themes.

Another poem from her most politically assertive period (from *The
Will to Change* and dated 1969) offers a miniaturized version of these
issues. "Our Whole Life" both dramatizes and proposes a relationship
between language and political status:

> Our whole life a translation
> the permissible fibs
>
> and now a knot of lies
> eating at itself to get undone
>
> Words bitten thru words
>
> meanings burnt-off like paint
> under the blowtorch
>
> All those dead letters
> rendered into the oppressor's language
>
> Trying to tell the doctor where it hurts
> like the Algerian
> who walked from his village, burning
>
> his whole body a cloud of pain
> and there are no words for this
>
> except himself
>
> 　　　　　　　　　(*FD*, 133)

The seeming randomness of the technique—the absence of punctuation, the participial nature of phrases, the infrequent verbs—makes
the poem, like so much else in Rich's work, seem entirely provisional.
In the whole poem there are but two real predicates, appearing in
subordinate clauses, and, at the end, a deliberately weak copulative.
The horror of pain is its permanence: it takes no verbs. Any translation is like a photograph, immortalizing a reality of which its form is
an inadequate imitation and that its articulating can hardly hope to
cure. The fecklessness of articulation is a dangerous recognition for a

poet who claimed earlier that "only where there is language is there world" ("The Demon Lover," *FD*, 84).

The search for integrity or wholeness may be doomed to failure, and closure itself an illusion. Our lives are broken; the wasteland offers little consolation or totality. As maps of wholes (and like lists, a form Rich favors), poems themselves are also like wire photos whose essence is division and particularity: an accumulation of dots amounting to only the appearance of an image. In "Waking in the Dark" Rich wonders:

> The thing that arrests me is
>> how we are composed of molecules
>
> (he showed me the figure in the paving stones)
>
> arranged without our knowledge and consent
>
>> like the wirephoto composed
>> of millions of dots
>
>> in which the man from Bangladesh
>> walks starving
>>> on the front page
>>> knowing nothing about it
>
>> which is his presence for the world
>>> (*FD*, 152)

Presence and representation, the relationship of reality to a linguistic understanding of it—these subjects have obsessed Rich since her third volume, *Snapshots of a Daughter-in-Law* (1963), in which she finally broke the bonds of conventional form and of conventional female roles as well. It was in the title poem that she first acknowledged those "permissible fibs" in her own life, which "Our Whole Life" raises to a communal, political level.

What to do with inadequate tools and how to find the right ones: these are Rich's early, breakthrough motifs. In "The Roofwalker" (1961), she portrays a life of daring self-exposure that is, at the same time, unchosen and therefore a passive submission to rules not of her own making. Again, she questions not only the adequacy of maps as guides to truth but also the purposefulness of any daring that is *merely* apparent. The poem treats poetry itself as a vehicle for the poet's life; work is never selected but somehow dictated. The poet tries to break free from passivity only to succumb to another, less terrifying passiveness. Her choice is not a real one, her vocabulary limited by the rules

of others: after identifying with the builders, she questions the worth
of her own metaphor:

> Was it worth while to lay—
> with infinite exertion—
> a roof I can't live under?
> —All those blueprints,
> closings of gaps,
> measurings, calculations?
> A life I didn't choose
> chose me: even
> my tools are the wrong ones
> for what I have to do.
> I'm naked, ignorant,
> a naked man fleeing
> across the roofs
> who could with a shade of difference
> be sitting in the lamplight
> against the cream wallpaper
> reading—not with indifference—
> about a naked man
> fleeing across the roofs.
>
> (*FD*, 49–50)

The poems of the sixties express discontent, sometimes without a clear
vision of alternatives: does the dangerous exertion of the roofwalker's
life outweigh the passivity of his or her not having chosen it? Would
she prefer reading about the experience to enacting a life of danger?
The balancing act required of both worker and speaker in the poem
is terrible, tenuous, and ultimately unfulfilling. But this has been all
along the condition of the speakers and characters in Rich's early poems, the ones praised by Auden and other early reviewers for their
good manners and their formal proprieties. Self-exploration comes to
mean, in Rich's career as in that of any major poet, a quest for an
adequate language, and "The Roofwalker," with its own vaguenesses,
exemplifies her difficulties during this period.

Rich's work appears, at first glance, to have moved away from the
graceful elegance of two early volumes to the more spare, jagged, and
free forms of the past two decades, and from poems about lovely
things and scenes to those about war, torture, and oppression. But
with the omniscience of hindsight one can see how the beginning contained all that followed. The characteristic early themes, presented
with mature prosodic assurance, are suffocation, alienation, and en-

tombment. The poems constitute defenses against outer threats and inner doubts. In "Storm Warnings," a girl shuns the fluctuations in the external and internal climates, her "sole defense" to "draw the curtains" (*FD*, 3); in "The Uncle Speaks in the Drawing Room," a bastion of refined order fears in troubled times "for crystal vase and chandelier" (*ARP*, 2–3). Aunt Jennifer, embroiderer of elegant tigers, is restrained by "the massive weight of Uncle's wedding band": the pride and strength of her tigers complement her life of frustrated confinement. At the awful price of her own freedom, sublimation has produced art: "When Aunt is dead, her terrified hands will lie / Still ringed with ordeals she was mastered by. / The tigers in the panel that she made / Will go on prancing, proud and unafraid" (*FD*, 4).

The people in *A Change of World* (1951) and *The Diamond Cutters* (1955) are elegant, passive, and will-less. The Griselda-like woman in "An Unsaid Word" "has power to call her man / From that estranged intensity / Where his mind forages alone, / Yet keeps her peace and leaves him free" (*FD*, 5). But she does not go foraging herself. A professor's wife can only begin to articulate her discontent: "I thought that life was different than it is" ("Autumn Equinox," *PSN*, 25). The tourists in those poems composed during a year in Europe are essentially out of place and barely in control: "We had to take the world as it was given . . . And always time was rushing like a tram / Through streets of a foreign city" ("Ideal Landscape," *FD*, 13). "Lucifer in the Train" wittily invokes the first traveler to an alien land for guidance:

> O foundered angel, first and loneliest
> To turn this bitter sand beneath your hoe,
> Teach us, the newly-landed, what you know;
> After our weary transit, find us rest.
>                               (*PSN*, 18)

The alienation in these poems is neither painful nor merely fashionable; rather, it inspires creativity and a set of formalist values: "Art requires a distance: let me be / Always the connoisseur of your perfection" ("Love in the Museum," *ARP*, 5); "Form is the ultimate gift that love can offer— / The vital union of necessity / With all that we desire, all that we suffer" ("At a Bach Concert," *FD*, 6). The human heart requires "proud restraining purity" to repair itself in a world of inevitable imperfection and disappointment. Art defends against invasions from without and threats from within. This youthful stoicism half-accepts the reality of human weakness yet holds out for an ideal landscape and an ideal form for poetry, however distanced. In poems like "The Roofwalker," Rich begins to abandon this last infirmity of the

Romantic mind, because she increasingly refuses to take the world as it is given. Her distaste for lapidary forms and for the calm betrayals and falsehoods of language gives way to her later, far from adolescent, rebellion against tradition. Just as she began to realize in her late twenties that the rules by which she was living a privileged life as a model Cambridge mother and faculty wife were false, that she *was* Aunt Jennifer, so to speak, so did she disavow the rules for poetry that enabled her to tell fibs in her first two books: "I had suppressed . . . certain disturbing elements to gain that perfection of order" (*ARP*, 89), she later admitted.

No wonder, then, that Rich's poetry became increasingly didactic and overtly concerned with the power of language to hide and to distort. One's whole life-as-translation necessitates an attempt, however arduous, to speak in the original tongue and to authenticate the true self. But how can the poet do this when language itself works against her?—her tools are the wrong ones. Even Gabriel, the eponymous angel of a 1968 poem, speaks no language and makes his annunciation with only his body. Silence has replaced such artful proclamations as older generations of poets or painters might have construed, and the relationship between speaker and listener reduces itself to a pitiful, desperate request:

> It's true    there are moments
> close and closer together
> when words stick    in my throat
> > *the art of love*
> > *the art of words*
> I get your message Gabriel
> just    will you stay looking
> straight at me
> awhile longer
>
> (*PSN*, 115–16)

The dangers of language painfully assert themselves in the failures of love, as (autobiographically) Rich recounts the breakdown of her marriage and the gradual avowal of her lesbianism; these linguistic traps are also connected, in the political poems of the Vietnam era, to more public forms of oppression. Increasingly in Rich's work, public and private spheres cease to have opposite meanings. Rather, they complement one another; Rich's feminist politics is condensed in one of the two epigraphs to *Diving into the Wreck* (1973), from George Eliot: "There is no private life which is not determined by a wider public life."

Gabriel's silences prepare Rich's readers for her more prolonged re-
fusals to hear or to repeat lies in her poetry. Between language and
silence, a poet must feel herself trapped by the strongest paradoxes,
as all language since Mallarmé has been haunted by the dream of the
blank page as the perfect, only untranslated, poem. Verbalization can
eliminate moral impulses, as Daniel Berrigan's remark reminds readers in the epigraph to "The Burning of Paper Instead of Children"
(*FD*, 116–19), a poem (1968) that succeeds both in asserting Rich's
frustrations with language and in finding a new language apposite to
her political discontent. "The Burning of Paper" is a paradigm for her
search for a poetic rhythm that will include prose, and for multiple
voices that are not her own but which she can appropriate into her
own.

Its three prose sections establish and clarify an argument. Narrative
and declaration, two of Rich's "modes," intersect with her free-form
poetic lines, her vehicle for contemplation. A neighbor, recollecting
memories of Hitler, tells her "there are few things that upset me so
much as the burning of a book" when their two sons are caught in
flagrante. His statement leads her to a string of autobiographical associations, involving her father's library, Dürer, Herodotus, The Book
of the Dead, and *The Trial of Jeanne d'Arc*: "love and fear in a house /
knowledge of the oppressor / I know it hurts to burn" (*FD*, 117). As
counter to "the oppressor's language," always necessary for communication, she posits "a tune of silence," in which music, chemistry, and
sensual contact can give "relief from this tongue." Muteness fascinates
Rich: she has inherited a staple of Romantic primitivism from Wordsworth and Whitman but continues to explore gradations of speech
and silence, from the fractured semiarticulate efforts of her "open admissions" students to her own sense of the availability and betrayals
that language makes possible. How can a poet find her tools? As she
plangently remarks in a later poem:

> I am afraid
> of the language in my head
> I am alone, alone with language
> and without meaning
> coming back to something written years ago:
> *our words misunderstand us*
> wanting a word that will shed itself like a tear
> onto the page
> leaving its stain
> > ("Tear Gas," 1969, *FD*, 198–99)

At this point in her life, "every act of becoming conscious," tied as it is to language and therefore bound to the inherent power structure, "is an unnatural act" ("The Phenomenology of Anger," 1972, *FD*, 169). In "The Burning of Paper" Rich quotes a student's moving essay, in all its eloquent incorrectness, as a simple antidote to the frustrated intellectual's meanderings:

> 3. *People suffer highly in poverty and it takes dignity and intelligence to overcome this suffering. Some of the suffering are: a child did not had dinner last night: a child steal because he did not have money to buy it: to hear a mother say she do not have money to buy food for her children and to see a child without cloth it will make tears in your eyes.*

(the fracture of order
the repair of speech
to overcome this suffering)
            (*FD*, 118)

David Kalstone has observed that the practical effect of the poet's parenthetical remark is to leave us unsure whether repairing speech will help to overcome suffering or whether the infinitive demands to be heard in counterpoint to the two noun phrases, with an implicit ellipsis: "it is necessary . . . to overcome this suffering."[4] In addition, the two different *kinds* of genitive, the first clearly objective ("the fracture of order"), the second far more ambiguous (is "the repair of speech" the process by which speech is repaired or the reparation that speech can make to order, and then to suffering?), enrich and connect the poem's political and linguistic dimensions. However ambiguous the poet's parentheses, and however awkward the student's grammar, the former takes a cue from the power of the latter's essay, ending her poem with the cool rhythm of prose exposition, a rhythm that weaves all the earlier motifs into a fugal stretto:

> 5. I am composing on the typewriter late at night, thinking of today. How well we all spoke. A language is a map of our failures. Frederick Douglass wrote an English purer than Milton's. People suffer highly in poverty. There are methods but we do not use them. Joan, who could not read, spoke some peasant form of French. Some of the suffering are: it is hard to tell the truth; this is America; I cannot touch you now. In America we have only the present tense. I am in danger. You are in danger. The burning of a book arouses no sensation in me. I know it hurts to burn. There are flames of napalm in Catonsville, Maryland. I know it hurts to burn.

(119)

Rich's obsession with listing and her habit of conjugating verbs for her readers, as at the end of "Diving into the Wreck" ("I am she: I am he . . . We are, I am, you are . . . the one"), support my hypothesis that she everywhere dreams of the possibilities of learning and teaching the primary rules of a new language. The drill-like nature of her recitations, instructing through repeating, suggests the poet's role as grammarian and linguist. But silence still attracts her, as it did her Romantic predecessors, because one can sometimes learn the lessons of the past more completely through hieroglyphs or unlinguistic signatures. Like Wordsworth's "The Ruined Cottage," the classic "archaeological" poem in which an interpreter reads the details of crumbled house and overgrown landscape as an extension of human biography, Rich's 1974 "From an Old House in America" (*FD*, 212–22) is the beginning of her latest phase, in which she reads history via the *liber naturae* and searches for details of life among prelinguistic evidence. In sixteen sections of unrhymed couplets, the poem telescopes history expansively, beginning at a summer house, from which the speaker reads the marks she finds as evidence of the "mostly un-articulate" lives, the ghosts present in "the humble tenacity of things," some useless, others mysteriously whole ("this pack of cards with no card missing"). It is the beginning of what might be called her Elizabeth Bishop phase, in which domestic details are first noticed, then pondered, then embraced, for what they say and what value they communicate. One may even detect, momentarily, Bishop's naive sense of wonder:

> Like turning through the contents of a drawer:
> these rusted screws, this empty vial
>
> useless, this box of watercolor paints
> dried to insolubility—
>
> but this—
> this pack of cards with no card missing
>
> still playable
> and three good fuses
>
> and this toy: a little truck
> scarred red, yet all its wheels still turn
>
> The humble tenacity of things
> waiting for people, waiting for months, for years
>
> (213)

From the objects of the house the speaker moves to its former inhabitants, placing her hand "on the hand / of the dead, invisible palmprint / on the doorframe," and reading old postcards, which give her an image first of the dead husband and wife, and then of a dead man (probably her late husband) in her own past. At the poem's center she builds to a vision of America and history, no longer envisioning only her life and house or the past of either:

> All my energy reaches out tonight
> to comprehend a miracle beyond
>
> raising the dead: the undead to watch
> back on the road of birth
>
> (215)

I return to this poem later in this chapter, in a discussion of Rich's use of antiphonal structures, but for the moment, I wish it to stand for her efforts to inhabit the realms of the dead, to revive them through a language that combines prelinguistic signs and the excitement of her own new humanism.

This is where her recent volumes begin. "Cartographies of Silence" rehearses the old ideas that speech can lie, language can deceive, and silence, far from being an absence, can strip bare, as in Dreyer's film *The Passion of Joan of Arc*. Rich knows this, wearily acknowledging, "it was an old theme even for me: / Language cannot do everything" (*FD*, 235). Now even muteness can deceive, as she ruefully admits in "A Woman Dead in Her Forties," an elegy about an independent WASP, a college dean who customarily foreswore intimacy in favor of the proud consolations of safe distance. To the establishment culture, pain and strong feeling go unmentioned because they are unmentionable, but Rich looks back to regret the deception of silence: "Most of our love took the form / of mute loyalty . . . We stayed mute and disloyal / because we were afraid" (*FD*, 255). Rich has always resisted the complacencies of accepted speech as well as those of conventional mores, but her refusal is even more notable as she passes into middle age. Her growing dissatisfaction with silence and with speech itself encourages her to bald statements of rejection: "these are words I cannot choose again: / *humanism   androgyny* / . . . / their glint is too shallow." (*FD*, 262–63). Or: "Old words:   *trust   fidelity* / Nothing new yet to take their place" (*FD*, 284). In the same poem ("For Memory"), she defines the difficulties of freedom as "daily, prose-bound, routine / remembering. Putting together, inch by inch / The starry worlds. From all the lost collections" (285). Thus, accumulation, one of her characteristic stylistic choices, receives its own justification in the psychological and moral arrangements she prefers.

Although she seems, as above, to disavow it, a delicate humanism has infused Rich's work at least since "A Valediction Forbidding Mourning" (1970), beneath the rage and anger that also inform the more thoroughly political poems. It is a humanism intimately connected to concerns for discovering truth in language and language as the proper vehicle for truth. In that earlier poem, two initial phrases open into a complete sentence, which significantly introduces a linguistic motif: "My swirling wants. Your frozen lips. / The grammar turned and attacked me" (*FD*, 136). Language assaults as well as corrupts, but the woman wants to control, rather than submit to, the only power she may own:

> A last attempt: the language is a dialect called metaphor.
> These images go unglossed: hair, glacier, flashlight.
> When I think of a landscape I am thinking of a time.
> When I talk of taking a trip I mean forever.
> I could say: those mountains have a meaning
> but further than that I could not say.
>
> To do something very common, in my own way.
>
> (137)

Making a last attempt to break through language to meaning, she resigns herself to, and in, an infinitive of expectation. The very "common"ness of the goal surpasses the assertion of individuality ("in my own way") as the single voice asks to speak for others.

This is the emotional tenor of many of her recent poems. Tenderness replaces terror; speaking for others allows her to speak for herself. The course of public life—the end of Vietnam, the gains of the women's movement—as well as the frank coming-to-terms-with her own homosexuality, may account for this new maturity. But the wisdom of middle age does not signal complacency. On the contrary, as the very fact as well as the content of *Twenty-One Love Poems* attests, patience is matched by the urgent desire to make up for lost time ("At forty-five, I want to know even our limits," *FD*, 237) and by future reckonings:

> and we still have to stare into the absence
> of men who would not, women who could not, speak
> to our life—this still unexcavated hole
> called civilization, this act of translation, this half-world.
>
> (239)

Rich would agree with Robert Frost's adage that poetry is what gets lost in translation; she has sought for a poetry that will not betray its sources but will accommodate the truths of silence through articulation. As she acknowledges in her *Love Poems*, "I fear this silence, / this inarticulate life," and her lover helps make "the unnameable / nameable" (240). Poetry begins, like politics, in the body, but Rich is able to "start to speak again," as she claims in a recent poem ("North American Time," *FD*, 324–28), precisely because, as for any post-Romantic poet, the powers of articulation must incorporate the truths and combat the delusions of muteness. She states her credo most forcefully at the end of "Cartographies of Silence," as much a map to the contours of her speech as a blueprint of the forms of rigorous silence:

> If from time to time I envy
> the pure annunciations to the eye
>
> the *visio beatifica*
> if from time to time I long to turn
>
> like the Eleusinian hierophant
> holding up a simple ear of grain
>
> for return to the concrete and everlasting world
> what in fact I keep choosing
>
> are these words, these whispers, conversations
> from which time after time the truth breaks moist and green.
>
> (*FD*, 236)

Although she complains obsessively that "in the matrix of need and anger" "the words / get thick with unmeaning" ("When We Dead Awaken," *FD*, 151), only language offers the sustaining, magical power to present and to animate: truth opens up, green and living, not through the unknown ceremonies of the mysteries but more mysteriously through the agency of metaphor and its appropriations.

Like any poet, of course, Rich relies largely on the various categories of figurative language, however one chooses to label them, to contain and then to augment her statements. More striking, though, is her ability to make out of imagery a discursive technique. As in "Waking in the Dark," part of which is quoted above, she realizes the differences between selfhood and "presence for the world" as versions of the contrast between integrity and partiality, pain and knowledge, and, most important, truth and its signifiers. Occasionally, Rich will develop an image into a conventional vehicle to convey discursive truths symbolically. Owing to its confusions, "The Roofwalker" is a relatively unsuccessful attempt at this, while the famous "Diving into the Wreck" (*FD*, 162–64) more strongly encapsulates in a narrative framework the motifs of exploration and submergence in what Conrad

termed the "destructive element." Although she is not especially playful with language—her didacticism would scorn the ingenious wit of
Nemerov and Merrill as unreliable or duplicitous—Rich occasionally
employs a central device (as in "The Burning of Paper") with an ironic
sense of its dimensions or, as in "Tear Gas" and "Storm Warnings" and
the more recent "Frame," submits the image of her title to various
examinations.[5]

Rich is, however, seldom comfortable with this strategy, the kind of
thing seen more frequently in Howard Nemerov or Richard Wilbur.
Instead, relying on an associationism the roots of which extend from
Wordsworth and native English empiricism through surrealism and
"deep image" poetics, Rich develops poems along strands of connection provided by imagistic contexts. Thus, the image serves a didactic
purpose, if by "didactic" one understands the lessons that the poet
both encloses and discovers through her associative structures. Rich's
middle period offers the most frequent use of such discursive images.
The occasional literalness of her procedure marks these images as the
tool of an intellectual more than of a lyricist. I have already given examples of an obsession with words, usually unacceptable ones, that occupy the speaker's consciousness; the beginning of the title poem in
*Leaflets* exemplifies this procedure:

> The big star, and that other
> lonely on black glass
> overgrown with frozen
> lesions, endless night
> the Coal Sack gaping
> black veins of ice on the pane
> spelling a word:
> > *Insomnia*
> not manic but ordinary
> to start out of sleep
> turning off and on
> this seasick neon
> vision, this
> division
> > (*FD*, 99–100)

From the obliquities of phrasing and unpunctuated syntax, a word
comes clear as the result of a waking consciousness and a pulling together of individual particles in a nocturnal scene. Not until the climactic seventh line does one hear a phrase without major assonance
or alliteration, as if Rich is suggesting that insomnia stands alone, vi-

sually and aurally, as the insomniac herself lies alone amid the eternal silence of infinite spaces.

More dense is the structure of "Ghazals: Homage to Ghalib," dated poems organized in couplets, which Rich claims in a note as "autonomous and independent of the others." The continuity and unity flow from the associations of images playing back and forth among the couplets in any single ghazal. The associative play allows the lyric and the programmatic sides of Rich's art to intersect; an expression of momentary feeling builds through a network, connecting private and public realms. Thus, for example, the second of three poems dated 7/26/68:

> A dead mosquito, flattened against a door;
> his image could survive our comings and our goings.
>
> LeRoi! Eldridge! listen to us, we are ghosts
> condemned to haunt the cities where you want to be at home.
>
> The white children turn black on the negative.
> The summer clouds blacken inside the camera-skull.
>
> Every mistake that can be made, we are prepared to make;
> anything less would fall short of the reality we're dreaming.
>
> Someone has always been desperate, now it's our turn—
> we who were free to weep for Othello and laugh at Caliban.
>
> I have learned to smell a *conservateur* a mile away:
> they carry illustrated catalogues of all that there is to lose.
>
> (*FD*, 107–8)

The last couplet, shocking conservative readers now as well as then, comes logically at the close of the poem, affirming a lesson that the speaker has developed through the preceding imagery. What looks at first like an imagist's perceptions, the stuff of an urban haiku, builds toward that final illustrated catalogue. The "image" of a dead black thing, trivial and unmourned, prepares us for the final illustration of loss. The dead mosquito connects to the black men addressed in the second couplet (as the door leads to a home), and thence to the fictive black men referred to in the fourth (who, as part of the baggage of traditional high culture, belong ironically among the adumbrations of the *conservateur*). The urban ghosts in the second couplet are tied to both the dead mosquito and the reversed white and black colors in the third, as the "images" in all but the fourth couplet suggest the major "theme," a mind contemplating images and their double adherence to

inner and outer realities. What, then, do we do with the seemingly
unconnected couplet, which contains no images? We should understand it, I suggest, through the logical associations it keeps with the
nonimagistic parts of the rest of the poem: to dream of reality is to
summon an image that "could survive" the distinction between aspiration and fact; such dreaming might remind us of *The Tempest*, where
it becomes part of the play's concern. That couplet also prepares for
the poem's final denunciation by poising daring, readiness, and futurity against defensiveness, timidity, and the protection of the status
quo.

One can discover the same impulse—to teach through images—in a
variety of Rich's poems. It is intimately connected with another impulse, the need to remain faithful to momentary passion and thought
and to turn away from her earlier static perfections to a form that will
accommodate swirling wants and volatile gestures. What often may
seem random, however, is rarely so, even when Rich uses methods and
motifs that come from film rather than from more static art. The mu-
seums, sculptures, and concerts of her first two volumes have given
way to "Snapshots" in the third, and then, in the middle books, to
"Leaflets," "Images," and "Shooting Script," in the last of which couplets break down to single lines, strung together. Even here, however,
the seemingly unconnected images are resolved by variations on images of circularity and return: a shell, the sea, the rhythm of the waves,
a dialogue, a monologue. Language and sound, give-and-take, reci-
procity and isolation, are all involved in these bits. From the very beginning of the first part of "Shooting Script":

We were bound on the wheel of an endless conversation.

Inside this shell, a tide waiting for someone to enter.

A monologue waiting for you to interrupt it.

A man wading into the surf. The dialogue of the rock with the
breaker.

The wave changed instantly by the rock; the rock changed by
the wave returning over and over.

The dialogue that lasts all night or a whole lifetime.

A conversation of sounds melting constantly into rhythms.

A shell waiting for you to listen.

A tide that ebbs and flows against a deserted continent.

A cycle whose rhythm begins to change the meanings of words.

A wheel of blinding waves of light, the spokes pulsing out from
  where we hang together in the turning of an endless
  conversation.

The meaning that searches for its word like a hermit crab.

A monologue that waits for one listener.

An ear filled with one sound only.

A shell penetrated by meaning.

(FD, 137–38)

The images demonstrate not only Rich's reliance on lists as a form of
poetic organization, but also her inheritance from the Blake of *The
Marriage of Heaven and Hell*, especially the Proverbs of Hell, which
prove how apparently unconnected fragments, in this case epigrams,
may embody deeper connections.

   Like Blake, Rich is a poet with a strong missionary zeal and a didactic fervor. It is instructive to consider how her poetic forms and the
techniques of her discursiveness derive from political obsessiveness
and, more specifically, from anger. It is anger, however, the correlative of which is love, as in a 1972 poem concerning the interconnect-
edness of personal grief and political structures, of the duplicities of
language and the necessity of attempts to tell the truth:

You show me the poems of some woman
my age, or younger
translated from your language

Certain words occur: *enemy, oven, sorrow*
enough to let me know
she's a woman of my time

obsessed

with Love, our subject:
we've trained it like ivy to our walls
baked it like bread in our ovens
worn it like lead on our ankles
watched it through binoculars as if
it were a helicopter
bringing food to our famine
or the satellite
of a hostile power

("Translations," FD, 169)

"Anger," Rich once remarked in conversation, "can be a kind of genius if it's acted on" (*ARP*, 111), and it is as a poet of and for anger that Rich has acted out her genius. Acting on anger establishes the necessary grounds for identity—emotional and poetic—from which other, gentler emotions may pour. In her earlier poetry, notably *Necessities of Life*, Rich duplicates the process outlined by Julia Kristeva in *Powers of Horror*: "I expel *myself*, I spit *myself* out, I abject *myself*, within the same motion through which 'I' claim to establish *myself*."[6] Rich has discovered an appropriate form, not a mere outlet, for her anger; in so doing, she creates a *self*, expelling and establishing simultaneously.

Aristotle calls anger the emotion closest to reason; the anger that gives birth to polemic should provide a strong basis for didactic poetry.[7] But most of us would agree experientially that anger frequently inhibits or prevents articulation: it may dam the wells of speech, or erupt with a fury that overflows all boundaries, but we seldom associate it with the formal control demanded by poetry. Rich herself, recognizing the ironic frustrations of working out of such an emotional impasse, has allowed this truth. Can the poet speak "words thick with unmeaning" in order to clarify, to reduce, and clearly to propound? Moreover, in performing their maneuvers, other great poetic haters like Blake and Pound usually work in forms more capacious than lyric, which give free rein to their emotions and counsels. Within the condensation of lyric, with its abbreviations of thought, intimacies of address, and suggestiveness of feeling, a poet seldom confines political advice, let alone full programs. Of the major political poets of our half of this century, Allen Ginsberg has followed the path pioneered by Blake and Whitman, while Robert Lowell developed out of his revised lyrics an extended commentary on the mirroring realms of public and private lives. But only Rich has radically redefined the scope and province of lyric, remaking it into a vessel solid enough to contain anger without bursting, and lucid enough to adduce political themes rationally. Emotions—rage, despair, hatred—that almost occupy the far side of articulation become an instrument as well as a subject.

The remainder of this chapter explores the poetic strategies, both the larger formal structures and the habits of syntax and style, that Rich has made her own. Three main tactics for organizing thought seem to have become comfortable for her, starting with her middle volumes. I label these list making, antiphony, and weaving; looking at them enables us to understand her particular brand of poetic teaching. The list is the technique of obsession, antiphony that of dialectic, weaving that of harmonious synthesis. Since critics have paid scant attention to Rich's methods, preferring to see her in the light of her political programs or their own, it may come as a surprise to discover that she is one of the most formally adept poets since Wallace Stevens.

Stevens might seem an unlikely name to utter in an essay that stresses Rich's turning aside from the strictly formalist lessons she learned from Auden, Frost, and Yeats, but she has herself given an explicit clue to her feelings for him in one of the "Blue Ghazals" from *The Will to Change* (1971), which is not included in her two *Selected Poems*. "You were our poet of revolution all along," she declares, and goes on to notice the "gaieties of anarchy," the disorder one finds in parades of political protest: "Disorder is natural, these leaves absently blowing / in the drinking fountain, filling the statue's crevice."[8] This homage to the poet of anarchy is juxtaposed with a reference to "the use of force in public architecture: / nothing, not even the honeycomb, manifests such control." As a connoisseur of chaos herself, Rich often takes a cue from Stevens in the very titles of poems: her "Script," "Snapshots," "Images," "Pieces," "Photograph," "Letters," and "Postcard" all betray a careful debt to the poet of "Prologues to What Is Possible," "Questions Are Remarks," "Asides on the Oboe," "Sketch of the Ultimate Politician," "Pieces," "A Postcard from the Volcano," "Extracts from Addresses to the Academy of Fine Ideas," "Prelude to Objects," and, above all, *Notes Toward a Supreme Fiction*.

Listing is a favorite form in contemporary American poetry.[9] Whitman, of course, is the seigneurial lister, with his exclamations, his resounding anaphora, greetings, collections of mementos and experiences, his use of inventory as the sole suitable mode for detailing the richness of the nation and the fullness of the self: "How can I but here chanting, invite you for yourself to collect bouquets of the incomparable feuillage of these States?" ("Our Old Feuillage"). From him have descended Williams, whose Dr. Paterson assembles the things of his world in book l of *Paterson*, and Ginsberg, with his breathy, impelling chants, apostrophes, and descriptions. But even Stevens reminds us in his titles, as in his techniques, of the need for notes, and of the two sorts of them: something elementary, in preparation for something else, and something tentative, experiential, and on-the-run. Like *The Prelude*, *Notes Toward a Supreme Fiction* in one way constitutes the whole of that fiction: it makes the very statement for which it was intended to prepare poet and reader. Lists, like notes, are provisional in two ways: they offer fodder, nourishment, what is required; and they may be temporary and, because forward looking, never adequate.

This provisional nature accounts for the frequency of lists in Rich's work. Wholeness, completion—of self or world—are unreal possibilities in our lives. And, especially after *Snapshots*, Rich's poetry adheres to the tentativeness of experience; her poems become ampler and more provisional as their lists duplicate the frustrated questioning from which they stem. "What burns in the dump today?" she asks in "Open-Air Museum" (*FD*, 63), casting a cold eye on the lapidary perfection of Richard Wilbur's "art" poems, or early Rich, or on the abstruseness of Stevens's "The Man on the Dump." The title poem of *Leaflets* defines the transitory nature of poems as political statements, testimonies to involvement, presence, and evanescence. They disintegrate like leaves, impermanent in a frenzied world. A leaflet is "merely something / to leave behind, a little leaf / in the drawer of a sublet room" (*FD*, 103).

Like others among her contemporaries, Rich relies on naming to identify the enemy: it is the first step in a political/poetic assault on norms that have failed. Obsession, hard to account for in any manifestation, may have been for a long time her prime impulse. Like a photograph, a list may represent an ever-changing reality, a vision always focusing on different arcs of a circumference. A list keeps vivid the horrors, as well as the lessons, of the past: to enumerate is to remind others of defilement and desertion, lest they forget: "These stays of tooled whalebone in the Salem museum— / erotic scrimshaw, practical even in lust." The questions of history, centering on reminders of its objects, reopen the wounds:

> The body has been exhumed from the burnt-out bunker;
> the teeth counted, the contents of the stomach told over.
>
> And you, Custer, the Squaw-killer, hero of primitive
>     schoolrooms—
> where are you buried, what is the condition of your bones?
>                                     ("Ghazals," *FD*, 108)

During her radical middle years, listing served Rich as a means of detailing lessons of history, accumulations within bourgeois society, and the fundamental ambivalence the poet feels when accounting for all the presences and absences in her world:

> What we've had to give up to get here—
> whole LP collections, films we've starred in
> playing in the neighborhoods, bakery windows
> full of dry, chocolate-filled Jewish cookies,
> the language of love-letters, of suicide notes,
> afternoons on the riverbank
> pretending to be children
>             ("Trying to Talk with a Man," *FD*, 149)

The same ambivalence that inspires momentary regret for abandoned objects occupies the central place in Rich's scenes of instruction, in which she accords sympathy to teacher as well as student, master and victim together. Consequently, in "Meditations for a Savage Child," where the prose passages from J.-M. Itard's diary about his failed experiment with the wild child of Aveyron are glossed by Rich's poetic interleavings, the inability to learn names is the clearest symptom of an inability to become civilized. Not just pleasure, but even a certain enlightened object fetishism informs her doctor's efforts; it is against this that Rich braces her subsequent lamentations:

> *There was a profound indifference to the objects of our pleasures and of our fictitious needs; there was still . . . so intense a passion for the freedom of the fields . . . that he would certainly have escaped into the forest had not the most rigid precautions been taken . . .*

In their own way, by their own lights
they tried to care for you
tried to teach you to care
for objects of their caring:

        glossed oak planks, glass
        whirled in a fire
        to impossible thinness

to teach you names
for things
you did not need

        muslin shirred against the sun
        linen on a sack of feathers
        locks, keys
        boxes with coins inside

they tried to make you feel
the importance of

        a piece of cowhide
        sewn around a bundle
        of leaves impressed with signs

to teach you language:
the thread their lives
were strung on

                        (*FD*, 179–80)

Rich's language exposes the fraudulence of even the commonest things, which she bitterly refuses to name: floor, pillow, book. She has the matter two ways at once. She lists things euphemistically but will not say them simply. She sympathizes with "Victor," the boy, but lavishes loving attention on all those nouns in the righthand column that culminate in that pathetically useless guardian of human literature and language itself.

One of the ironies of radical feminism is that after rejecting patriarchal stereotypes of female domesticity, the clichés of housekeeping-as-fulfillment, many women return to similar motifs—in their lived lives and in their literary work—with renewed and altered enthusiasms. Rich's recent poetry is filled with lists of what might have been condescendingly called in earlier days "women's subjects"—domestic life, indoors and out, attention to natural conditions of flora and fauna, a focus on traditional women's work, cooking and sewing—"a universe of humble things," she calls it in "Natural Resources," in which she adduces with touching simplicity the poet's role as archaeologist and builder:

> These things by women saved
> are all we have of them
>
> or of those dear to them
> these ribboned letters, snapshots
>
> faithfully glued for years
> onto the scrapbook page
>
> these scraps, turned into patchwork,
> doll-gowns, clean white rags
>
> for stanching blood
> the bride's tea-yellow handkerchief
>
> the child's height penciled on the cellar door
> In this cold barn we dream
>
> a universe of humble things—
> and without these, no memory
>
> no faithfulness, no purpose for the future
> no honor to the past
>
> (FD, 262)

Ordinariness has always made its claims on Rich's attention, but nowhere more effectively than in these recent poems. Precisely because

patriarchal society demands individual striving, and because power inevitably torments, she has increasingly seen social life as a collective
stay against individual assertions, and personal life as itself a collective
experience.

So, in "Transcendental Etude," the study and practice of life do not
involve a preparation for a competitive, virtuoso performing career
with its false glamour, but something more common. The end of the
poem contains Rich's most moving list, a composition of objets trouvés
by a woman who walks away "from the argument and jargon" and
begins an assemblage of fragile, delicate things:

> Vision begins to happen in such a life
> as if a woman quietly walked away
> from the argument and jargon in a room
> and sitting down in the kitchen, began turning in her lap
> bits of yarn, calico and velvet scraps,
> laying them out absently on the scrubbed boards
> in the lamplight, with small rainbow-colored shells
> sent in cotton-wool from somewhere far away,
> and skeins of milkweed from the nearest meadow—
> original domestic silk, the finest findings—
> and the darkblue petal of the petunia,
> and the dry darkbrown lace of seaweed;
> not forgotten either, the shed silver
> whisker of the cat,
> the spiral of paper-wasp-nest curling
> beside the finch's yellow feather.
> Such a composition has nothing to do with eternity,
> the striving for greatness, brilliance—
> only with the musing of a mind
> one with her body, experienced fingers quietly pushing
> dark against bright, silk against roughness,
> pulling the tenets of a life together
> with no mere will to mastery,
> only care for the many-lived, unending
> forms in which she finds herself,
> becoming now the sherd of broken glass
> slicing light in a corner, dangerous
> to flesh, now the plentiful, soft leaf
> that wrapped round the throbbing finger, soothes the wound;
> and now the stone foundation, rockshelf further
> forming underneath everything that grows.
>
> (FD, 268–69)

"Will" has resounded through so much of Rich's poetry, as both word and concept, that its denial here must strike a reader as a sign of a major shift in attitude. But even when she embeds the eternal within the transient, or the transcendent within the elemental (her version of Blake's program of seeing a world in a grain of sand), Rich remains a student, and a lister, of that which endures in fragility and strength. Flying up, sinking down, things retain their power to capture her attention and to focus her energy.

Listing, or enumeration, the trope of obsession, is one kind of didactic habit; antiphony, question and answer, the trope of dialectical exploration, is another. As in "Meditations for a Savage Child," quoted earlier, Rich often maintains a double allegiance; even at her angriest, as feminist critics have observed, her dream of burning the male enemy is a charitable one, directed not at murder but at transformation (see "The Phenomenology of Anger," *FD*, 165–69). Not even John Ashbery's double-columned poems manifest so strong a didactic stance, insistent on doubleness, as Rich's stichomythia, her passages resembling Socratic dialogues that go nowhere. Part 14 of "From an Old House in America" (*FD*, 220) is a naked conversation, "he said" versus "she said," questions without answers, rendering human relationships into a stalemated battle with no advancement. Conversation with no place to go, no resolution, appears once again in "Natural Resources" (*FD*, 258) in a reconstructed interview between a male correspondent and a female poet. "Can you imagine . . ." [x or y] he inquires, to which she "wearily" answers, "yes," she can imagine separate worlds of men and women. In both of these cases, Rich alights on the oldest technique out of Greek drama to portray irresolvable conflict. The nakedness of confrontation, so perennial a subject in Rich's work ("A Marriage in the Sixties," "Trying to Talk with a Man," "A Valediction Forbidding Mourning," "Leaflets," "The Phenomenology of Anger," "Rape," "Re-Forming the Crystal") demands its appropriate form for presentation. These mock catechisms, especially when leading to no resolution, convey the frustrations as well as the imaginative reachings out, in Rich's effort to confront, learn from, and teach the opposition.

Only two ways out are possible, and one is unlikely: a synthetic resolution to such dialectic maneuvers or confrontations. On rare occasions, in the hallucinated conjugations ("I am she, I am he . . .") that begin to coin a new language, Rich's speaker may construct a new idiom that breaks the bonds of gender and consequently the bondage of sexual exploitation. But another way, implicit in the forms of her longer poems, is more sympathetic: what I have labeled the technique of weaving, a way of interlacing voices, echoes, or motifs in poetry, creates a whole from distinct and separate elements. Individual readers will decide whether the resulting fabric is an organic unity or a crazy quilt of bits and patches, joined only by Rich's indomitable will. The medley, a genre Rich hit upon in the breakthrough title poem in *Snapshots of a Daughter-in-Law*, allows her to build for, or in, a poem a composite identity comparable to the composite selves that she accumulates in her pictures of the new woman she writes about and becomes. The recent poem "Culture and Anarchy" (*FD*, 275–80) proceeds chunk by chunk, verse paragraphs sprawled on the left- and right-hand margins, a first person voice interspersed with italicized fragments from nineteenth-century women's letters and diaries. It significantly opens at a rural house, as a descriptive poem echoing "Tintern Abbey" ("Daylilies / run wild, 'escaped' the botanists call it / from dooryard to meadow to roadside") before spreading open a list of accumulated objects:

> Rainy days at the kitchen table typing,
> heaped up letters, a dry moth's
> perfectly mosaiced wings, pamphlets on rape,
> forced sterilization, snapshots in color
> of an Alabama woman still quilting in her nineties,
> *The Life and Work of Susan B. Anthony.* . . .
>
> (275)

Naming, stitching, quilting—these activities continue throughout the poem, as if to account for, duplicate, and counter what she calls the "anarchy of August," but culture and anarchy often look complementary rather than antagonistic:

> Anarchy of August: as if already
> autumnal gases glowed in darkness underground
> the meadows roughen, grow guttural
> with goldenrod, milkweed's late-summer lilac,
> cat-tails, the wild lily brazening,
> dooryards overflowing in late, rough-headed
> bloom: bushes of orange daisies, purple mallow,
> the thistle blazing in her clump of knives,
> and the great SUNFLOWER turns
>
> (276–77)

The luscious elements are gorgeously presented, and flow trippingly from the tongue, now in perfect iambs ("autumnal gases," and so on), now cemented by alliteration ("grow guttural / with goldenrod") and slant or internal rhymes (milkweed . . . lilac . . . wild lily; brazening . . . late . . . daisies). Rich has focused her diction as well as her energy, aligning quotations from women's history against a natural foreground of her own detailing and against the implied contrast in her title borrowed from Matthew Arnold.

This doubleness proves, as it were, the unity suggested in the poem's last citation, a letter from Elizabeth Cady Stanton to Susan B. Anthony: *"I should miss you more than any other / living being from this earth . . . / Yes, our work is one, / we are one in aim and sympathy / and we should be together"* (280). Human identity is plural, collective, and although Rich's primary interest is in woman's identity, one can make the legitimate leap from gender to species since Rich herself had done so in "Diving into the Wreck" and "The Stranger." Boundaries blur, as she suggested in the title poem of *Necessities of Life*; even prose and poetry sit squarely together or, rather, inhabit one another's realms. In "The Burning of Paper," prose assumed the rhythms and condensation of lyric, and in "Culture and Anarchy" the very decision to print prose excerpts in poetic lineation, as above, forces readers to hear in those triple-stressed lines a rhythm appropriate to formal, public, and lyric pronouncement instead of to private address. Public-private, outer-inner, prose-poetry, self-other: all the old dichotomies break down, no longer through mere fiat but through the weaving of filaments of language into a unity.

Weaving and listing are sometimes alternatives to one another; the obsessive, hallucinated naming of enemies or victims makes for a monolithic, toneless articulation, whereas the interlacing of figures naturally embeds would-be opposites in one another's limits. But like the woman in "Transcendental Etude" "who survives to speak / new language," Rich has from her middle years onward absorbed the lessons of Penelope, sequentially weaving and unweaving, accumulating through lists that she then proceeds to unravel, trying to bring meaning and language, which she opposed to one another in "Tear Gas," into new coordinations with one another. The 1967 poem "Postcard" (*PSN*, 137), with its Stevensesque title, opposes the "dream of language / unlived behind the clouds" to the "hacked" bronze image of Rodin's Orpheus, paralyzed in silent pain. The perfect, because frozen, sculpture, a summary of all the works of art that appeared in Rich's early volumes, represents the primal poet as if petrified by the horrible force of his own song. Language kills, but it can also release, as her later work reveals. Even "Tear Gas," in the same volume, uses tears as a leitmotiv to balance desire and the inadequacy of desire in a search for sufficiency. The tears of the title, provoked during a political demonstration, combine with "tears of fear" and "tears of relief" on the public and private fronts as the speaker seeks "a way of saying" that will include, as well as cure her of, her laments. Once again, a strettolike conclusion picks up the earlier strands:

> things I have said which in a few years will be forgotten
> matter more to me than this or any poem
> and I want you to listen
> when I speak badly
> not in poems but in tears
> not my best but my worst
> that these repetitions are beating their way
> toward a place where we can no longer be together
> where my body no longer will demonstrate outside your
>   stockade
> and wheeling through its blind tears will make for the open air
> of another kind of action
>
> (I am afraid.)
> It's not the worst way to live.
>
> (*FD*, 200)

The simplicity of declaration acknowledges the usefulness of fear and counters the parenthetical, sotto voce statement made in shame or embarrassment. From an aside to a full articulation, from a muttered, private grief to a public conversion of fear to bravery, Rich's poetry produces a program for the discovery of sufficiency.

It does so nowhere more straightforwardly than in "Images for Godard," a radical linking of the political director to the seemingly hermetic, private Wallace Stevens. Again, the implied conjunction produces a woven alternative to a direct confrontation of the political and personal realms inhabited by the poet. Looking toward a lighted screen and attempting to shed light on her own life, the poet is living entirely in the present (how different a response to film from that of James Merrill in "Scenes of Childhood," where home movies trigger a Proustian recollection of lost worlds). All the infinitives expressing unfulfilled desires that Rich favors in this period—"to know," "to see," "to love"—inhabit the central sections of the poem, rehearsing the reflections of private life off the screen in the depiction of life upon it. Both the images and the naked sentiments of the poem's ending make the strongest case for Rich as Stevens's heir:

> Interior monologue of the poet:
> the notes for the poem are the only poem

the mind collecting, devouring
all these destructibles

the unmade studio couch the air
shifting the abalone shells

the mind of the poet is the only poem
the poet is at the movies

dreaming the film-maker's dream but differently
free in the dark as if asleep

free in the dusty beam of the projector
the mind of the poet is changing

the moment of change is the only poem
(PSN, 171–72)

Like film, a poem consists of a linear sequence of moments that change. Justification by feeling is not, however, artistically valid, because feeling does not organize art, however much it may inspire it. Like any major poet, Rich is searching throughout her radical period for the appropriate form of feeling—of discontent, wonder, and anger—and she discovers it in her technique. Saying merely "this is my thought" gives neither coherence nor credibility to speech, but combining the resources of notation, listing, and imaging, through a texture interwoven of various strands makes the drive to the city limits of language a feat of heroic exploration.

Antiphony is an easy means to structure provocation and response. The 1983 "Education of a Novelist" (*FD*, 314–17), like "Meditations for a Savage Child" and "Culture and Anarchy," offers a meditation on italicized lines from Ellen Glasgow's autobiography, but by the end the poet acknowledges her own resemblance to the novelist. Quotation becomes a linguistic appropriation, as one self merges with another that originally seemed merely a reflection. This dialectic—thesis and antithesis synthesized through an absorption of one voice into another—has been an American habit at least since William Carlos Williams's Dr. Paterson, and owes something to the more fractured, spasmodic medleys of voices in *The Cantos* and *The Waste Land*. But Rich differs from her male predecessors in committing herself to a personal merging of identities instead of focusing on vaster, communal voices. She would not say with Whitman, "I am great. I contain multitudes," but rather "I am contained by them." Like the speaker in the 1968 "Planetarium," thinking of Caroline Herschel, she might say: "I am bombarded yet    I stand," where bombardment includes the "direct path of a battery of signals" (*FD*, 116) and the more indirect (or, in her subsequent label, "untranslatable") pulsations that she attempts first to absorb, then to translate, then to retransmit.

If all this sounds curiously like the male stereotypes of woman as first the absorber, then the deliverer of life, it shows only that Rich has succeeded as much in rethinking and reformulating the clichés of identity as she has in employing domestic activity and details from rural life as the new ground for woman's identity. New presbyter may be only old priest writ large, but in Rich's case intelligence and artistic variety empower those images to teach an audience to see this woman as a renovated chameleon poet. "I am an American woman," she announced in "From an Old House in America" (1974), by which she means also all women, and just as "any woman's death diminishes" the composite speaker, so does she gain strength from the union of others: "I never chose this place / yet I am of it now" (*FD*, 216) echoes Rich's earlier passivity and her fortitude. The artistic weaving of strands becomes equivalent to the psychological and political solidarity with the miners and "raging stoic grandmothers" in "Natural Resources" (1977), but its roots lie deep in Rich's earlier work.

Unlike Stevens, progressively contenting himself with less, Rich in many ways affirms Blake's proverb that nothing less than *all* will satisfy. Her demands for sufficiency increase proportionately with her battle for self-realization and political change, via an expansion of her own person to include those of others. The early poem "Double Monologue" poses the problem succinctly:

> To live illusionless, in the abandoned mine-
>     shaft of doubt, and still
> mime illusions for others? A puzzle
>     for the maker who has thought
> once too often too coldly.
>
> Since I was more than a child
>     trying on a thousand faces
> I have wanted one thing: to know
>     simply as I know my name
> at any given moment, where I stand.
>                                    (*PSN*, 55)

Defining the self by withdrawing and fixing limits is one way, but Rich chooses the other way, of pushing beyond the boundaries and participating in other lives. To transform the enemy for his rebirth, to identify the enemy within: the goal is one of Keatsian empathy, hard won with pain and struggle. The title poem of *Necessities of Life* states the dilemma: either the self has a rigid identity, in which case it is a "small, fixed dot," "a dark-blue thumbtack / pushed into the scene," or else it loses itself under the onrush of other lives:

> After a time the dot
>
> begins to ooze. Certain heats
> melt it.
>       Now I was hurriedly
>
> blurring into ranges
> of burnt red, burning green,
>
> whole biographies swam up and
> swallowed me like Jonah.
>               *(FD, 55)*

Invoking and absorbing such various presences as Wollstonecraft, Wittgenstein, Godard, Louis Jouvet, and Caroline Herschel in the poems of the late sixties, Rich confronts the challenge of the past to identify foreign elements within herself, to share female weakness and strength, and to teach us—this is her stunningly original theme—the dangers as well as the solaces of empathy. Reaching beyond the sexes in an effort to understand sexuality, her poetry urges readers to accept the bisexuality of the psyche. Animus and anima, as yolk and white of the one shell, are interwoven: all identity is shared. The theme that I have called "original" is so, really, only for lyric poetry; it is a staple of modernism, especially within the longer and more congenial forms that Eliot, Woolf, and Joyce mastered. As Calvin Bedient has recently noted in his study of *The Waste Land*, "one of the assumptions of modernism is that every individual contains the blueprints of all the rest. 'We have other lives,' says wispy Lucy Swithin in Virginia Woolf's *Between the Acts*."[10]

Of her recent poems, perhaps "Transcendental Etude" best demonstrates Rich's techniques for teaching us the worth of multiple selves. Starting with the title, which prepares us for music as subject and formal principle, the poem works its weavings into a resonant whole, always so naturally as to seem inevitable. Concluding with the list of objets trouvés quoted earlier, the poem retains firm control at the same time that it consciously abjures all "mere will to mastery" (words with special consequence throughout Rich's work) in favor of communal identity. But throughout, the poet nimbly offers assurances that oppositions can in fact yield to deeper syntheses. These polarities—beginning and ending, love gained and love lost, study and mastery, fragility and endurance, flying up and sinking down—all exist, in the words of the 1978 "Integrity," a poem about the uneasy truce between anger and tenderness, "as angels, not polarities" (*FD*, 274).

Like a Romantic nature lyric, according to the classic formula of M. H. Abrams,[11] "Transcendental Etude" begins with a specific situation in time and place, moves to a long, meditative, and thoroughly didactic middle part concerning women's love, and ends with the catalogue as a trope appropriate to "vision" and "a whole new poetry." What most impresses is the continuity between and within the individual sections, which are both seamless and cut off from one another by the conventional signs of lineation and spacing. The musical title must be taken as a clue to the poem's method and to its central image, one that is ironically invoked and shunned at the same time.

The opening description—of late summer in Vermont—establishes a scene and a rhetoric of dialectic. The poet watches deer run frightened from her car, and then thinks ahead to autumn's hunting season when "they'll be fair game for the hit-and-run hunters." Above the apparent contrast between the observed and the envisioned scenes, however, lies an uneasy resemblance, since the poet already has startled the deer with her own vehicle. The paragraph ends with an implicit reworking of "To Autumn" and "Sunday Morning":

> But this evening deep in summer
> the deer are still alive and free,
> nibbling apples from early-laden boughs
> so weighted, so englobed
> with already yellowing fruit
> they seem eternal, Hesperidean
> in the clear-tuned, cricket-throbbing air.
>
> (*FD*, 264)

Nowhere else does Rich so easily capture Keats's sense of nature's inevitable process, of boughs early-laden but seemingly eternal, and of our own deception, like that of the bees who think warm days will never cease.

Having established the polarities and complementarities—twin scenes of humans and deer, an apparently eternal summer moment already absorbed by its own "yellowing"—the poem proceeds to contrast the "fragility of all this sweetness" in the "green world" with both the "fake Vermont" that has been sentimentalized, photographed, and developed, and the "sick Vermont" of poverty and violence, which tourists never see. What "persists," in other words, is the very fragility of nature, whereas human desecration, abrupt and transforming, may turn out, after all, to be superficial. And once more suggesting Keats, she ends this paragraph with a section bringing into focus the eternal beneficence of natural foison:

> I've sat on a stone fence above a great, soft, sloping field
> of musing heifers, a farmstead
> slanting its planes calmly in the calm light,
> a dead elm raising bleached arms
> above a green so dense with life,
> minute, momentary life—slugs, moles, pheasants, gnats,
> spiders, moths, hummingbirds, groundhogs, butterflies—
> a lifetime is too narrow
> to understand it all, beginning with the huge
> rockshelves that underlie all that life.
>
> (265)

Death and life, the minute and the expansive, the "dense" and the "momentary," stone and light, a narrow lifetime and the "huge rockshelves" underlying everything mingle in neo-Romantic lushness.

These sensuous oppositions, observed through a landscape, prepare the poet for her more overt didacticism, the human application of her perceptions, in the middle section, which wonders about the relationship between study or practice and transcendence or perfection: the title comes to refer to more than music. Humans do not have the luxury of choice: "No one ever told us we had to study our lives, / make of our lives a study, as if learning natural history / or music" . . . "And in fact we can't live like that: we take on / everything at once before we've even begun / to read or mark time." Birth dislocates woman from mother, and loss, a wrenching apart, becomes the ground note of existence. So what we have, her metaphor continues, is a text as "counterpoint": "trying to sightread / what our fingers can't keep up with, learn by heart / what we can't even read. And yet / it *is* this we were born to" (266).

Turning away from virtuoso performers (her version of Prufrock's rejection of heroism), mistrusting the false glamour of theatricality, the poet allies herself instead with the quiet, anonymous audience, responding to the music, "hearing-out in her blood / a score touched off in her perhaps / by some words, a few chords, from the stage" (266). Just when it seems, however, that she is reaffirming the old stereotypes of the passive, responsive nature of woman, Rich steps back to consider the moment of a new kind of daring, a "severer listening, cleansed / of oratory," the unavoidable detachment (a repetition, within the poem, of the earlier traumatic "wrenching-apart" from the mother) from old solaces:

> No one who survives to speak
> new language, has avoided this:
> the cutting-away of an old force that held her
> rooted to an old ground
> the pitch of utter loneliness
> where she herself and all creation
> seem equally dispersed, weightless, her being a cry
> to which no echo comes or can ever come.
>
> (267)

The language of music ("ground," "pitch," "echo") interweaves itself with the images from nature with which the poem began ("cutting-away," "rooted") to expand and extend the figurative base of the poem.

Turning from the moment of loss, the poet continues to mingle the languages of nature and music as she ecstatically claims the joys of women's love as "a sudden brine-clear thought / trembling like the tiny, orbed, endangered / egg-sac of a new world." From this recognition comes a new birth, a new music, a new nature ("as, after the heat-wave / breaks, the clear tones of the world / manifest: cloud, bough, wall, insect, the very soul of light"), a "whole new poetry" (268).

Such is the list of the "finest findings" that ends the poem; although *assemblage* has replaced music as the primary metaphor, the actual and implicit terms of the rest of the poem continue through its didactic conclusion, quoted earlier. The "sherd of broken glass" recalls the helicopter's wings at the end of "Snapshots of a Daughter-in-Law"; the contrast of danger and salving repeats the end of "Necessities of Life," where the speaker faces the daring invitation of the world and goes out "trenchant in motion as an eel, solid / as a cabbage-head" (*FD*, 56). Taking her cue from objects of the world, the woman here "becomes" what she finds, complementing the world and becoming herself a complementary principle that reconciles oppositions like danger and safety: various, ephemeral, but also solid and enduring, she becomes the stone foundation, itself an echo of the "rockshelves that underlie all life," with which the poem had begun.

Rich has succeeded in many of her recent longer poems, like "Transcendental Etude" (one might cite as well "The Spirit of Place," "Turning the Wheel," "In the Wake of Home"), in combining metaphoric structures and naked statement and in doing justice to the complexities, even the contradictions, in human feeling, speech, and identity.

Even in shorter poems, where overall structure is less important than immediate utterance, she has found appropriate formal and syntactic gestures for her didacticism. One might even conclude that these gestures literally create, or at least embody, her didactic impulses. What even sympathetic critics like Helen Vendler object to in Rich's prose polemics (the rhetoric of sentimentality intermingling with the rhetoric of violence) and hostile ones like Alexander Theroux can refer to as the "hacking didacticism" of Rich's purpose,[12] is transformed through her poetic utterance by techniques of declaration, definition, and rhetorical variety that enable her to convert the expression of private opinion into a generalized, humane empathy.

From the start, Rich has been a poet of generalization and definition: to categorize and to conclude are the intellectual's habits, and one sees these deployed confidently throughout the poetry:

> These are the things that we have learned to do
> Who live in troubled regions.
> > ("Storm Warnings," *FD*, 3)

> To work and suffer is to be at home.
> > ("The Tourist and the Town," *FD*, 14)

> > For to be young
> Was always to live in other peoples' houses
> > ("The Middle-aged," *FD*, 15)

> Inhuman patience is the true success.
> > ("Rural Reflections," *FD*, 32)

These neatly epigrammatic early statements may be undermined by the political and emotional turbulence of Rich's subsequent radicalism, but the form of direct statement as an act of definition, creating the distinctive articulations in Rich's poems as speech-acts, remains. Thus, in "The Fact of a Doorframe," "music is suffering made powerful" (iv); or in the recent "For Memory": "freedom is daily, prose-bound, routine / remembering" (*FD*, 285); or in "Hunger": "The decision to feed the world / is the real decision" (*FD*, 231); or in "Turning the Wheel": "Nostalgia is only amnesia turned around" and "What rivets me to history is seeing / arts of survival turned / to rituals of self-hatred" (*FD*, 306–7). Some of the definitions are merely emphatic tautologies, others genuine. These examples, few among many, suggest not only a form for many of Rich's memorable utterances—"X is Y"—but also a habit of mind not unlike that of the more classically pedagogic Howard Nemerov. The attempt "to get something right in language" means that Rich will not shun the power of simple aphorism as part of her poetic arsenal.

On the other hand, the simple definitions are more powerful as the result of their place in longer, more disheveled works. One sign of the relative unease in so many of the early poems is, ironically, the unalleviated quality of the sureness: the poet hardly exposes the mind "in the act" of finding what will suffice; instead, the poems are *all* conclusion, with little tentativeness, exploration, or emotional variety. The middle period, the one that angered so many readers, in fact presents a Rich who is poetically if not politically gentler, because her epigrams come in the midst of exploration. Verbs of "wonder," of thinking, of imagining, fill these poems, as in the conclusion of "Leaflets," with its simple present tense and anapestic rhythm: "I am thinking how we can use what we have / to invent what we need" (*FD*, 104). Or others, culled almost at random:

> I know the inmates are encouraged
> to express themselves
> I'm wondering how
> ("Essential Resources," *FD*, 202)

>                  I wonder
> what it is to be cast in bronze
> like the sender
> ("Postcard," *PSN*, p. 137)

> I'm wondering
> whether we even have what we think we have
>                  ("Hunger," *FD*, 230)

> I can't know what you know
> unless you tell me
> ("For Memory," *FD*, 284)

These present tense declarations give the strongest evidence for what I have called Rich's original theme: the attractions and dangers of empathy, for which another word is imagination. These are contained as well in the appropriation or inclusion of other voices in her latest, ventriloquistic pieces where Willa Cather, the architect Mary Jane Colter, Ellen Glasgow, and others speak both in their own words and through the invented ones of the poet.

The 1973 "Re-Forming the Crystal" exhibits all the poetic-didactic gestures I've suggested throughout this chapter, and deserves quotation in full:

I am trying to imagine
how it feels to you
to want a woman

trying to hallucinate
desire
centered in a cock
focused like a burning-glass

desire without discrimination:
to want a woman like a fix

Desire: yes: the sudden knowledge, like coming out of 'flu, that
the body is sexual. Walking in the streets with that knowledge.
That evening in the plane from Pittsburgh, fantasizing going to
meet you. Walking through the airport blazing with energy and
joy. But knowing all along that you were not the source of that
energy and joy; you were a man, a stranger, a name, a voice on
the telephone, a friend; this desire was mine, this energy my energy; it could be used a hundred ways, and going to meet you
could be one of them.

Tonight is a different kind of night.
I sit in the car, racing the engine,
calculating the thinness of the ice.
In my head I am already threading the beltways
that rim this city,
all the old roads that used to wander the country
having been lost.
Tonight I understand
my photo on the license is not me,
my
name on the marriage-contract was not mine.
If I remind you of my father's favorite daughter,
look again. The woman
I needed to call my mother
was silenced before I was born.

Tonight if the battery charges I want to take the car out on
sheet-ice; I want to understand my fear both of the machine and
of the accidents of nature. My desire for you is not trivial; I can
compare it with the greatest of those accidents. But the energy it
draws on might lead to racing a cold engine, cracking the frozen
spiderweb, parachuting into the field of a poem wired with dan-

ger, or to a trip through gorges and canyons, into the cratered
night of female memory, where delicately and with intense care
the chieftainess inscribes upon the ribs of the volcano the name
of the one she has chosen.

(*FD*, 205–6)

The alternation of poetry and prose is not surprising, but as in "The
Burning of Paper Instead of Children," the prose itself resonates with
strong rhythms that repeat and expand single images and motifs
within the poem. The alternation calls attention to itself—what, one
might ask, are the reasons for printing part of this as lineated poetry,
part as prose with justified margins? For one thing, the "poetic" seg-
ments deal with present issues, while the first prose passage recollects
past time and the second anticipates the future. I discuss further the
importance of fragmentation, ellipsis, and verblessness later in these
pages: poetry means "presence" and the present tense is Rich's vehicle
for wonder, as in the unpunctuated opening, which gives a perpetually hallucinated quality to her "imagining," and in her turning away
from all "images" of the represented self in the third section (e.g., the
photo, the name, the reminder).

A personal reformation requires an imaginative re-forming and a
formal response to the demands of empathy: sexuality and imagination inhabit the same field of energy in the first section (desire "focused like a burning-glass" is the first image of crystallization) and in
the second, where "the sudden knowledge . . . that the body is sexual"
opens a sequence from knowledge to "fantasizing" to the energy of
anticipation. Each of the prose sections builds from simpler to more
complex structures, as the listing of possibilities shows the workings of
the imagination. Additionally, where the first prose chunk works
largely with fragments, the second deploys complex sentences, which
culminate in the aggressive listing of possible outlets for imaginative
energy. As an experiment in reformation, the poem builds itself up
from an initial act of wonder through a contemplation of past eagerness, possibility, and daring to a commitment to self-exposure. As part
of a personal and poetic program it occupies (along with the stylisti-
cally more conventional "Diving into the Wreck") in Rich's oeuvre a
place similar to that of the odes to Psyche and Melancholy in Keats's.
Imagining an act of daring—in poetry—is equivalent to performing it.
The final image invoking the ancient priestess and her victim-votary
certainly recalls the goddess Melancholy, who admits her suitor to her
temple only to have him hung among her cloudy trophies through a
comparably suicidal act of imaginative adventure. The poem's various

crystals—the burning-glass, the telephone, thin ice, frozen spider-web—all give way to the one implied, unmentioned crystal: the ball for predicting the future that becomes the prophet's medium as the poem is that of the energized poet.

"Re-Forming the Crystal" exemplifies Rich's technique as well as her ideology. It combines the tropes of listing and weaving that I have already mentioned. Its hallucinated quality is presented more variously than the comparable obsessions of "I Dream I'm the Death of Orpheus" (*FD*, 119–20) with its anaphoric "I am a woman ... a woman ... a woman" threading through the imaginary occupation of a movie script. Its concision matches the more narrative organization of "Diving into the Wreck," which also relies on anaphora as a structural principle and an equivalent of mental attention, and the insistent choral quality of the end of "Tear Gas," with its prayerful reiteration of need and fear building to the relief of a conclusion: "(I am afraid.) / It's not the worst way to live." Rich's poetry is a poetry of repetition: its assertive verbs express the demands of self on the world, as in "Splittings" (1974), with its antiphonal strands "I choose" and "I choose not" woven into the refusal of division and separation implied by the title. Here, in fact, the language of choosing, in its insistent repetition, is made part of a specifically educational program ("Yet if I could instruct / myself, if we could learn to learn from pain," [*FD*, 228]). Rich's lessons to her implied and actual audiences always derive from an effort of self-instruction: "I choose to love  this time  for once / with all my intelligence," she announces at the end, her self-admonitions having been rehearsed, heeded, and cured.

This means that unlike an equally didactic poet of a more conventional bent, Rich conducts monologues rather than lectures, even when maintaining the pretense of direct address. She can construct epigrams as cogent or pithy as those of Auden and Nemerov, but more often she replaces the elegance of that sort of compression with speech acts that will do justice to her sense of a momentary, incomplete reality. Not only does she rely on action or contemplation in the present tense, and simple copulas for her acts of definition, but she also typically constructs passages around elliptical, verbless, unpunctuated phrases, relying on infinitives, which reproduce the tentativeness of experience and the eagerness of expectation. Beginning with her strongly felt and argued political poems of the late sixties, this is her characteristic mode. The first part of "Pieces" (1969), subtitled *Breakpoint*, resembles the seemingly fragmented listings of "Ghazals" or "Shooting Script":

The music of words
received as fact

The steps that wouldn't hold us both
splintering in air.

The self witheld in an urn
like ashes

To have loved you better than you loved yourself
—whoever you were, to have loved you—

And still to love but simply
as one of those faces on the street

(*FD*, 130)

Each of the first three couplets reflects another aspect of fragmentation: the pastness of words uttered, the incapacity to defy natural laws
like gravity, the imprisonment of the true self within its shell. The last
two counter the failure and inhibitions implicit in the first three with
infinitives of eager expectation, tinged with the implicit nostalgic understanding that such expected love was inadequate to seal the inevitable ruptures. From no verbs to infinitives: there is no hope within
the present moment, and the despair is all the more plangent for what
I take to be gentle echoes of the "Ode on a Grecian Urn": both the
vase in line 5 and the updating of Keats's empathic address to the
young lover in the second stanza of his poem: "For ever wilt thou
love."

"Words," as Rich announces in "Our Whole Life," are only "bitten
thru words"; in that poem, discussed earlier, only the illusion of integrity exists during one's whole life, and Rich's poetics has sought an
irresistible means of defining the partiality of the self-in-experience
through the nervousness implicit in such jagged poetic forms. Rich
was committed to the infinitive as early as "Double Monologue"
(1960), with its opening query: "To live illusionless, in the abandoned
mine- / shaft of doubt, and still / mime illusions for others?" (*PSN*, 55).
All of these constructions, which try to remain faithful to the immediacy of experience, are by definition elliptical, relying on a grammatical equivalent of T. S. Eliot's "indirection," demanding completion by
a responsive reader. Thus one finds "is it possible to live illusionless?"
with its hopeful "yes," and its resigned "no"; or the determined opening of "Face to Face," with an implicit "I have been lucky" before its
literal first line:

Never to be lonely like that—
the Early American figure on the beach
in black coat and knee-breeches
scanning the didactic storm in privacy

(*FD*, 76)

And in the resilient conclusion of "Shooting Script" (1970):

Now to give up the temptations of the projector; to see instead
the web of cracks filtering across the plaster.

To read there the map of the future, the roads radiating from
the initial split, the filaments thrown out from that impasse.

To reread the instructions on your palm; to find there how the
lifeline, broken, keeps its direction.

To read the etched rays of the bullet-hole left years ago in the
glass; to know in every distortion of the light what fracture is.

To put the prism in your pocket, the thin glass lens, the map of
the inner city, the little book with gridded pages.

To pull yourself up by your own roots; to eat the last meal in
your old neighborhood.

(*FD*, 145–46)

The infinitive is the form for readiness, expectation, and exploration.
This ending duplicates the ending of the 1962 "Necessities of Life,"
quoted earlier, with its more conventional "I'll dare inhabit the world
. . . I have invitations," and it prepares for the exploratory "Diving into
the Wreck" with its conventional narrative framework. But the infinitives gird the speaker between decision and event; she is all breathless
determination and eagerness, as if declaring: "I vow to give up the
temptations; it is fitting to reread the instructions on your palm; you
had better be ready to put the prism in your pocket; it is time to pull
yourself up by your own roots."

Infinitives, fragments, grammatically incomplete units that nevertheless encourage full apprehension, have become virtual signatures
in Rich's work. Significantly, these fragments, bits, or shards tend to
cluster at the opening or close of a poem. It is as if we have caught a
speaker in midthought or, rather, as if she has taken us by surprise,
demanding our attention. The arresting opening of "The Phenomenology of Anger" could easily be rewritten, and is certainly to be un-

derstood in part, as a simple statement: "The freedom of $x$ is not the freedom of $y$." Instead, Rich gives us the following:

> The freedom of the wholly mad
> to smear & play with her madness
> write with her fingers dipped in it
> the length of a room
>
> which is not, of course, the freedom
> you have, walking on Broadway
> to stop & turn back or go on
> 10 blocks; 20 blocks
>
> but feels enviable maybe
> to the compromised
>
> curled in the placenta of the real
> which was to feed & which is strangling her.
>
> (FD, 165)

The phrasal nature of this stanza, relegating its metaphor to a subordinate clause while withholding an independent clause, and its unpunctuated lineation both arrest and deceive us: this is especially true of the dramatically ambiguous "which," guarding the pass between the confined patient and the ambulatory, sane addressee, but also bringing the two into an uncomfortable resemblance while keeping them apart. Since the entire poem both constructs and undermines logical oppositions, the apparent randomness of the form of the opening definition prepares us for the speculations that follow.

I take this stylistic tactic as a synecdoche for the job of the entire poem. Poetry, addressed in and symbolized by "The Fact of a Doorframe," the 1974 poem that stands as the title piece in the latest selection from Rich's complete work, serves, according to its central image, to support, to build, to divide:

> *Now, again, poetry,*
> *violent, arcane, common,*
> *hewn of the commonest living substance*
> *into archway, portal, frame*
> *I grasp for you, your bloodstained splinters, your*
> *ancient and stubborn poise*
> *—as the earth trembles—*
> *burning out from the grain*
>
> (iv)

The poem, which starts with an ellipsis from title to first line ("The Fact of a Doorframe ... means there is something to hold"), bears witness to the fear that Rich explains in her foreword to the latest anthology—"that the walls cannot be broken down, that these words will fail to enter another soul"—the fear that lies behind the fractured utterances in poems like "The Phenomenology of Anger." She has concerned herself for more than twenty years with images about building and joining:

> I long to create something
> that can't be used to keep us passive:
> I want to write
> a script about plumbing, how every pipe
> is joined
> to every other
>             ("Essential Resources," *FD*, 202)

> And I think of those lives we tried to live
> in our globed helmets, self-enclosed
> bodies self-illumined gliding
> safe from the turbulence
>
> and how, miraculously, we failed
>             ("The Wave," *FD*, 205)

> A city waits at the back of my skull
> eating its heart out to be born:
> how design the first
> city of the moon? how shall I see it
> for all of us who are done
> with enclosed spaces, purdah, the salon, the sweatshop loft,
> the ingenuity of the cloister?
> ("The Fourth Month of the Landscape Architect," *PSN*, 225)

It is not, therefore, inappropriate for Rich to focus her readers' attention onto syntactic and grammatical arrangements that bolster those images. Words fail, words support: a doorframe steadies and also gives one leave to thrust one's "forehead against the wood." The implicit doubleness of the infinitive (the very idea of action without temporal specificity) and the ambivalence of her expressive means justify Rich's hopefulness, the part of her disposition encouraged to think of radical change as the complement to her frustrations, conscious as she is of the pitfalls, dangers, and failures of all attempts to communicate.

Rich is predominantly a poet of the present tense: even her infinitives, suggesting purpose or futurity, ring with present determination. And the present tense typically provides the time and language of instruction. Direct or implied address demands the immediacy of lyric; presence is actual, even when represented by the wire-dot photograph of a man in pain. Temporal continuity may be an equivalent to personal integrity, something hoped for but difficult to know, and some of Rich's most touching poems admit a preference for small moments to anything grander. The teacher, when addressing her students or audience, is still mostly addressing herself; the lessons of the past encourage a reformed faith for the future, as in the touching "From a Survivor," addressed to her husband shortly after his death. If the arts of teaching and learning demand an absorption of the past as preparation for the future, this delicate, unembellished piece may stand as a paradigm of educational technique.

It, too, is a poem of statement:

> The pact that we made was the ordinary pact
> of men & women in those days
>
> I don't know who we thought we were
> that our personalities
> could resist the failures of the race
>
> Lucky or unlucky, we didn't know
> the race had failures of that order
> and that we were going to share them
>
> Like everybody else, we thought of ourselves as special
>
> Your body is as vivid to me
> as it ever was: even more
>
> since my feeling for it is clearer:
> I know what it could and could not do
>
> it is no longer
> the body of a god
> or anything with power over my life
>
> Next year it would have been 20 years
> and you are wastefully dead
> who might have made the leap
> we talked, too late, of making

which I live now
not as a leap
but a succession of brief, amazing movements

each one making possible the next
(*FD*, 176–77)

Figurative language is reserved for the lines about the dead man's body and the final simile comparing life to a leap and a succession of moments, but even these sections barely rise to the level of poetic revelation. As in so many of Rich's poems the appearance of the lines, separated, grouped, isolated on the page, adds an emotional frisson that calls attention to single lines or clusters; these poems would lose much of their effect if printed as simple, justified prose. And yet in spite of such bareness, its relative flatness, its seemingly unpoetic structure, "From a Survivor" movingly exemplifies the didacticism to which Rich has laid claim. Its progress is a temporal one, its three sections neatly focused on past, present, and future. The survivor is also a surveyor, examining a temporal terrain and commenting rationally but sympathetically on the eagerness of youth, in its self-deceiving confidence, to "resist the failures of the race," then coolly appraising the legacy of the past to the present, and finally looking hopefully forward to a conditional future that includes the present, but that looks backward just as the first section treated the past in terms of the couple's youthful expectations for future successes. The temporal configurations provide the poem with both a formal organization and a controlling hope: they are Rich's equivalent of the string of days embodied in Wordsworth's "My Heart Leaps Up" that stand as epigraph to the Intimations ode: "And I could wish my days to be / Bound each to each in natural piety."

As the time changes through the poem, so does the social or human focus: the first third places the young marrieds ("we") ironically against a background of the race to whom they mistakenly feel themselves superior; the second section makes the first and only extended apostrophe to the dead husband; the third part, just as it resurveys past and present ("we talked," "I live") in terms of the future ("next year"), also reconsiders the pronominal terms of the past two parts ("we," "you") before settling squarely into a final clause depicting the woman alone, accommodating herself to solitude, middle age, and all the compromises that define what we call maturity.

Emotionally, at least, the lessons of the poem have neatly progressed from the ironies of youthful illusions overturned, through an acceptance of a realistic commitment to another person that is possible only because of his death and her growth, to a confident statement of forward progress. Gradually stripping herself of imagined superiority, of a godlike husband and her own inflated sense of his powers, of the larger community ("race") and the smaller unit of the marriage, the speaker finds surest confidence and happiness through deprivation and loss. Knowing what to make of a diminished thing, she has learned to profit from disaster. The act of self-instruction is all the more delicate for gradually eliminating the very verbs of knowledge at the moment of clearest insight: after "I don't know . . . we thought . . . we didn't know . . . we thought . . . I know," the final eight lines present their lessons unobtrusively and confidently, doing away with the apparatus of instruction and thinking, and relying instead on the sure knowledge implicit in a direct statement, all the more powerful for coming late.

In her early poem, "The Middle-aged," observing the phenomenon proleptically, Rich concludes an evaluation of the lessons and compromises of age touchingly: "All to be understood by us, returning / Late, in our own time—how that peace was made, / Upon what terms, with how much left unsaid" (*FD*, 15). In "From a Survivor" Rich revises her earlier poem, as she depicts her own private arrangements in public (the later "pact" echoes the earlier "peace" and "terms"). She makes a truce with a dead man and her own dead, past self and attends to future arrangements. She learns, because she has earned them, the satisfactions of difficult ordinary happiness: happiness ordinary in and because of its difficulties. And what she learns she teaches, through the clarity of simple speech in "From a Survivor" as well as through the more complex structures of later poems like "Transcendental Etude." For a poet normally thought of as political and polemical, even recklessly uncontrolled, Rich teaches gently: her best poems seldom hector or lecture. Like any good teacher she resorts to an arsenal of instructional weapons that includes a larger percentage of patience, even when wild, than aggressiveness. As a poet, she has forged a technique out of simple speech as well as more ornate figurations. Her recent long poem, *Sources* (1983), a retrieval and replanting of her own roots, ends with a moving definition of the knowledge she seeks, and a defense of the methods of articulation that she long ago wielded:

> There is no definite knowing, no such rest. Innocent birds, deserts, morning-glories, point to choices, leading away from the familiar. When I speak of an end to suffering I don't mean an-

esthesia. I mean knowing the world, and my place in it, not in order to stare with bitterness or detachment, but as a powerful and womanly series of choices: and here I write the words, in their fullness:

powerful; womanly.[13]

# SIX

# The Sacred Books of James Merrill

As recently as fifteen years ago no one would have thought to make James Merrill the central figure in a book about discursive poetry. Perhaps at that time such a book itself would have been inconceivable. But it now seems incontrovertible to many readers that Merrill's achievement in *The Changing Light at Sandover* has permanently altered the course of American poetry for the rest of our century. This encyclopedic work—whose Ouija board mechanics are familiar to most readers of poetry—has subsumed and redefined all the standard genres of poetry and the techniques of versification that Merrill inherited from his teachers. How shall we label it? Epic, diary, *Kunstlerroman*, *Bildungsroman*, autobiography, myth, scientific tract? It is of course all of these. But it is primarily as a modern georgic, a manual of instruction not in the limited Virgilian spheres of sowing, reaping, and bee-keeping but in the more expansive emotional realities of human life, that I wish to consider it. For all of its commerce with other worlds and its maneuverings with a crackpot mechanism that embarrasses readers in the same way that Yeats's spiritualism disappointed Auden ("how southern California!"), this thoroughly didactic poem returns readers to Horace's *prodesse et delectare*. Or, as one of the dead human spirits remarks after a particularly grueling lecture of which sense has yet to be made:

IT'S A CLOSED CIRCLE    A BOCCACCIO
WE 8 AMID TIME'S HOWL SIT TELLING TALL
TALES TO AMUSE & AMAZE & WITH LUCK INSTRUCT US ALL
(324)[1]

Before 1976 Merrill had already amused and amazed his readers with his exquisitely poised poems, diaries of love and loss, testaments to the objects in a privileged life, or to scenes from shimmering landscapes. From the start, no one doubted his mastery of verse technique; indeed, the mastery became a cudgel with which to beat him for having chosen (as if one could choose) cold perfection rather than intense, self-revealing honesty. Thus, even the *New York Times* condemned the awarding of the 1972 Bollingen Prize to Merrill, criticizing the foundation for making an award in politically troubled times to a genteel poet. This animosity simply found other excuses for its own defense after the Ouija board poems began to appear in 1976; readers who previously scorned the objets d'art and the exotic settings, the delicate observations and baroque syntax, the polite reticence and the layered diction of Merrill's volumes through *Braving the Elements*, then took offense at his choosing nothing less magisterial than the subjects worthy of conventional epic: the nature of the universe, conceived both macro- and microcosmically; the future of the planet; God's plan for his creatures and their survival; free will and its absence; and the artist as modern hero in the depiction and transmission of a divine scheme.

Perhaps the least generous reviewer said of *Mirabell*, the second part of the trilogy, that it shows "not stylish hijinks but uninspired plodding . . . ontological data is transmitted to the gullible. . . . Aside from its selective summary of western thought, *Mirabell* is an intellectual sham . . . the poetry is as inartistic as the content is fatuous, the structure is haphazard."[2] Not only hostile critics have aimed their barbs; even Merrill's friends have been taken aback by or have misappreciated his gifts and have misinterpreted his achievement. Thus, Calvin Bedient reviews "Ephraim": "Misunderstanding his gifts, James Merrill has written a long, a very long poem [little did he know what was yet to come] . . . the epic size is too coarse and ambitious for him."[3] Or Judith Moffett, acknowledging *Sandover* "a masterwork of great eccentricity," still betrays her preference for the essentially lyric Merrill, when she calls book 4 of *Mirabell* "an agreeable respite from straight instruction."[4] Most recently, Robert von Hallberg, in a book in which one might hope to find detailed analyses of Merrill's newfound discursiveness, summarily dismisses *Sandover*: "the seriousness of the poem is not in its didacticism . . . of all his contemporaries, Merrill is least likely to write a long, earnestly didactic poem." Von Hallberg is bound to be disappointed with *Sandover*, since he labels Merrill's predominant tones "arch" and "camp" and finds that "for Merrill, energy, invention, and ornamention—not signification—are what make poetry."[5] The case of Merrill proves more forcefully than that of any other recent poet that energy and invention, which *make* poetry itself, also create the signification of the work. Extractable messages there may be aplenty in *Sandover*, but meaning is the grace beyond the reach of art.

A long, earnestly didactic poem is, fortunately for our age, its audience, what Merrill has written. He has certainly not lacked for patient, sympathetic analysts of his achievement: David Kalstone, Helen Vendler, and Stephen Yenser, among others, have paved the way for an understanding of his life's work.[6] A brief remark in an essay by

Charles Berger points in the direction followed in this chapter: writing specifically of *Mirabell*, but referring, I think, to the entire trilogy, Berger places Merrill squarely within the boundaries established not only by his contemporaries but also by his predecessors: "[it is a poem] within a modernist tradition that continues the ancient function of the epic as a vehicle for instruction. For an age that prided itself on renouncing Victorian didacticism, a not inconsiderable amount of modernist verse epic is devoted to lecturing the reader, either by foregrounding aesthetic touchstones or by outright preaching."[7]

All discussions of *Sandover* necessarily involve a summary of its action and methodology, although any attempt to paraphrase its "story" will be baffled in part by the complications ingrained in its time schemes, the changing voices of its characters, and its constant shiftings through space and within history. Judith Moffett's explication is a convenient reference point for beginners, but the following paragraphs set a stage for my own commentary.

The trilogy details a lengthy series of contacts, via a Ouija board, with voices from beyond this world. Merrill and his longtime companion David Jackson, having moved to Stonington, Connecticut, in the first year of their friendship (1954), began their experiments the following year and made contact with Ephraim, whose communiqués form the substance of part 1, "The Book of Ephraim," accumulated over twenty years and printed by itself in Merrill's 1976 volume, *Divine Comedies*. Ephraim instructs his human friends JM and DJ, "scribe" and "hand" respectively, in a universe where reincarnation—modeled loosely on the oldest systems of orphic mysteries that make their classic appearance in Plato and Virgil—brings people back to earth until they have been sufficiently prepared to enter a complex, purgatorial, otherworldly hierarchy through which they rise toward final peace. "Ephraim" is also, however, the book containing the largest percentage of "lived" life, mingling as it does JM's and DJ's experiences in Stonington and Europe with accounts of other travels to the Orient and the western United States and with descriptions of Merrill's failed and lost novel (which he describes also in "The Will," another poem in *Divine Comedies*) and contemplations about love and art.

"Ephraim" is the most human of the volumes, not just because the Ouija apparatus contains the most human voices, but also because Merrill's naturally lyrical impulse is still in the foreground. Those emotions attendant upon elegy—reflections of personal loss, the accommodations of the self to diminished energies, and the looming prospect of further lessening and death itself—are the starting point for his tentative explorations of other subjects and poetic modes.

The book is divided into twenty-six sections, A to Z, corresponding to the alphabet on the Ouija board; *Mirabell*, or "Books of Number," is arranged around mathematical units, from 0 to 9, each of the ten parts having ten subsections; and *Scripts for the Pageant*, the last and longest of the books, has the simplest organization, its three parts headed YES, &, and NO, after the three other major figures on the board. "Ephraim" ends with hints of two voices that will speak more loudly in the subsequent volumes. In section U, a strange figure interrupts with a command: "MYND YOUR WEORK." At the very end, a starry version of *das Ewigweibliche* asks, "Why do you no longer come to me?" She will develop into the feminine half of Merrill's godhead, especially in *Scripts*. The former figure, however, anticipates the voices of *Mirabell*, a series of legionary formulas who become bats and offer JM a different kind of instruction in part 2.

The lessons of *Mirabell* are at once more complex and less varied than those of "Ephraim." It is a poem of "science," or the popularized science that Merrill learns both from his tutelary spirits and from his readings in Konrad Lorenz, B. F. Skinner, Lewis Thomas, and subatomic particle physics. And it also enlarges considerably the numbers of instructors speaking from the other world: first, there are two major human figures, W. H. Auden and the poet's Greek friend Maria Mitsotaki, both recently dead, who act as intermediaries, themselves part-teachers and part-students to the lessons of Mirabell and the other bat figures. By now explaining the universe in both microcosmic and macrocosmic terms, these offer considerable correction of Ephraim's doctrines. Discussions of molecular structures and genetic recombination alternate with a history of the cosmos that includes two unsuccessful creations (Mirabell and his crew are the remains of the second of these, centered on the myth of Atlantis) before our own. Now, instead of "simple" reincarnation, Merrill paints a picture of a giant research laboratory (the R/Lab) in which God and his workers, like Santa's elves, work to undo earlier mistakes, to thin out and perfect the human race. At one point, on page 143, Mirabell announces that "THE SCRIBE'S JOB IS TO HELP SPEED ACCEPTANCE" of the work of the aristocratic "Five," God's special emissaries who have included, in various incarnations, Akhnaton, Nefertiti, Montezuma, Homer, and Plato. Their "v" work—for "five," *vie*, and "vital"—goes on, while they are themselves reincarnated throughout history as scientists, artists, and other leaders.

Just as "Ephraim" ends with a foretaste of *Mirabell*, the second volume prepares its readers (and, of course, its writer, the major student of these visions) for the fullest lessons of *Scripts*. Ten final lessons, in reverse order, repeat, as a kind of refresher course, the book's lectures on culture, man's soul, the nature of weather and heaven, and the relationship of the living and the dead. At the end, after the count- down, a new voice intrudes: the angel Michael, one of God's four special viceroys, announces (276) that "GOD IS THE ACCUMULATED INTEL- LIGENCE IN CELLS SINCE THE DEATH OF THE FIRST DISTANT CELL." The macrocosmic and microcosmic are brought, at last, into a symbolic harmony, and Merrill has readied us for *Scripts*.

*Mirabell* was published in 1978, *Scripts* in 1980, the entire trilogy, with a coda, "The Higher Keys," in 1982. Since we know that he made his first contact with the spirits in 1955, we have an epic that has oc- cupied the largest part of Merrill's creative life. And even though the actual composing of "Ephraim" took less than the twenty years of its experiencing, what we seem to have throughout the trilogy is a simul- taneous increase in the speed of writing and the size of the output. *Scripts* is the longest of the books, with the largest cast of characters and the greatest amount, as well as percentage, of unvaried lectures in the uppercase letters of the board's speakers. Everything has pre- pared for this; just as Mirabell and his crew have corrected the half- truths and mistakes of Ephraim, so here, too, former lessons are seen in a new light and from a different perspective (e.g., on page 311 Mir- abell is "Poor Mr Chips / And his preparatory school— / Behind us now").

*Mirabell* is a book of Stonington, assembled in the bicentennial sum- mer of 1976 but actually composed subsequently during the dictation of *Scripts* in Athens. The last lessons of *Scripts*, ten under the supervi- sion of Michael ("YES"), a middle five ("&"), and the negative or op- posing lessons ("NO") by Gabriel, the dark, or "shy" brother, are given to JM and DJ in their Athens house and simultaneously to a group of human figures centered around Auden and Mitsotaki (or WHA and MM as they are most often labeled), whom the poet imagines seated in the old nursery of his ancestral house, for which the epic has been named. A return to Sandover and childhood accompanies an advance- ment in learning: nursery becomes schoolroom, the mirrored world of the living humans' room in this book that makes the most of dou- blings, and reflections of all sorts, in its methods. A mirror has been used as a prop throughout the Ouija experiments, so that the disem- bodied voices may in some way "see" themselves reflected; for exam- ple, the original cover of *Divine Comedies* presented a silvered frame, and the epigraph to "Ephraim," from *Paradiso* 15, quotes Cacciagui- da's reference to "that mirror in which your thought is revealed even before you think it." Finally, mirrored reflections constitute the sub-

stance as well as the design and the incidental details in the entire epic.
A complex truth, composed of variations on all the themes, lessons,
metaphors, and formulas elucidated by the speakers from beyond,
emerges; "murky blocks / Of revelation" (297–98) clarify themselves,
as the overarching structure of the whole is revealed at last.

Michael's lessons proceed from his aphorism that "THE MOST INNO-
CENT OF IDEAS IS THE IDEA THAT INNOCENCE IS DESTROYED BY IDEAS"
(321); he orchestrates a dialogue among the four angels (Raphael and
Emmanuel, representing land and water, complement Michael and
Gabriel, light and fire, the two more important elements), and various
representatives of the Five, concerning God and his handiwork. God
himself is heard at the end of Michael's lessons (360) in a reminder of
cosmic fragility. Gabriel, the "negative" force, representing fire, destruction, time itself ("the forbidden, the forgotten theme" [438]),
takes as the text for his ten sermons an aphorism to balance Michael's:
"OF ALL DESTRUCTIVE IDEAS THE MOST DESTRUCTIVE IS THE IDEA OF DE-
STRUCTION," and begins to promise nuclear destruction as part of a
thinning process to improve the race. But it turns out (much is revealed, to the surprise of scribe and his readers alike) that man, God's
third child, is destined for survival, as Gabriel reveals in lesson 8:

> GOD CREATED HIS THIRD CHILD & GAVE THE COMMAND: LET IT
>   SURVIVE AND LET THERE BE NO ACCIDENT,
> FOR I CAN NO LONGER ABIDE SUCH PAIN. WE OBEYD.
> THE SCRIBES, MUCH AS GOD, NOW COMMAND: OUR V WORK, LET IT
>   SURVIVE. LET NO ACCIDENT PAIN IT, OR ITS READER TO DISBELIEF.
>                                                              (473)

As in Michael's last lesson, God speaks again in lesson 10 of "NO," com-
manding JM to execute his own "v" work, this poem, out of Michael's
light and Gabriel's darkness. The standard end of autobiography, we
know, is the decision to compose; Merrill's penultimate stance in *Sandover* is his determination, the major decision in the generic life of the
writer of epic, to make his major pronouncement.

The poem ends with revelations, farewells, and celebrations, which
I discuss in more detail later. Its coda, however, returns to the writing-
speaking self, in the most personal touch of all. Shared identities,
masks put on and taken off, strippings of veils as well as illusions to
reveal truths, have constituted the bulk of the epic's lessons. Of all the
doublings and redoublings revealed throughout *Scripts*, perhaps the
most significant comes after the assurance that the four angels are
"THE SUPREME MOMENTS OF THE FIVE" (552). Ephraim announces that
he is really an incarnation of Michael, or, in the poem's typography-

typology, M/E. They both, in other words, are versions of their author, the "me" of James Merrill, who after his lessons, his transcriptions, and his creations, arises in the final moment to deliver a performative utterance. The poem ends with its own imagined reading, in the old ballroom, before an audience of literary precursors (and in the room at Athens before DJ and a friend whose wife has recently died and assumed her place on the other side), with JM the cynosure, treating his friends to his, and their, individual and collective lives. He ends with his beginning; the coda returns to the opening of "Ephraim," making a full circle and coming simultaneously to a stop that virtually asks us all to begin again:

> Both rooms are waiting.
> DJ brighteyed (but look how wrinkled) lends
> His copy of the score to our poor friend's
> Somber regard—captive like Gulliver
> Or like the mortal in an elfin court
> Pining for wife and cottage on this shore
> Beyond whose depthless dazzle he can't see.
> For *their* ears I begin: "Admittedly . . ."
>
> (559–60)

As a didactic poem, *The Changing Light at Sandover* prompts the following questions, for which I hope to furnish answers in the following pages: What are the subjects and who are the students of instruction? What poetic-educational methodology do the teachers within the poem, and Merrill the author without, employ to drive their lessons home? What drama of instruction does the poem provide from the students' point of view?

Apart from its nominal theses, to which it may be easily reduced (a warning against a population explosion; an urging to thin and improve the race qualitatively as well as quantitatively; a defense of science, music, and poetry as privileged modes of creation and understanding), the epic seeks to explain four subjects that have occupied Merrill's work since the beginning. In this, the poem represents a change not so much of topic as of technique. These are the four things that alone seem to distinguish the human species from its predecessors and its angelic superiors: affection, appearance, language, and time. At the intersection or within the permutations of these four the poem discovers its own highest energies and Merrill his own "v" work.

Critics like von Hallberg think of Merrill as primarily a love poet who has misapplied his true talent in *Sandover*. I would say that, on the contrary, his commitment to the bonds of human affection is nowhere in his work more consistently and variously present than in his epic. The manifold varieties of love and the roles or masks one plays and wears in defining the grounds of one's relationships exist in the drama of *Sandover* in dizzying array: filial love, sexual fancy, marital bonds, and friendship are all woven not only into the poem's action but also into its very subject matter, as the various lecturers give as much attention to these topics as to reincarnation, black holes, and nuclear physics. The last lines of the coda, quoted above, remind us that in Merrill's work the ascent to spiritual revelation is rooted in personal affection, Yeats's foul rag-and-bone shop, and returns to it at the end. Even the theoretical justification for homosexuality, which occupies part of the lessons in *Mirabell*, derives from Merrill's free use of the facts of his own life; the celebration of a silver anniversary with David Jackson (*Scripts*, 352–59) fits into the scheme of Michael's affirmative lessons, balancing the first meeting with Ephraim years before, at the start of their relationship, and announced in section A of the first poem as "The Book of a Thousand and One Evenings Spent / With David Jackson at the Ouija Board / In Touch with Ephraim Our Familiar Spirit." At the end, the poem is read for the very real person in one room, even more, perhaps, than for the imagined dead seated in their serried ranks.

Although Ephraim, here paraphrased by JM, claims that "huge tracts of information / Have gone into these capsules flavorless / And rhymed for easy swallowing" (9), the supposed lessons of the first book are, especially in retrospect from the forbidding heights of the other books, not strenuous or hard to take at all. Apart from reports about the bureaucracy and its operations for the guidance, control, and rebirth of souls below, "Ephraim" offers little in the way of abstruse thought. At the time, however, it all seems heady indeed: Ephraim drops the bombshell about *A Vision*: "POOR OLD YEATS / STILL SIMPLIFYING" (14), and his students are dubious of their own capacities:

> We'd long since slept through our last talk on Thomist
> Structures in Dante. Causes
> Were always lost—on us. We shared the traits
> Of both the dumbest
>
> Boy in school and that past master of clauses
> Whose finespun mind "no idea violates."
>
> (14)

The reference to Henry James is more than a gratuitous compliment: Merrill's true subject in "Ephraim" is every individual's accommodation to love's demands and challenges, the rewards as well as the losses exacted by human relationships—a subject, in other words, appropriate to James or Proust. The first book educates Merrill in the art and necessity of "being sufficiently imbued with otherness" for artistic as well as personal growth.

Harold Bloom rightly corrects the powerful illusion of Merrill as an elegiac poet.[8] Lamentation and loss are indeed among his obsessive concerns, but ultimately, as his Dantean title suggests, everything is converted to good: there are no real catastrophes in the trilogy, as even the dead return to the living via the board. The product of art commemorates and eternalizes (such is the oldest defense of art as the regime of Mnemosyne) and the very processes of art keep the dead with us, making them even more available than they were in life ("I can't pretend to have known Wystan terribly well in *this* world," Merrill let drop in an interview).[9] Merrill's access to otherness comes from his board but also from the foiled attempts at writing a novel, the characters of which are thinly veiled portraits of other people in his life and characters in the poem (JM, Ephraim, DJ's parents), and from (to quote a touchstone from an earlier poem, "An Urban Convalescence") "the dull need to make some kind of house / Out of the life lived, out of the love spent."[10]

The whole *Changing Light at Sandover*, even its title, is that house. As Merrill announced proleptically at the end of *Water Street* (1962), celebrating his move to Stonington: "If I am host at last / It is of little more than my own past. / May others be at home in it" (*FFN*, 118). The major theme—time's passing—will be discussed later in this essay. It is significant here at least to remark the way in which Merrill's poetry, with its painterly fascination with shimmering light, joins space and time, making of them a single continuum. In the trilogy, the supposed solidity of place gives way to an imagined "other" space, itself a partial recollection from the poet's childhood; otherness is metaphorically present in those unseen rooms in Stonington and Athens. Likewise, beneath the flowing currents of time lurks a depth that the poem constantly sounds in order to test, coming up, after all, with something rather solid. One can be finally at home in the past. The early poem, "A Tenancy," quoted above, predicted (perhaps not accidentally) the title of the epic itself in describing a new rooftop room in the Stonington house:

> A changing light is deepening, is changing
> To a gilt ballroom chair a chair

Bound to break under someone before long.
I let the light change also me.
The body that lived through that day
And the sufficient love and relative peace
Of those short years, is now not mine.
Would it be called a soul?

(FFN, 117)

Of course it would. Beneath the doubleness of "changing" in its transitive and intransitive senses lies the depth of Merrill's poetry. The
world is a vale of soul making in which "otherness" fulfills rather than
diminishes the apparently infinite capacities of the self for incorpora-
tion and expansion. The revelation is made in another way in that
poem which purports to discover a name for the epic now completed.
Visiting David Jackson in Key West, Merrill thinks about real estate (a
house DJ has just purchased) and his *real* estate, his poetry: both ventures, like life itself, are legitimately joint: "*Our* poem, now. It's signed
JM, but grew / From life together, grain by coral grain. / Building on
it, we let the life cloud over" ("Clearing the Title," *FFN*, 358). All authorship, all ownership is shared.

The authority of "Ephraim" is likewise splintered, divided, mutual,
and that of the other two volumes even more so. Multiplicity—
whether in the vocal polyphony of the board, the veiled and reflecting
identities of characters, or the couplings of ordinary mortals—is the
key to individual identity. Doubtless Merrill would agree with a comment of Buckminster Fuller: "Unity is plural and at minimum two."
In "Ephraim" this unity is largely represented in the relationship of
JM and DJ; indeed, as if to anticipate and forestall any secular reader's
objections to the poem's blarney, Merrill describes a visit to an insight-
ful psychiatrist, who analyzes the Ouija phenomenon as a "folie à
deux":

"Harmless; but can you find no simpler ways

To sound each other's depths of spirit
Than taking literally that epigram
Of Wilde's I'm getting damn
Tired of hearing my best patients parrot?"

"Given a mask, you mean, we'll tell—?"
Tom nodded. "So the truth was what we heard?"
"*A* truth," he shrugged. "It's hard
To speak of *the* truth. Now suppose you spell

It out. What underlies these odd
Inseminations by psycho-roulette?"
I stared, then saw the light:
"Somewhere a Father Figure shakes his rod

At sons who have not sired a child?
Through our own spirit we can both proclaim
And shuffle off the blame
For how we live—that good enough?" Tom smiled . . .

(30)

Ephraim may be more than an embodiment of the childless couple's
shame; as their creation, JM's and DJ's child, he is "a projection"

Of what already burned, at some obscure
Level or another, in our skulls.
We, all we knew, dreamed, felt and had forgotten,
Flesh made word, became through him a set of
Quasi-grammatical constructions which
Could utter some things clearly, forcibly,
Others not. Like Tosca hadn't we
Lived for art and love?

(31)

The art emanating from their love, Ephraim is the very proof of its
existence:

Ephraim's revelations—we had them
For comfort, thrills and chills, "material."
He didn't cavil. *He* was the revelation
(Or if we had created him, then we were).
The point—one twinkling point by now of thousands—
Was never to forego, in favor of
Plain dull proof, the marvelous nightly pudding.

(31–32)

The ambiguity inherent in the opening genitive phrase is made explicit two lines down, and suggests the mutuality or dialectic in Merrill's brand of teaching and creation. Ephraim *makes* revelations, and
himself constitutes revelations of the inner lives of his recipients, who
are also his creators. Student and teacher exist in a configuration always changing.

Precisely because of their relative youth, "the Rover Boys at thirty"
begin their lessons at an elementary level; Ephraim, it will turn out, is
the kind of teacher best suited to their particular needs because of the

"tone / We trusted most, a smiling Hellenistic / Lightness from beyond the grave" (15). It is no coincidence that the first lessons contain not only information about the sensuous experience of the dead at their various elevations but also appropriate epigrams about the wisdom of the senses: "TAKE . . . / FROM SENSUAL PLEASURE ONLY WHAT WILL NOT / DURING IT BE EVEN PARTLY SPOILED / BY FEAR OF LOSING TOO MUCH" (15). From relative lightheartedness to increasingly somber lessons, *Sandover* expands its lectures according to the lives and needs of its protagonist composers. Toward the beginning of *Scripts*, Merrill acknowledges the outward spiralling and the polyphony, and even assays a visual equivalent of multiplicity by adopting two separate typefaces:

> Moving, as we've done since *Ephraim*, from
> Romance to Ritual, and from the black
> Fustian void of *Mirabell*, against which
> At most one actor strutting in costume
> Tantalized us with effects to come,
> And the technician of the dark switchboard
> Tone by tone tried out his rainbow chord;
> Now, with light flooding auditorium
> (Our room, seen from the far side of the mirror)
> And stage alike, why need we—just because
> It "happened" that way—wait till end of scene
> For Wystan and Maria's mise en scène?
> Why not now and then incorporate
> What David and I don't see (and they do)
> Into the script? Italics can denote
> Their contribution. So—ready or not:
>
> (319)

In "Ephraim," however, romance predominates; as the lovers approach late youth they learn, to their horror, of future separations, which Merrill characteristically rationalizes as the price of separateness that inevitably accompanies even happy relationships. Told by Ephraim that he is now in his last mortal life but that DJ has a few to go, JM bravely protests:

> Ephraim, this cannot be borne. We live
> Together. And if you are on the level
> Some consciousness survives—right? Right.
> Now tell me, what conceivable delight
> Lies for either of us in the prospect
> Of an eternity without each other?

. . . . . . . . . . .

His answer's unrecorded. The cloud passed
More quickly than the shade it cast,

Foreshadower of nothing, dearest heart,
But the dim wish of lives to drift apart.

(25)

To the "thesis" of togetherness and the "antithesis" of separation, Merrill ends this section (J) with a complex synthesis of truths:

Times we've felt, returning to this house
Together, separately, back from somewhere—
. . . . . . . . . . . . . . . . . . .
Felt a ghost of roughness underfoot.
There it was, the valentine that Maya,
Kneeling on our threshold, drew to bless us:
Of white meal sprinkled then with rum and lit,
Heart once intricate as birdsong, it
Hardened on the spot. Much come-and-go
Has blackened, pared the scabby curlicue
Down to smatterings which, even so,
Promise to last this lifetime. That will do.

(25)

"Together, separately": the words, like the human pair, sit squarely beside one another, conjoined but at the same time opposed in meaning and divided by a single comma.

Neither unity nor separation, paradoxically, seems to exist without the other; especially in the deepest communion does isolation inevitably intrude. Chekhov's epigram—"If you don't want to feel alone, never get married"—could well stand for the central truth learned by the couple throughout the epic. Their threshold valentine has both resisted and fallen prey to time's depredations. The heart hardens in order to endure; the smatterings, relics, or shards will suffice as a stay against confusion. Is the emblematic valentine (a gift from a friendly witch) stronger or weaker for all the come-and-go? Is the heart solidified or fragmented into merely vestigial outlines? Can the heart be worn down but not worn out? The answers, as always in Merrill: yes and no.

The book longest in the making, "Ephraim" also offers a hero who, by the end, has not only learned but also changed. Whatever Ephraim and other occasional voices have dictated, JM's principal knowledge has been of his own present lot, a lot endured during twenty years.

Brief allusions to Strato, a Greek lover, remind us, as they remind JM himself, of the fleeting nature of infatuation, the way one sometimes outgrows or abandons lovers, or is abandoned by them, and of the attraction of opposites: "However seldom in my line to feel, / I most love those for whom the world is real" (51). The peripheral characters, seemingly tangential, are all mirrors in which the hero can see himself reflected, accurately or with some distortion ("We represent / Isms diametrically proposed" says "the figure in the mirror" to the fictive Sergei in section T [69]). People augment one another as well: the self, filling with otherness, increases spiritually as well as otherwise: "David and I lived on, limbs thickening / For better and worse in one another's shade" (41). Self-increase through the experience of love is matched by self-diminution, a subject Merrill tackled bravely in "The Thousand and Second Night" in *Nights and Days* (1966), where the crisis of middle age is symbolized by a temporary paralysis of half the speaker's face, and by the geographical schizophrenia of Istanbul, half-European and half-Asian. The "self-effacement" there is repeated and revised at the end of "Ephraim," section Y, which elegantly measures the self in terms of both growth and loss;

> And here was I, or what was left of me.
> Feared and rejoiced in, chafed against, held cheap,
> A strangeness that was, and was not, had
> All the same allowed for its description,
> And so brought at least me these spells of odd,
> Self-effacing balance. Better to stop
> While we still can. Already I take up
> Less emotional space than a snowdrop.
> My father in his last illness complained
> Of the effect of medication on
> His real self—today Bluebeard, tomorrow
> Babbitt. Young chameleon, I used to
> Ask how on earth one got sufficiently
> Imbued with otherness. And now I see.
>
> (89)

The "chameleon" poet—is this but another name for schizophrenia? Are the masks we wear excuses for the deep, unyielding, and imageless truth of identity? Or do they, rather, constitute that truth?

Significantly, JM absorbs the lesson of otherness after a passage concerning DJ's visit to his aged parents at a senior citizens' retreat in Arizona. Once again, Merrill mitigates the relative horror of the longest and dreariest journey with an acceptance of its compensations:

So far they've escaped the worst, or have they?—
These two old people at each other's gnarled,
Loveless mercy. Yet David now evokes
Moments of broadest after-supper light
Before talk show or moon walk, when at length
The detergent and the atrocity
Fight it out in silence, and he half blind
And she half deaf, serenely holding hands
Bask in the tinted conscience of their kind.

(88)

His understanding of the various roles the self cons or enacts comes
as a result of the example of two old people. Are love and lovelessness
the same thing? Is it the visit to DJ's parents that prompts JM's recollection of his own father at the end? As the affirmations and coinci-
dences of the trilogy mount, one finds everywhere syntheses and identity where one first suspected dichotomies and opposition. Singularity
is increasingly lost as identity is paradoxically formed.

One other section near the end of "Ephraim" speaks movingly of
the hero's *education sentimentale* with Merrill's typical combination of
opposing tones and gestures. In section X, having first considered the
latest scholarly theories about Giorgione's palimpsest painting, *La
Tempesta* (in a passage that follows a gorgeous Venetian episode that
includes a storm), Merrill undertakes a contemplation of all phenomena flowing beneath or within apparent realities, and of the very relationship of appearances to absences that actually point to endurance,
such as the supposed "absence" of his own mother from the poem.
She, he announces, has been present in every line, in one feminine
manifestation or another (the conversion of the raw material of life
into the subjects of art will occupy his more theoretical musings in the
next two parts of the trilogy), including some of the women from the
failed novel. Then the poem modulates to the lives—real? imagined?—of those figures, and at last Merrill contemplates the inadequacy of words to capture feeling.

First, those of his characters, but then his own:

What I think I feel now, by its own nature
Remains beyond my power to say outright,
Short of grasping the naked current where it
Flows through field and book, dog howling, the firelit
Glances, the caresses, whatever draws us
To, and insulates us from, the absolute—
The absolute which wonderfully, this slow

December noon of clear blue time zones flown through
Toward relatives and friends, more and more sounds like
The kind of pear-bellied early instrument
Skills all but lost are wanted, or the phoenix
Quill of passion, to pluck a minor scale from
And to let the silence after each note sing.

So Time has—but who needs that nom de plume? I've—
We've modulated. Keys ever remoter
Lock our friend among the golden things that go
Without saying, the loves no longer called up
Or named. We've grown autumnal, mild. We've reached a
Stage through him that he will never himself reach.
Back underground he sinks, a stream, the latest
Recurrent figure out of mythology
To lend his young beauty to a living grave
In order that Earth bloom another season.

Shall I come lighter-hearted to that Spring-tide
Knowing it must be fathomed without a guide?
With no one, nothing along those lines—or these
Whose writing, if not justifies, so mirrors,
So embodies up to now some guiding force,
It can't simply be written off. In neither
The world's poem nor the poem's world have I
Learned to think for myself, much. The twinklings of
Insight hurt or elude the naked eye, no
Metrical lens to focus them, no kismet
Veiled as a stern rhyme sound, to obey whose wink
Floods with rapture its galaxy of sisters.

(84–85)

This lengthy excerpt suggests the economy as well as the magnitude of Merrill's technical skills. The moment of quiet contemplation, which may take place in part aboard a plane returning from Europe to America, alludes to motifs prevalent in part X and throughout "Ephraim" generally: language and silence; protection from and access to "the absolute"; mirrors as embodiments as well as reflections of power. It also acknowledges time's power to change, and the individual's maturation through (in both senses) time. Foretelling still greater statements of creative and emotional independence in the later books, the passage seems to bid farewell to Ephraim, who is not at any rate a major figure in the book's final quarter, as JM decides to go it alone, without mystery or guide.

The technique of the passage defines Merrill's particular brilliance, in its stylishness and in its relationship to the nature of shared identity. Where Howard Nemerov's puns correspond to his sense of interrelatedness in the world and of the relation between world and self, Merrill's usually possess an even deeper human application. Thus, the "naked current" applies both to electricity and to the fictional stream in the ill-starred novel, which is mentioned in the previous paragraph. The "absolute" metamorphoses neatly into the "abso-lute," an archaic instrument, and "the quill of passion" into a *nom "de plume"* while even the "keys" become agents of both musical and architectural release. By the time one reaches "I . . . we" one knows that the bold ambivalence is intentional: JM and his fictional equivalent Sergei, or JM and DJ, both pairs possibly referred to, insist on the shared nature of all identity, as does the very following line, which is interrupted by one of Merrill's favorite rhetorical devices at a moment when he finds the intensity of revelation too difficult to maintain, and his natural reticence overwhelms him. Never one for final statements (even the end of *Sandover* eschews stasis and makes a gesture of recommencing), Merrill deflects a climax, and undercuts his rapturous starry finale with an abrupt descent into the reality of the flesh:

> Muse and maker, each at a loss without the
>
> —Oh but my foot has gone to sleep! Gingerly
> I prod it: painful, slow, hilarious twinges
> Of reawakening, recirculation;
> Pulsars intuiting the universe once
> More, this net of loose talk tightening to verse,
>
> And verse once more revolving between poles—
> Gassy expansion and succinct collapse—
> Till Heaven is all peppered with black holes,
> Vanishing points for the superfluous
> Matter elided (just in time perhaps)
> By the conclusion of a passage thus . . .
>
> (85–86)

The final elision, ending the entire section, is Merrill's way of suggesting the fluidity of time and space and also of bringing his matter to conclusion. The delicacy of the detail, starting with the implied but unstated relationship of muse and maker who need one another, through the exactness of diction (e.g., "peppered with black holes"), dramatizes the way Merrill's method always serves his vision. The mind awakens as the body sleeps; when the body resumes its own life, the forced conceits of the earlier stanzas give way to a different tone and to a different poetic gesture as well. After lines of hendecasyllables, Merrill subsides delicately into two perfect, but distinct, pentameter terza rima units, making his verse tighter and turning his attention away from the superfluities of self-analysis, which elide at last into section Y ("Years have gone by") over a mimetic bridge between pages.

This passage shows how Merrill can harness his lyric gifts (condensation, wit, tightness of imagery) to the traditional concerns of elegy (change, loss, abandonment), and to the ongoing movement in a narrative that is fast becoming an epic. At times this wit seems to permit him to evade direct statement, condensing his wisdom into volatile, explosive puns that barely contain his energy. But at others his didacticism seems less diffident, indeed more difficult, as the multiple meanings of words and phrases, the convolutions of syntax, are replaced, if only for a moment, with the delicacies of direct statement. In the passage above, as at every stage of his self-understanding, JM experiences both gain and loss, refusing to accept any lesson as final or binding. His very humor protects him against heavy-handed confessions but also constitutes part of his education. Life and the "other" life, the single self and its twinned opposites, sobriety and lightness, multiple suggestions of a single word, all constellate around a center: a solar or atomic model for self-presentation expands, in the next two books, as Merrill begins to develop a loftier theory of selfhood tied to more abstruse theories of history, science, and cosmology. His sentimental education, guided by Ephraim, will soon be augmented by lessons concerning one's place in a very crowded universe. From "Ephraim," with its combination of "so much facetiousness," "matters of life and death" (section C), and bravery in acknowledging the future (DJ "must cope / With the old people, who are fading fast . . . / But that's life too. A death's-head to be faced"), Merrill moves to *Mirabell*, opening with the deaths of DJ's parents.

Subtitled "Books of Number" and arranged decimally, *Mirabell* is in its scope hardly mechanical at all. Although it nominally concerns God B's greenhouse plan for the universe, and the nature of the atom and its fission, the most interesting of its educational topics are language and manners, hardly the stuff of a scientific epic. Just as "Ephraim" 's true subject was love, although its nominal theme was reincarnation, in *Mirabell* chemistry and physics are excuses or, as JM realizes early in the book, metaphors for deeper truths. This purgatorial volume connects the facts of the physical universe to the myths of reincarnation to, at last, Merrill's genuine subject, the nature of language and the poet's special use of it.

The poem begins reluctantly, tea-tabling as it were ("Oh very well, then. Let us broach the matter / Of the new wallpaper in Stonington"). This will hardly be the "matter" of the remainder of the poem, even though the wallpaper does have symbolic connections to Mirabell and his bat legions. JM is, he hopes, finished with visits from the other world and the compositions entailed to it:

> And that will be the end, we hope,
> Of too much emphasis upon possessions
> Worldly or otherwise. No more spirits, please.
> No statelier mansions. No wanting to be Pope.
> Ephraim's book is written now, is shut.
>
> (99)

But after the deaths of the Jacksons and their burial in Athens beside Maria Mitsotaki, JM and DJ contact Ephraim for "sense, comfort and wit," the very qualities he brought and epitomized in the earlier book. What they now learn surprises them: Ephraim tells JM that he will be a vehicle for revelation: "WHEN THEY CHOOSE / A SCIENTIFIC OR ARTISTIC BREAKTHRU / THE VEHICLE EXPERIENCES HIS WORK / UNIQUELY & THE RESULT IS . . ." (108). The breakdown here ("masterpiece" is the implied finale of the line) itself signals a revelation of sorts, and the news is strange. New voices demand poems of science. "Ugh," JM replies, but upon reconsideration realizes that science can as easily become the subject (and, in another sense of the word "become," the techniques) of poetry. He might as well be hearing the voice of Yeats's spirits, who said, "We have come to bring you metaphors for poetry."

JM is initially repelled, as much by his own congenital incapacity as by any distaste for science's obfuscation, until he realizes that he has nothing to lose and everything to gain:

> Not for nothing had the Impressionists
> Put subject-matter in its place, a mere
> Pretext for iridescent atmosphere.
> Why couldn't Science, in the long run, serve
> As well as one's uncleared lunch-table or
> *Mme X en Culotte de Matador*?
> Man by nature was (I'm paraphrasing)
> Ignorant. The man of science knew
> Little, could therefore be enticed to learn.

Finally the few of more than common sense—
Who but they would be our audience!

(109)

Given both a subject and a ready-made, updated sort of epic audience,
fit but few, he studiously sets himself to the task, reading books written
in what seems a foreign tongue:

>                                 Opaque
> Words like "quarks" or "mitochondria"
> Aren't *words* at all, in the Rilkean sense of
> House, Dog, Tree—translucent, half effaced,
> Monosyllabic bezoars already
> Found in the gullet of a two-year-old.
> Whereas through Wave, Ring, Bond, through Spectral Lines
> And Resonances blows a breath of life,
> Lifting the pleated garment. The day will come . . .
> The day has never gone. Proton and Neutron
> Under a plane tree by the stream repeat
> Their eclogue, orbited by twinkling flocks.
> And on the dimmest shore of consciousness
> Polypeptides—in primeval thrall
> To what new moon I wonder—rise and fall.

(110)

Passages like this show JM's readiness for future discoveries about the
nature of human language (or, rather, this shows his understanding,
at an advanced level, of the uses of our speech) as a bridge between
mathematical formula and the unstated, or unstatable, deep, imageless truths. Finally, as a grace note to the book's opening, JM is con-
fronted by his Greek-American goddaughter, a living embodiment of
the abstract "two-year-old" mentioned above, who comes upon her
distracted poet (that her name is Urania must count for something)
with a pertinent question that sets him going: " 'Noné (godfather), /
What's matter?' I face her, and almost know" (111).

Matter is his subject, and to continue the child's play pun, his dilemma. Looking at childlike wonder and responding to it as a mirror
image of something within himself, JM now becomes the child pupil
of lecturing masters sterner than Ephraim ever was. As he hears the
opening lessons about God B and his complementary or adversary
principle Chaos ("which employs feeling"), and adjusts to words like
*power*, *science*, and *atoms*, JM decides both defensively and cunningly

that "all this Flame and Fall / Has to be largely metaphorical" (114). And indeed, in the mirrored world of correspondences that seem to increase geometrically, all truth turns out to be metaphorical, just as all potential subjects, from the atom to the cosmos, seem to tell the same story. At the very start of "Ephraim," when JM thought mistakenly that "the baldest prose reportage was called for," to get as much meaning to the widest possible audience, he considered setting his visions into a novel. Now, at last, having buried both his failed novel and his delusions about the writing of fiction, he tackles different formal questions, but everything leads to the same end: a scheme of complex harmony for the atom, the self, and the entire universe.

After Matthew Arnold, it is hardly news to report the supplanting of religion by art in the modern world. Merrill glorifies poetry, along with music and science, as guides to a new age, or not so new actually, since God's basic cosmic rules—survival, no accidents, evolution—are supplemented by the suggestion that poetry will win out. Still, in no comparably long poem about such disparate matters can one find such consistent reflections on the province of human language and its poetic uses as one does in *Sandover*. As if answering those hostile critics who have complained of his "mere" technique, Merrill now offers contemplations as well as examples of language heightened to full resonance. As "MANS TERMITE PALACE BEEHIVE ANTHILL PYRAMID" (118), language offers an alternate subject to the pseudoscience that JM, himself forestalling his fears by sharing them, refers to as the junk, the allegory, "the whole horror of Popthink" (136) in the epic. Literary criticism itself comes to play an increasing part in the epic, almost as if to suggest its own self-consciousness. So the spirits acknowledge W. H. Auden for his "wonders" ("HIS SINGLE FLAW HE NOW KNOWS: THE MISMARRIAGE / OF LYRIC TO BALD FARCE SO THAT WORK BECAME A PASTIME" [143]), who then reminds readers of Merrill's own worries about a possible reception:

> WE MY BOY DRAW FROM 2
> SORTS OF READER: ONE ON HIS KNEES TO ART
> THE OTHER FACEDOWN OVER A COMIC BOOK.
> OUR STYLISH HIJINKS WONT AMUSE THE LATTER
> & THE FORMER WILL DISCOUNT OUR URGENT MATTER.
>                                         (147)

Dante, says Auden, was lucky to have lived in a gullible age (in "Ephraim," JM concludes that whereas the doctrine of the day demanded a Hell, Dante's Paradiso was "pure show-and-tell"), Merrill less so. For this reason, the subject of language and the nature and uses of metaphor may be said to be more important than the nominal scientific hooks on which the poet hangs his hat.

Like any post-*Prelude* epic, *Sandover* wrestles with its own formation and takes as part of its subject matter the enterprise of its own composition. In one important way, at least, Merrill's dilemma is the exact opposite of Wordsworth's: the Romantic poet sought a theme, somewhat vainly, before falling into a self-justification that became his epic subject. The comforts of blank verse afforded his meanderings a rhythm right from the start, although he had no clear direction. Merrill receives his subject, which is supposedly dictated, given to him as a bequest, while he contemplates the appropriate speech forms and metrical bases for the best conveyance of his truths. *Mirabell* concerns style in obiter dicta and in its overarching concern with language as humankind's surest way to divinity.

It is no wonder that in a work so formally various one finds the characters thinking of their language. Early on, Mirabell gives a clue to the book's form: just as humans use a decimal system, the fallen angel-bats were attached to fourteen as a sacred number (their earthly sites numbered fourteen); JM remembers this later on when he tries to find "a line, a meter that effectively / Distinguishes them from us." Auden helps him out:

> Don't you agree
> We *human* characters should use this rough
> Pentameter, our virtual birthright?
> THE 5     MOST FITTING     So fourteeners might
> Do for the bats? NOT SKITTERY ENOUGH
> WHY NOT MY BOY SYLLABICS? LET THE CASE
> REPRESENT A FALL FROM METRICAL GRACE
> Wystan, that's brilliant!
>
>                                    (240)

Again, in the countdown last lessons Auden lends a hand after JM reminds Mirabell of "how slow" the mortals are to absorb his lessons. The poetic fun and games here are not gratuitous but brilliantly coincident with a vital truth just proposed. Since the backward-numbered lessons dramatize the "convalescence" of the mortals and also a stripping-away process that MM and WHA experience as they prepare to reenter this world in different forms, Mirabell asks: "IS NOT THE SOUL / IN ITS TRANSIT & CHANGE LIKE THE PSYCHE IN DAILY LIFE? / DO U NOT, ALONE, WEAR ONE FACE? WITH OTHERS, ANOTHER?" A truth universally acknowledged throughout Merrill's poetry is here augmented by a commentary from Auden, which devolves upon his own changes at this moment:

SPIRIT & SOUL MY BOY    LIKE GEIST & SEELE
DON'T CONFUSE EM! READY FOR THE TRAILER?
AHEM: IF LANGUAGE IS THE POET'S CHURCH
LET US CONSTRUCT
A TO Z AN ALTAR LIKE AN ARCH
GROUNDED ON NUMBERS    DRAT    WHAT RHYMES WITH UCT?
ON NUMBERS    HMM    I TWITCH IN MY RED GOWN
LIKE AN OLD CARDINAL WHOSE LATIN'S GONE
NO DOUBT THE STRIPPING PROCESS . . .

(252)

WHA, stripping and stripped but clothed like a cardinal, suggests another version of all duplicities: rhyme taken from him, he can no longer make quite as much "human" sense of the world because his own elevation demands a corresponding loss of poetic power.

Both masks and rhymes present truth through a combination of revelation and concealment. As at other points in the trilogy, Merrill can even suggest a rhyme when he hasn't actually made one, thereby implicating the reader in the creative process and reminding him or her that absence and presence are hardly diametrical opposites. "ALL THINGS," says Maria Mitsotaki to her "ENFANTS / . . . ARE DONE HERE IF U HAVE TECHNIQUE" (104), and what surprises most pleasantly in *Mirabell* is Merrill's submitting his technical skill to the demands of theme. Voices interrupt and blend with one another more thoroughly, but with appropriate concern for station (there are no accidents, as the book reminds us). But what does one say about the following moments? Toward the beginning, Maria is cut off as she begins to comfort DJ:

LIFE TERRIFIES ALL ALL BUT THE UTTER FOOLS
But you're . . . not living, and still terrified.
OF THEM AS U ARE    I HAVE MORE TO LOSE
Literally? I BELIEVE SO    THEY CAN USE
FI    *Censorship*

(128)

Has the revelation been made? To the extent that one fills in the "RE," it has, but the reader, like the scribe, must compensate for the initial loss; breakthroughs alleviate breakups. Later, Maria creates a void that she proceeds to fill, after a significant pause:

I ALWAYS WANTED A MONKEY    So did I—
Perhaps next he'll turn into one? JM
AREN'T U ASHAMED OF YR MONKEY    My animal nature?
Not a bit. O LET ME MAKE THE JOKE:
—SHINES?

(171)

Even more problematic is the striking "phantom rhyme" (what might
be termed an exemplary "trope of absence") in Chester Kallman's lament when he learns he is to be reborn as a black African:

> AH LIFE    I FEEL THE LASH
> OF THE NEW MASTER    NOTHING NOW BUT CRASH
> COURSES    What does Wystan say? TO PLATO?
> HAVING DROPPED ME LIKE A HOT    O SHIT
> WHAT GOOD IS RHYME NOW

(184)

The incidental charm of much of these poetic shenanigans is com-
plimented, and also warned against, by Robert Morse, a Stonington
friend who dies in the middle of the trilogy and assumes a place in the
other world in *Scripts*. Toward the end of *Mirabell* he makes an earthly
appearance strolling into the Water Street house where he reads the
*Mirabell* transcripts. E. F. Benson babytalk precedes sterner admonitions in terza rima whose fluency is exceeded only by its appropriate-
ness:

> "Ah, lads, it's taxed

> My venerable beads. Me giddy fwom
> Uppercut of too much upper case.
> (A weak one, if you please. Most kind. Yum-yum.)

> Everything in Dante knew its place.
> In this guidebook of yours, how do you tell
> Up from down? Is Heaven's interface

> What your new friends tactfully don't call Hell?
> Splendid as metaphor. The real no-no
> Is jargon, falling back on terms that smell

> Just a touch fishy when the tide is low:
> 'Molecular structures'—cup and hand—obey
> 'Electric waves'? Don't *dream* of saying so!

—So says this dinosaur whom Chem 1A
Thrilled, sort of. Even then I put the heart
Before the course . . . " And at the door: "Today

We celebrate Maria's Himmelfahrt
And yours. You're climbing, do you know how high?
While tiny me, unable to take part,

Waves you onward. *Don't look down.* Goodbye."
—Answered with two blithe au reservoirs,
He's gone. Our good friend. As it strikes me, my

Head is in my hands. I'm seeing stars.

(256)

Dying and knowing it, Morse reminds JM and his readers of the salient connections among metaphor, truthfulness, and jargon at a moment that celebrates the glories of JM's artistic enterprise and Morse's
own death in a tone redolent of small town intimacies and paradisal
ascents. The "Feast of the Assumption" includes a prediction of the
*other* Maria's own reincarnation: all is doubleness, from the Dantean
ending couched in an American cliché to the way Merrill adduces poetic truths in common diction ("the real no-no is jargon"), proving his
methods effective while asserting the basis of an aesthetics.

Dante and E. F. Benson speak together through Merrill's fluent ventriloquism. Adept at mimicry, he can sound the depths of emotion and
wit while sounding like any one (or several) of the masters whose vocal
lessons he has absorbed. *Mirabell* allies this mimic art to lessons about
the creative relationship between the individual self, or conscious ego,
and the unwilled multiplicity of voices and influences that rise from
the inner depths of an artist's share in the collective unconsciousness.
For all the poetic fireworks and technical showing off in Merrill's
work, the trilogy pays a remarkable homage to individual lack of identity (another version of Keats's chameleon poet). Rather than striving
to forge a distinctive voice and style, Merrill often seems, like Stravinsky, to be most master when most sedulously a student of others. In
pastiche one finds truest originality, in a crazy quilt the most singular
figure.[11]

The collaborativeness of art is a central lesson in the epic's method,
DJ and JM together receiving, recording, and rearranging their sig-
nals from beyond. But much literature, according to the developed
myths of *Mirabell*, seems to be communal: "TSE DOWN ON CERTAIN /
SUPERSTITIOUS SCRIBES    WE HAD TO APPOINT RIMBAUD    HE WROTE /
THE WASTE LAND    WE FED IT INTO THE LIKE-CLONED ELIOT" (219) an-

nounces Mirabell; likewise, Dante sat and listened to a defrocked mendicant priest, who was really one of the bat legions. Some few poems, like the Homeric epics as well as *The Waste Land*, are prewritten, but even Merrill's friend Hans Lodeizen, dead for twenty-five years, was cloned so that his poetic talent could be recycled into JM's own masterpiece. All this may mean in simpler terms that any poet absorbs the manifold events of his life as influences upon his work, and Hans Lodeizen may be, JM contemplates, "the key / This opus began and will end in" (221). But in the trilogy the stakes are bigger: a major dialectical force is the conflict between the fiction of creativity and the fact of responsiveness.

Just as the individual is paradoxically small and complex, so does Merrill become frustrated by the realization that his work may not really be his own:

> And maddening—it's all by someone else!
> In your voice, Wystan, or in Mirabell's.
> I want it mine, but cannot spare those twenty
> Years in a cool dark place that *Ephraim* took
> In order to be palatable wine.
> This book by contrast, immature, supine,
> Still kicks against its archetypal cradle
> LESS I SHD THINK BY CONTRAST THAN DESIGN?
> A MUSE IN HER RECURRENT INFANCY
> PRESIDES AS U MY DEAR WERE FIRST TO SEE:
> URANIA BABBLING ON THE THRESHOLD OF
> OUR NEW ATOMIC AGE     THE LITTLE LOVE
> AT PLAY WITH WORDS WHOSE SENSE SHE CANNOT YET
> FACE LEARNING     Very pretty, but I'd set
> My whole heart, after *Ephraim*, on returning
> To private life, to my own words. Instead,
> Here I go again, a vehicle
> In this cosmic carpool. Mirabell once said
> He taps my word banks. I'd be happier
> If *I* were tapping them. Or thought I were.
>                         (261–62)

This anxiety prompts Auden's correction (quoted in chapter 1) about the relative smallness of the "self" in artistic creation. Will the poet have nothing on which to pride himself?

Everything seems either inherited, inherent, or ghost-written. Merrill's art dazzles while it defers humbly to the authority of others. Weaving himself into the "unbroken chain" of power scribes (121) who include Homer, Dante, and Proust, he both submits to their presences and manages to carve out a space for himself. This ambivalent process finds its strongest correlative throughout this central book in his developing theory of metaphor. As a bridge, the idea of metaphor separates and connects formula on the one side and revelation on the other, just as any single metaphor abridges items otherwise separate. The poet's tool, acknowledged by Aristotle as the first and only rule for genius, distinguishes human discourse from scientific and divine languages.

JM demands clarity where obfuscation seems inevitable:

> Superhuman powers like these
> We want as mentors, not as servants, please!
> How should you speak? Speak without metaphor.
> Help me to drown the double-entry book
> I've kept these fifty years. You want from me
> Science at last, instead of tapestry—
> Then tell round what brass tacks the old silk frays.
> Stop trying to have everything both ways.
> It's too much to be batwing angels *and*
> Inside the atom, don't you understand?
>
> (122)

And this demand for a stylistic clarity is equivalent to one for easier lessons; JM hopes that "tomorrow all will be lucid, crystalline: / No opposition graver than between / Credulity and doubt" (125). Between credulity and doubt, JM sits on the horns of a dilemma: metaphor, one might say by analogy, sits between tautology and scripture and consequently serves the poet as he himself serves and gradually transcends his otherworldly teachers.

As fact and fiction are twin sides of a single coin, or perhaps two words for a single truth, so all artistic language is by nature double. The spirit says to JM: "U HAVE NOW HEARD SOME OF OUR LEGENDS & TAKEN THEM WITH / A GRAIN OF SALT    DISMISSD THEM AS MERE METAPHOR    & YET / NO MORE DIRECT METHOD SEEMS TO WORK" (146). Metaphor and legend are teaching tools of the highest order, and necessary since the bat speakers know and constitute formulas: their normal discourse is a divine computerese, as they are merely mechanisms of the Research Lab. Imaging forth is like telling tales: both activities help to dramatize fact. Speaking of "black holes," the bat must resort to metaphor (" 'Vulgar' though it is, and 'negative'?" JM inquires): "HOW ELSE DESCRIBE (WITHOUT THE FORMULAS / EVEN WE LACK) WHAT IS TO US A RIDDLE?" (149–50). Several pages earlier, Mirabell for the first time employs a device that he will continue to use self-consciously to remind his human audience of the artifice in even the most colloquial of human speech:

> CAN U IMAGINE (METAPHOR) A BLACKSMITH ALLOWD TO
> SHOE IN GOLD? NOT PRACTICAL    TOO SOFT    TOO FANCIED BY
> MAN.
> BLACKSMITH: PATRON    HORSE: REPRESENTATIVE    & SHOE: THE
> SOUL
> BORN INTO WHATEVER EARTHLY LIFE. THE SYSTEM U KNOW
> OF REINCARNATION MERELY GIVES US THE SAME OLD HORSE
> RESHOD
>
>         (144–45)

One may recall Merrill's earlier worry in "Ephraim": "Since it had never truly fit, why wear / The shoe of prose? In verse the feet went bare" (4). The metaphor itself allies those two seemingly unrelated but in Merrill's work intimate subjects: soul making and verse making, or perhaps souls and soles. In small as well as large ways, the writing of the poem enacts a process of self-formulation. (Later, in *Scripts*, a pun on "lines" makes the same connection between art and life: celebrating their twenty-fifth anniversary, DJ gives JM a small ring, and JM replies "I've no gift but these lines the years / Together write upon my face and yours" [353].)

All art, especially the mysteries of music and language, assumes a high place in Merrill's religious evaluations. In the second final lesson (numbered nine in the reverse process), Mirabell discursively suggests the prominence of poetry to the new age:

> WE HAVE PULLD DOWN THE SUPERANNUATED CHURCH
> & RAISED AN ALTAR TO THE NEW HOUSE GODLET: PURE REASON
> NOT IN THE VOLTAIREAN SENSE BASED ON KNOWLEDGE MERELY
> BUT REASON RUN THRU THE FIRES OF MAN'S CLONED SOUL    A
> NEW
> ENERGY, A NEW THERMOSTAT WILL HEAT & LIGHT MAN'S HOUSE.
> NOW METAPHOR IS THE RITUAL OF THIS NEW REASON
> & OF WHAT RITES? THE RITES OF LANGUAGE    IF THERE ARE STILL
> 3
> MAJOR FAITHS THESE ARE NOW SCIENCE, POETRY & MUSIC
> & THE REVEALD MONOTHEISM OF TODAY IS LANGUAGE.
> THAT OF SCIENCE: FORMULA    OF POETRY: METAPHOR
> OF MUSIC: NOTATION    IN EACH THE VIBRANT RINGING LIGHT
> FILLD WITH COLOR!
>
>         (239)

That this reference to the "rites of language" immediately precedes JM's discussion with Auden about the meter appropriate to the bats' speech and the latter's suggestion that syllabics "represent a fall from metrical grace" merely puts to work the very theorem that Mirabell has just given. Decisions that seem arbitrary, in other words, like the choice of a verse form, must have a rational explanation: "sensational effects have subtle causes," Merrill once observed ("Pola Diva," in *The Fire Screen, FFN*, 209).

At the dramatic center of *Mirabell* lies the excitement of names and name giving, as Stephen Yenser has suggested.[12] At the start of book 7, the humans learn that the sacred "Five," known under some incarnations as Akhnaton, Nefertiti, Plato, Homer, and Montezuma, were really "called" something else:

> we've heard
> That the five "names" originally given
> For *the* Five—Torro, Von—weren't after all
> Word made flesh but formula made word,
> Bestowed upon the R/Lab by God B
> (Who, lacking human volubility,
> *Has* no word for His own power and grace;
> Who, left alone, just falls back on flimflam
> Tautologies, like *I am that I am*
> Or *The world is everything that is the case*):
> Five formulas which only then—the solo
> Instrument emerging nakedly
> From the Lab's thumping tutti—took the live
> Twin aspect of Akhnaton-Nefertiti,
> A double soul, firstborn among the Five.
>
> THEY LIVED, ACCOMPLISHD THEIR V WORK, MISJUDGED &
>    DIED     GOD B
> FASHIOND THE OTHER 3 & THESE 5 SOULS ARE UNIQUE. MY
> TRANSLATION OF THEM INTO NEUTRAL (M) NAMES CONFUSED U
>
> (223)

Some poets share Nemerov's obsession with the primal human creative act, Adam's naming of the animals. Even Merrill, who generally seems more interested in other linguistic problems, puts naming at the heart of human intellection. God's names are all species of translation; in heaven, truth exists because language does not. Where tautology and formula alone communicate, neither humanity, passion, nor discourse is possible.

Above all, Merrill is a poet of manners, not mannerisms. In the same way one would call Proust a recorder of a social scene, Merrill's very enterprise is premised on the possibility of language as a means of social action. In an interview he once allowed that "manners for me are the touch of nature, an artifice in the very bloodstream,"[13] and one of the prominent didactic truths of *Mirabell* is the crucial relationship of manners to language. The voice quoted above belongs to OO, one of Mirabell's own teachers, who reminds DJ that "MATH ENCAPSULATES COMPLEX TRUTHS WHICH AS WITH OUR 1ST / MEANINGLESS TO U & THERE4 FRIGHTENING VOICES MUST / BE RENDERD INTO YR VOCABULARY OF MANNERS" (224).

*Mirabell* dramatizes, as I have suggested, a reciprocal schooling. Just as the title character continues the epic lessons concerning nature, history, and the universe, so is he himself introduced and welcomed to the world of human manners, in which language and social gaffes such as interruption are intimately connected. Even the issue of "voice" comes to stand for the problem of tone in, or of, voice.

At the start of book 2, the voice-number known still as 741, "our school's / New kindergarten teacher," suggests the neatest symbols for division: punctuation comes to the board, and in addition to the letters, numbers, "Yes," "&," and "No," heretofore their sole resources, hand and scribe now have hyphen, period, comma, and so forth, those interruptors of free and automatic letter-mongering that can distinguish between, by dividing, speakers' voices. Mostly, however, these "tinkering symbols [are] known / Not in themselves, but through effects on tone." Grateful and delighted, JM cannot quite bring himself completely to address his spiritual teacher: "Is it still Bezel—I can't say that name / But you know who I mean: are you the same?" (129). The voice 741 (later Mirabell) and his kind are mathematical formulas requiring exposition through metaphor for acceptance by human minds. At the same time, Mirabell is the pupil of his human contacts, who can instruct him in the bonds of human society, namely manners.

The promotion of Mirabell through humane courtesy continues in book 3, and once again revelation succeeds a breaking. First 741 confesses that "THIS WORLD OF COURTESY" has slowed down the learning process; then,

> Breaking off, the cup strolls round the Board
> As who should take a deep breath before speaking:
>                 NOR WD I HAVE COME TO LOVE U
>                                          (155)

Illuminated and animated by the human scribes, 741 has "ENTERD A GREAT WORLD   I AM FILLD / WITH   IS IT MANNERS?" Immediately following, he begins a defense of homosexuality as a recent product (four thousand years ago) of God B to encourage arts and mind. JM demurs, reminding him that "certain very great / Poets and musicians have been straight." The answer is cut off: "NO DOUBT   BUT 4000 YEARS AGO GOD B REALIZ / *Censorship*." And once more the break heralds a remarkable transformation: JM urges 741, the erstwhile bat, to speak for himself, not for God, and his kindness encourages the number to assume a new form. Maria announces simply, "MES ENFANTS HE HAS TURNED INTO A PEACOCK" (157).

Mirabell receives his name in book 7, right before the countdown review of lessons; the entire book, symbolically, operates structurally on the principle of breaking, humanizing, and revealing that the smaller moments above prepare us for. JM defends Mother Nature before 741, who relegates what he calls "physical densities" to a relatively trivial position when weighed against "soul densities." Something happens, however, to 741's pronouncement about this maternal figure:

> BUT SHE DOES NOT ALWAYS COMPLY AS U YRSELVES WILL SEE
> WHEN SHE COMES TO U
>> Here the cup sweeps—is swept?—clear off the Board
>> Into the wings, a single violent swerve.
>
> (231)

Maria now reveals that poor 741 was caught in midsentence and was "HAULED OFFSTAGE BY A HOOK LIKE A BAD TAP / DANCER ON AMATEUR NIGHT." Everyone seems to JM "so anti-Nature"; indeed, MM and WHA want to leave for a smoke. Gradually abandoned, by his spiritual friends and then by DJ, who goes off to Boston for a medical checkup, JM is left alone with his thoughts, and in a setpiece of seven eight-line stanzas, he conjures up Mirabell's name, significantly in the middle of a contemplation about his own mother, the nature figure throughout all of his work. What renders the naming so lovely is that it comes almost as an aside, or perhaps as an illumination in the midst of his Yeatsian consideration of the polarity of mind and nature:

> Once out of nature, a mercurial
> Inch, look back! Sea, jungle, alpine snow,
> Buff desert far below
> Alternate by "turns" as in a music hall.
> So distanced, it could be the way
> Of our own world, as the fops in Congreve knew
> With their strut and plumage—ah! mightn't Mirabell do
> For our peacock's name?—
>
> (232)

His heart contracting in terror, fearful of what may have happened to his own mother whom he is telephoning long distance, JM gets through at last as the line clears, the phone is answered, and Mother Nature resumes earthly communication.

The newly named Mirabell is restored to his human benefactors and in a mannerly exchange redons his peacock finery (234). A single "please" makes possible the restitution of appearance to voice (although "seen" only by WHA and MM), and a second "please," like the audience's applause for Tinkerbell in *Peter Pan*, brings back Ephraim as a special treat to the audiences on both sides of the mirror. The stage is set, and the manners have affirmed polite discourse: Mirabell now begins the last lessons. Addressing his peacock by name for the first time, JM asks, after a thoughtful pause, whether he approves of his fancy name, to which Mirabell replies:

> INDEED
>
> IT QUITE SUITS THE PERSON U HAVE MADE OF ME    HAS
>   SOMETHING
> OF THE MIRACLE? THE MIRAGE? & SURELY OF THE PLUM!
> NOW B4 US LIE OUR TEN RECUPERATIVE LESSONS
>
> (236)

The mastery of politesse purges the spirits of their formulas by giving them names. It reassures the living by producing a lively, loving commerce with the other world in which the achieved manners are a hard-won victory and an assurance of future communication. The appearance of the angel Michael at the end of *Mirabell* prepares DJ and JM, as well as Auden, Maria, and the reader, for the sterner stuff of *Scripts* with its headier revelations. Politeness has healed Mirabell of numbers; it has humanized through naming and through metaphor. Language is the province of the humans, and it has its intellectual analogue in Keatsian negative capability, another term for the polite willingness to remain content with partial information without any irritating, vulgar groping after personal truth or gain. Although JM acknowledges a wish for "the feather of proof," he has been too polite to ask, and the reward for this self-effacing kindness will be the grander assurances of the heavenly pageant. His legacy, according to Mirabell, for having endured gaps and breakups, will be restitution and wholeness:

> WE & YOU MOVE IN OUR FIELD TOGETHER
> (THERE! STITCHES OUT WHERE THE SCAR'S LIPS MEET INVISIBLY)
>   AH

WITH WHAT REGRET THAT WE CAN NEVER SAY: CAREFUL DEAR
   FRIENDS
DO NOT TAKE THAT FALSE STEP! OR IN ANY WAY PROTECT U
WHO ARE OUR LOVED ONES    WD THAT WE CD LEAD U TO THAT
   LOST
VERMEER THAT MANUSCRIPT OF MOZART OR LEAVE U SIMPLY
A LITTLE GLOWING MEDAL STRUCK IN HEAVEN SAYING: TRUE

> Dear Mirabell, words fail us. How banal
> Our lives would be, how shrunken, but for you.

(258)

Having been naturalized, the manners will never be relinquished; Michael's chilling last words invite JM and DJ to a meeting of equals:

I HAVE ESTABLISHED YOUR ACQUAINTANCE & ACCEPT YOU. COME
NEXT TIME IN YOUR OWN MANNER. SERVANTS WE ARE NOT.

(276)

These angels, unlike the bat-spirits, engage in mannerly exchanges of information; the trilogy has moved from a human spokesman in Ephraim, through a subhuman group of tutors (Maria reminds JM on page 123 that the bats "HAVE NO MANNERS   THEY WERE NEVER MEN"), to an even higher politeness in the last volume.

Having performed his services, and been educated in turn by his human masters, Mirabell retires at the end of his volume to dreams of former human glories ("AT NIGHT COME HOME / SLIP INTO MY MIRABELL ROBES & DREAM OF THESE OLD TIMES," 264), as he will be reabsorbed into sheer number. JM, for his part, has internalized Mirabell along with his lessons; since all identity, in Merrill's fables, is composite, absorption and reflection complement one another as narrative and structural devices in the epic. All appearance belongs to the human world, just as all metaphor does, and it is a signal fact of the trilogy that the world of appearances, what seems truth to us, demands the fiction of appearances in the other, invisible world. Things invisible to mortal sight are made through fiction and the fictional apparatus of mirror and board into the stuff and the very metaphor of the educational plan, as Maria had earlier reminded her students (152): the heavenly friends, realizing that sheer emptiness terrifies more than anything else, take on appearances in order to placate their worldly hosts. In the following section (4.4), JM reminds himself that Mirabell is neither "person, not a peacock, not a bat; / A devil least of all—an impulse only / Here at the crossroads of our four affections" (173). Human love generates imaginative invention, which then redounds backward to its source through the complementary mechanism of metaphor: appearance and affection, the two constituents of human uniqueness, are joined through metaphor, the agency of human language, to render the entire experience a field of vision and feeling, as Mirabell continues JM's thought: "OR MAKE OF ME THE PROCESS SOMEWHERE / OPERATING BETWEEN TREE & PULP & PAGE & POEM" (173).

The four friends, two on each side of the board, "nucleate a kind of psychic atom" (191), but the hooks of connection, as JM realizes, do not stop at four; "all things alive touch" the two humans, while, at the same time, the "atom's precarious inviolability" is Mirabell's major theme. Fusion and fission, on both nuclear and psychological levels, are themselves twinned throughout the poem's development. Pairs of opposites, pairs of reflections: some tensing one another, others shadowing, all "enact the deep capacities for good / And evil in the atom" (192). And of these polarities art is the finished product, surviving "by feeding on its personages' lives" (218). This is why Mirabell and his cohorts retreat at the end of his volume; they have fulfilled and, in their turn, been fulfilled by their encounters with the humans. The peacock touchingly reminds JM in the penultimate final lessons that "WE / ACCUMULATE THRU U A KNOWLEDGE THAT MUST HENCEFORTH BE / PART OF US IN A REALM BEYOND THE GREAT GOLDFRAMED MIRROR" (257). Book 8 as a whole ends by stressing the limits of love, symbiosis, imagination, and of all dualities; mannerliness, as a gauge to human behavior, enforces the reticence required by the passage quoted earlier ("BUT WE & YOU    WE & YOU MOVE IN OUR FIELD TOGETHER," 258).

*Scripts for the Pageant* initially looks like the fussiest and the least "shrunken" of the epic's three parts; it turns out to be the simplest and most lucid. The level of social politeness is highest; deference is accorded inevitably to Michael and then to Gabriel as natural superiors, even though God B's plan is for "A GOOD COMPANY AND A FRIENDLY PLACE" (293), where all the participants share in talent and intelligence. At the same time, the language of the angels sounds orotund, distant and icy, with more ritual in their communiqués. So we have regressed to a formal scene of instruction, although the students are considerably more adult than they were when they first contacted Ephraim. (Merrill's implicit educational philosophy seems to recommend seminars for freshmen, followed by sterner, more advanced lectures for upperclassmen.) But this is also the volume of healing and cementing, which neatly and elegantly sews up the seams between life and death, form and matter, God B and nature, between, in fact, all dualities. Speaking from a didactic standpoint, one may appropriately label it the volume of synthesis. Having learned that "INTELLIGENCE . . .

IS THE SOURCE OF LIGHT" (296), Merrill includes larger tracts of scientific and philosophical information throughout his *Paradiso*. The lectures are unalloyed and unleavened, but humor is not entirely absent; indeed, this volume betrays the richest variety and depth of human feeling throughout the epic.

More than just preaching, *Scripts* continues to enact, even as it explains, a process of education. Once again, I am less interested in its nominal subject—destruction and preservation, the central opposition created by time—than in its metadidactic constructions and its depiction of learning as a process of absorption, forgetting, and reminiscence. Its pedagogic assumptions and dramatic encounters ally Merrill with the other important mythographers of education in the Western tradition that extends from Plato and includes such recent avatars as Keats and Wordsworth. Maria Mitsotaki makes an important revelation in the middle of the volume; after the five middle ("&") lessons, she lets JM and DJ know how she and Auden took part in the archangel Michael's first term lectures:

> THEN CAME THE MIRACLE: THOSE LESSONS READIED
> DURING YR MONTHS APART ENFANTS WERE BY
> A WAVE OF MICHAEL'S HAND WIPED FROM OUR MINDS
> TO BREAK UPON US STAGGERINGLY ONE
> BY ONE. MIRACLE 2: THE MIDDLE FIVE
> ENDED, 'WE WILL NOT DECEIVE OUR SCRIBE.
> NOW TELL THEM' And it all came flooding back!
> THAT VERY INSTANT
>                         NEED WE STRESS MY DEAR
> THE EXQUISITE REVERBERATIONS HERE:
> EARTH LAY OPEN LIKE A BOOK TO READ
> & THERE OUR POEM SLEPT     LOCKED IN A SEED.
> NOW GEORGE & ROBERT ARE ALREADY 'AT'
> THE NEXT 10 LESSONS ON INHERENT, NON
> BIOLOGICAL LIFE ENERGIES
> And when the time comes will they too forget?
> & BE REMINDED & AMAZED
>
>                              (414–15)

We have witnessed a paradigm for all creation, which is also allied to the myths of recollection and reincarnation in the *Republic*, the *Aeneid*, and the Intimations ode of Wordsworth. Language is in a literal way the "characters" of Merrill's poem, not just because the board and its figures sit squarely at the center of the poem's fable but also because his entire dramatic purpose in *Scripts* derives from his linguistic credo that all is translation.

If knowledge and poetry, all language in fact, are species of translation, then one should not be surprised to discover revelation and unmasking as the climax to the epic. The simple organization of *Scripts* around "Yes," "&," and "No" is easier than those of its predecessors, and its cast of multiple characters turns out, at the end, to be smaller. Identities overlap, extended from and into one another, as they had increasingly done throughout *Mirabell*. Multiplicity, as a principle of organization, diminishes to unity, as breakings and strippings leave the heroes of the epic with clarity in their perception and human alliances. People may be reborn as elements, or cloned into others, or simply absorbed by the living; the principle of metamorphosis reduces rather than expands the human cast. Thus Mirabell comments on the upcoming death of the scientist George Cotzias:

> THESE RETURNS TO THE ELEMENTS ARE NOT
> SAD OR SINISTER BUT IN FACT SAINTLY ELEVATIONS.
> NEXT TO THE STATIONARY AFTERLIFE OR STEP BY STEP
> BUREAUCRATIC UPWARDNESS GIVEN TO MOST, A RETURN
> LIKE OUR FRIENDS' IS A NEAR-MIRACULOUS REPLENISHMENT:
> THEY WILL BE JOINING THE ARCHANGELS OF EARTH & WATER.
> THEY HAVE LONG BEEN CHOSEN
>      Becoming—stripped of personality—
>      Part of what those angels know and are?
>          OF THE DOMINIONS CHEM & VEG
> THEY WILL BE OF THE RULING ORDERS
>      But with no way for us to get in touch.
>                THEY WILL MAKE THEMSELVES
> KNOWN TO U BOTH    THEY WILL CHARGE U WITH ENERGY & WAIT
> TO LEAD U TO THEIR MASTERS
>      Localized—here Daphne in young leaf?
>      There the chalk face of an old limestone cliff?
>            AH THEY WILL RIPPLE     THEY WILL
> JOLT THRU THE WAVES OF TREES & WARPS OF EARTH     THEY WILL
>   CARRY
> MESSAGES IN THE GRAIN OF ROCK & FLOW IN THE GREEN VEINS
> OF LEAVES, FOR THOSE 2 GODS' VAST NETWORK KEEPS THE GLOBE
>   INTACT
>      Like "Adonais"—all of life imbued
>      With the dead's refining consciousness.
>                                    (309–10)

The dead, as Eliot said, "are . . . that which we know,"[14] and Merrill's underlying reduction, following an apparent proliferation of entities, suggests as seamless a web for human identities as for his updated version of the nine Muses, who appear as both individuals and a cluster, symbolized by the woven garland they may either carry or drop (400–404). All are versions of Psyche or Nature, the female half of the dual governing principle; the Muses "ROAM THE DIMLY VAULTED BRINE- / ENCRUSTED CHAMBERS MAN CALLS BRAIN" (401), occupying internal and external space. JM begins to get the picture when he asks: "Is the cast / Much smaller than we'd thought? Does our quick-change / Michael double as—DJ: Ephraim?" (405). It is a prediction of a truth, although at the time, in the middle of the book, only perplexity attends them:

> In spite of broad hints liberally strewn
> Throughout, as to tomorrow afternoon,
> Crescendo and confusion leave unheard
> —By us at least—the clarifying word.
> It's like those 18th century finales
> (Which might have lasted well into our age
> Had not Rossini laughed them off the stage):
> A thousand whirling thoughts confuse the head.
>
> (405)

Just as Raphael and Emmanuel, also called Elijah and Elias, angels of earth and water, are twins; and as Gabriel and Michael are twin sides of God's primary impulses; as even Nature is God's twin—so all identities are at least double. Ephraim is Michael, as indeed all of the "5" are angelic representations, and Maria turns out at last to have been Plato in disguise. The unmaskings have returned us to a simpler world indeed.

Simple but not unitary. At the heart of Merrill's method and his universe is the principle of duality, which one might call manichaean or simply a version of dichotomy with a didactic flourish. For every force, an equal or opposite counterforce: to God, nature; to Michael, Gabriel; to creation, destruction; to light, fire; to "idea," "thought"; to space, "black holes" and so forth. To every yes there is a no, to every gain a loss, to all forward movement some kind of negative resistance. *Scripts* carefully depicts and resolves these dichotomies and in so doing justifies thinking of Merrill as an apocalyptic heir to Shelley. As an earnest of the ambiguous resolution of contraries upon which the volume depends and of its didactic methods, one may take the anniversary scene that occurs before the last of Michael's ten "positive" lessons. A silver anniversary for DJ and JM is celebrated on the other side of the board by Strauss and Hofmannsthal, and on this side by gift giving and listening to a recording of *Der Rosenkavalier*. Strauss even composes a fifth last song for Flagstad, which seems to be appropriately mimed by the ventriloquist Michael. Following the song, with a request to "compose a silent harmony," the schoolroom empties and the mortals are left to their wonder:

> Our black wick smoulders over melted ice.
> In and out of numbers 9 to 1
> Weaving like a drunk, the cup comes down
> To earth: SPORTSWEAR    BOYS CLOTHING    WATCH THE STEP!
> WOW    DID U FEEL OUR TOUCH UPON YR HANDS?
> JM: Not I. DJ: I felt . . . a chill?
> YES    FOR MY DEARS WE TOUCHED U & CAN STILL
> ALMOST: AS RS SAID, ROSEPETAL SKIN
> OR BABIES' BOTTOMS Were we somehow *in*
> The mirror for that hour? U WERE INDEED
> Literally?—but by now we know
> Where that will get us. Tutti: YES & NO
>
> (358)

Simultaneity rather than opposition occurs to JM again at the end of part 1, as they consider the negative lessons yet to come. DJ worries that Gabriel will "have some negative / Interstellar static" but JM asks him to think

>                    of what other meanings
> The word "negative" takes on in *Ephraim*;
> X-ray images, or Maya's film
> In which the widow turns into the bride.
> Tricks of the darkroom. All those cameras clicking
> In Venice, on the bridge. For now a new bridge—
> Can it be crossed both ways?—from Yes to No
> Is entering the picture. DJ: So
> Is Venice, if our plans firm up. JM:
> By which time, from the darkness you foresee,
> Who knows what may develop milkily,
> What loving presence?
>
> (362)

Not a simple opposition, but rather a continuum of possibilities along the arc from "Yes" to "No" and back again, or through all the characters of the board.

Such synthetic reduction to simple first principles is possible only at the highest level. We regain the simplicity of truth only after our individual and collective experiences with difficult complexity. The move toward a higher innocence, a reintegration of faculties within and without, puts Merrill in the company of all poets, from Plato to Wordsworth and Blake, who seek the possibility for reintegration and harmony following fall, breaking, and dissonance. Once more, a general truth is carried via a scientific metaphor. George Cotzias lectures on the atom, in the middle lessons:

> LORDS, WE HAVE KNOWN
> OF THE ATOM SINCE AKHNATON. WE KNOW AS WELL
> ITS PARTS AND POWERS: THAT FLUTTER, THAT HEARTBEAT
> OF ATTRACTION & REPULSION. ON SUCH WINGS
> CAME GOD.
>                 NOW IN THAT WHIRL IS A REVERSE WHIRL
> MAKING, AS IN THE BEATEN WHITE OF EGG,
> FOR THICKENING, FOR DENSITY, FOR MATTER.
> YES, FROM THIS OPPOSITION, WHICH HOLDS SWAY
> NO LESS WITHIN MAN'S SOUL, LORDS, CAME THE FIRST
> MINUTE PASTE THAT WAS GOD'S MATERIAL.
> IN SHORT: THE ELEMENTS FROM A 'WHITE' SOURCE
> RESISTED THOSE OF A 'BLACK' OR 'SHADOW' FORCE.
>
>                                                     (396)

Slightly farther on, Psyche makes a human application of the same principle:

> WE DESCENDED WITH OUR BROTHERS, EVEN AS MADAME SAID,
>     CARRYING TOOLS FROM THE GALAXIES,
> GOD BIOLOGY AND I, TWINS. OUR BROTHERS WISHED US WELL &
>     STILL DO.
> OUR WORK WAS TWOFOLD: HE, CREATION OF MATTER, THE
>     ARCHITECT. MY HUMBLE SELF, THE DECORATOR? AND SOMETHING
>     A BIT MORE SUBSTANTIAL:
> 'SISTER, BEFORE I CALL FORTH INHABITANTS OF THIS PLACE, LET US
>     PLAN.
> WHAT POINT IS THERE IN AN IMMORTAL BEING (THOUGH LESS,
>     MUCH LIKE OURSELVES) IF HE CONTAINS NOTHING NEW, NO
>     SURPRISE, TO CALL HIS OWN?
> LET US DIVIDE THE FORCE OF HIS NATURE, JUST AS WE WILL MAKE
>     TWO SIDES TO ALL NATURE,

FOR IN DUALITY IS DIMENSION, TENSION, ALL THE TRUE GRANDEUR
WANTING IN A PERFECT THING.
SISTER, TAKE COMMAND OF HIS . . . RESISTANCE? HIS 'UNGODLY'
SIDE. MAKE HIM KNOW DARK AS WELL AS LIGHT, GIVE HIM
PUZZLEMENT, MAKE HIM QUESTION,
FOR WOULD WE NOT LIKE COMPANY?'

(408)

What became in Plato and Yeats symptoms of man's divided and in-
ferior nature here attests to his equality to the gods themselves. In
opposition, as Blake knew, resides true friendship, and only with resistance can genuine progress or even complexity adhere. Psyche, although in some ways the negative principle, speaks for man and for
life when she summarizes: "DEATH IS THAT RESISTANT FORCE DEFINING
THE FORWARD MOTION OF LIFE" (410).

In the economy of Merrill's universe, nothing is ever lost; all is
translated, and consequently even apparent tragedy may convert to
gain. The human character suffers deprivation, loss, even "waste, self-
hatred, boredom," which he calls in *Mirabell* (187) the metaphorical
equivalent of black holes. These are merely the twinned negatives to
those positive forces in the comedian's bag of opportunities for conversion, substitution, and restitution. Every loss can become an asset,
and like any sentient being, JM is divided between elegiac sentiments
and the artist's inevitable greed to make sense of his life by recycling
its events and his friends in his own version of the R/Lab: his own
mind. What happens to Robert Morse is a touching paradigm of the
techniques of restitution—both for the individual soul and the poet
who can pull the strings even when he feels himself most the puppet
of higher forces.

Robert Morse dies in the middle section ("&") right after the death
of George Cotzias. GK (*K* is the Greek letter equivalent to our *C*) immediately makes himself useful through the board, meeting Auden
and Maria and preparing to join the elemental powers with them. But
Morse is a more purely human figure, a private friend whose death
hurts deeply even as JM acknowledges its usefulness:

A sense comes late in life of too much death,
Of standing wordless, with head bowed beneath

The buffeting of losses which we see
At once, no matter how reluctantly,

As gains. Gains to the work. Ill-gotten gains . . .
Under the skull-and-crossbones, rigging strains

Our craft to harbor, and salt lashings plow
The carved smile of a mermaid on the prow.

Well, Robert, we'll make room. Your elegy
Can go in *Mirabell*, Book 8, to be
Written during the hot weeks ahead;
It's only fiction, that you're not yet dead.

(376)

Thus the piratical appropriation of the dead by the living. Morse himself comes to represent a fully human response to the hocus-pocus of
heavenly lab work. Neither an intellectual himself nor one having too
much of what the spirits label "Jew" density, he is the complete amateur; consequently he serves as something like the boys' (whom he often addresses as "lads") surrogate in the other world, where he is himself schooled by the help of a small centaur-unicorn creature, a
remnant of the second creation, who attaches himself to this charming
master. As JM and DJ steel themselves for Gabriel's negative rejoinder
to Michael's positive lessons, they approach both rebirth and separation with sadness. One of the bat legion announces the forthcoming
appearance of Gabriel, and instills in his listeners a regret for future
partings:

LORD GABRIEL GRACIOUSLY APPEARS WITH GREAT COMPANY
THIS HOUR TOMORROW. WILL THAT ALL GOES WELL. THESE LAST
 VISITS
SEE YR V WORK THROUGH, YR DEAR ONES SOON AFTER ON THEIR
WAY.
MY LEGIONS RING WITH PRAISE. I SALUTE YOU AS MY MASTERS.
     You mustn't! We've just sat back while they—
                    Gone.
     SIRS? Uni, did you see something then?
     A FLASH    A SHADOW    LIKE A STORM AT NIGHT
     Clear skies now? BLANKNESS    FOR WE WORK IN BLANKNESS
     Ah, Uni, we're about to lose our friends.
     IT WAS A MIXED GIFT, GOD'S IMMORTALITY.
     MY MASTER SAYS WE TOO MUST PART
     MAY I ADMIT I AM NOT HAPPY?
     Nor are we at that prospect. WELL    WE GRIEVE
     TOGETHER    BLESS OUR NATURES, TEARS!

(429)

The economy of Merrill's world allows us to see gains in loss and losses in gains. Thus, Morse's death restores him to a wholeness, as his moving account of it tells:

LET ME RECONSTRUCT MY 'DEATH' FOR YOU
After more thought, I HEARD A VOICE 'HE'S GONE'
AND LOOKED DOWN AT MY OLD FRIEND: MEAT & BONE.
LOOKED UP: THE SKY! ALL STARS! NO FEELINGS. FAINT
UNCONNECTED DAUBS OF THOUGHT LIKE PAINT
WERE FORMING ME AS IMAGE IN MY MIND.
'ROBERT, REMEMBER THIS, REMEMBER THAT'
THE THOUGHTS SAID TILL THEY SMOOTHED INTO A SOLE
UNBROKEN ONE: 'THAT LIFE IS OVER, LEAVE IT.'
BY THEN THE IMAGE OF MY SELF WAS WHOLE,
THE STARS INVISIBLE—where Self itself
Had blacked out Heaven?

(498)

Hole is perhaps another name for whole; integrity requires a release, a subtraction. And as counter to this, Merrill describes Morse's rebirth as a musical prodigy in Minnesota, heir to Mozart, in "The Higher Keys," where he is progressively removed from JM's field while, sense by sense, his new embryo grows. The growth blots out the old image in the world of "appearances" symbolized by the other world and its reflections in this one. Just as Morse's death restored him to wholeness and to access to former friends, so now birth becomes, in an updating of *The Picture of Dorian Gray*, the ultimate loss. In a remarkable 180-degree turn Merrill encourages tears at what appears a last parting. The angel Raphael administers the final command:

NOW WITH YOUR STRONG LITTLE FOOT, A KICK! SOUND
NUMBER TWO:
DOWN THROUGH LIVE CAVES & TUNNELS HER CRY COMES TO
YOU.
The tiny figure winces at the cry
And squeezes its face shut despairingly.
NOW 4/5 BABE, YOUR LAST BUT ONE
GIFT RECEIVE FROM ME, THIS GUN
Eyes open. Fingers curl about the flute—
A "blow-gun" (witty Raphael)—TO SHOOT
MUSIC INTO THE WORLD'S EARS FROM YOUR HEART.
REMEMBER YOUR NAME, TOM, AND START!

> Again the kick. The mother's cry. One glance
> From Raphael and the portrait . . . is no more.
> A pinch of dry, used color dusts the floor.
> Faint sanguine plots a newly primed expanse.
> *Raph.* DUST    DUST TO DUST    GO, G O
>                                    And gravely he
> Goes also. Blackout in the nursery.
>
>                                          (539)

Of course, nothing is finished in Merrill's universe. Neither is there final truth, reduced to axiom or expanded to infinitely multiple identities, nor is there final parting from loved ones. Ephraim had earlier reprimanded JM and DJ for their attempts to interfere with some of the simpler reincarnation tricks (he warned them to LOOK LOOK LOOK YR FILL BUT DO DO DO DO DO NOTHING), and they had to demonstrate considerable self-restraint, while walking through Kew in 1956, not to peer into a thousand baby prams in search of the lately reborn Charles Merrill. On the other hand, they get a green light to arrange a rendezvous with Maria-Plato in her next incarnation as a Punjabi adolescent in Bombay, in 1991. So although the board restores the dead to the living, they learn only that death hardly resolves ultimate questions.

Robert Morse's rebirth, the eradication of his picture as well as of his own memory, reminds us that all along *Scripts* has dramatized an educational program that stresses the equality of teacher and student, and the equal roles of knowledge and forgetting. Another indication of Merrill's two-sided response to any issue, his pedagogy in *Scripts* summarizes the processes of attending, questioning, remembering, and inventing dramatized by the techniques of the previous books. These constitute the grounds of his didacticism. That the hero is no longer young, but less supple and receptive than he was when he first contacted Ephraim, makes the effort all the more heroic. He must contend not only with the boredom and wastefulness of middle age but also with its increasing forgetfulness; perhaps the worst insult of age is its loss of immediate memory, a stripping process shown at the start of *Scripts* while JM sits alone in Stonington during the February composition of *Mirabell*. Tired, unwinding with a drink, he wonders whether he has caught the "immunity to Time / On which our peacock plumed himself":

> Evenings, I imitate Sergei, alone,
> Unwinding with a stiff drink. Solitaire.

A meal of leftovers.
At most some laughter on the telephone

With friends I seem to miss but not invite.
A letter to DJ. Or one from him
Read over. A last highball
And bed. Tonight is every blessed night.

(Wait, I did things! Went to hear *Thaïs*—
Or was it *Dialogues des Carmélites*?
Went even to California . . .
Here are the stubs. Where are the memories?)

And what if this immunity to Time
On which our peacock plumed himself should prove
Mortal and contagious?

                                        (311–12)

The immunity can become the surest evidence of suffering, as time's
flow betrays the adult into ignoring its passage. For this, as well as for
other reasons, the return to the childhood home as a partial scene of
instruction for the last lessons appropriately defies time by allowing
JM to retreat in part to his origins: learning, best accomplished *in*
childhood, now takes place on the other side of the board within a
scene redolent *of* childhood, although all the students there are now
fully grown adults, but waiting for rebirth. Adult/child, life/death,
Athens/Sandover: the pairs both parallel and join each other. Even
schooling is plural, as the seminar and the twin typefaces prove, at the
same time that it is singular: JM imagines "*a high hedge*" around the
whole estate that "*stands for the isolating privilege / Of learning*" (320). In
such isolation inheres strongest communal response and growth.

  All along, JM as character and Merrill as poet have fluctuated between a childlike responsiveness and a more active grappling with the
signals, lessons, lectures, and tales delivered from the board. *Scripts*
moves, in its dramatic form, to the final breaking of the glass, an ab-
juring of some of the Ouija board apparatus and its hocus-pocus (although this continues in the coda but without the mirrored reflections
and help from WHA and MM); this represents an attempt to stand
alone, to speak with adult voice and one's own authority. The whole
volume readies JM for his final reading at the end of the coda. Auden
gives him the "form" for this part of the poem, and JM replies gratefully:

> Talk about a grand
> Design! Why didn't that occur to me?
> ENFANT FISHING FOR COMPLIMENTS? Not at all.
> An empty glittering's our only haul
> Without Wystan and you to drive the school
> Into these nets. Alone, I'm such a fool!
> YES PARSIFAL, IN ONE SENSE I AGREE
> U'VE ON YR SIDE UTTER NEUTRALITY,
> NO MADE TO ORDER PREJUDICES   NO
> BACKTALK   JUST THE LISTENER'S PURE O!
> NULL ZERO CRYING OUT TO BE FILLED IN:
> FOR ALL TOO SOON CONFRERE U MUST BEGIN
> TO JUDGE   TO WEIGH WHAT'S CAST INTO THE SCALES
> *Me* weigh *their* words?
>
> > (328)

His time will come, although he now stands back from judgment (earlier he had forced himself to make sense of the "murky blocks / Of revelation" [297–98] from *Mirabell*). Auden warns him that "FEELING'S THRONE [may] PROVE AN ELECTRIC CHAIR" and JM takes the challenge reluctantly:

> *Don't.* Give us time to get beyond
> —We whom at each turn sheer walls of text
> Sweep from one staggering vista to the next—
> That listener's *Oh.* Discriminate, respond,
>
> Use our heads? What part? Not the reptilian
> Inmost brain—seat of an unblinking
> Coil of hieratic coldness to mere "thinking".
> Yet *it* branched off, says fable, a quarter billion
>
> Years ago. A small, tree-loving snake's
> Olfactory lobes developed. Limbs occurred
> To it, and mammal warmth, music and word
>
> And horror of its old smelled-out mistakes
> —Whose scent still fills the universal air?
> PLUG AWAY ENFANT   YOURE GETTING THERE
>
> > (332)

The "oh" of wonder is equivalent to the "O" of number: part of learning and responsiveness is the stripping away continually enforced upon the about-to-be-reborn, and even upon the living adult coming

to terms with his own wintry prospects, an image that has already appeared chillingly in *Mirabell*:

> DJ YR DEAR HAND IS A MAGIC WAND
> JM THE STRIPPING IS THE POINT YR POEM WILL PERHAPS
> TAKE UP FROM ITS WINTRY END & MOVE STEP BY STEP INTO
> SEASONLESS & CHARACTERLESS STAGES TO ITS FINAL
> GREAT COLD RINGING OF THE CHIMES SHAPED AS O O O O O
>
> (211)

Completion is a loss that one can live through, that is, both survive
and profit from; the formation of a personality involves a stripping,
symbolized by Robert Morse's birth-as-loss, by the x rays that treated
both MM and GK in their final illnesses, and as far back as "Ephraim"
by the returns, after death, of souls to their earthly habitats merely to
erase whatever taint of humanity remained.

In the return to origins, childhood, primal myths of creation, *Scripts*
offers at last the fullest incarnation of *das Ewig-Weibliche*, who sounded
her seductive note at the end of "Ephraim" and who has taken the
guise of Maria (WHA and MM are called "father of forms and matter-
of-fact mother" in book 2 of *Mirabell*). Nature-Chaos-Psyche, the complementary half of God B, speaks to and for man; as an inspiring principle she is also a figure from the realm of recollection. WHA sees her
as "the chateleine of Sandover" and wonders what heavenly emanation she most resembles:

> *Wystan, peeking, does a double take:*
> *Somewhere on Earth he fancies he has seen*
> *A face so witty, loving, and serene*
> *—But where? Some starry likeness drawn by Blake*
> *Perhaps for 'Comus'? or the one from Dante*
> *Of Heavenly Wisdom? This, then, is the third*
> *And fairest face of Nature (whom he'll come*
> *To call, behind Her back of course, Queen Mum).*
>
> (407)

As a figure anticipated by dream and literature, Nature herself takes
a mother's side against the more anxious and fearsome pronouncements of God the father; she speaks, throughout, not so much for
chaos, the negative part of her nature, as for human emotion as the
generative principle, along with language, of human salvation.

For this reason, Merrill's allusion to the dream of Dante's mother,
recounted by Boccaccio, occupies a prominent, resonant place toward
the start of the volume. Coming paradoxically from George Cotzias,

the quintessential man of science, the dream attests to the similarities
of fable and fact, hindsight and prediction, intuition and science. The
methods of poet and physician turn out to be almost identical, and the
passage recalls the earliest Lucretian image, in "Ephraim," of the physician's use of honey-coated pills to enable the patient to swallow corrective truths:

> Do I remember, he goes on, the dream
> Of Dante's mother, from Boccaccio?
> She saw a peacock in a laurel tree,
> Beak snipping the clustered berries—down they fell
> Until the skirt she held outspread was full—
> And woke in labor. Taking up the theme,
> Moving past Lesbia's sparrow, Poe and Keats,
> Coloratura wood-note understood
> By Siegfried, thumb licked clean of dragon's blood;
> Past twittering parliament, past the "little bird"
> Who speaks to instinct with a paraclete's
> Ghostly cackle, we attain the sphere
> (Justice?) where Dante saw the letter M
> Become an Eagle made of ruby souls
> Which sang to him. What of the Phoenix, then?—
> Its blaze our culture-watchers doze before,
> Never quite making out the infra-vulture.
> Of Senator X who vowed Vietnam would "rise
> Like a Tucson" from the ashes—? A short pause,
> Then George: "You won't laugh if I tell you I
> Also get these voices, these vocations?
> Over the years, each time I've undergone
> A general anesthetic, the same one,
> A woman's, cold yet not unloving, fills
> My head with truths about the cosmos—truths,
> Jimmy, too deep, too antilogical
> Ever to grasp, short of the odd detail
> Clutched on waking. Once, the phrase 'black holes'
> (And this was long before black holes made headlines)
> Stayed with me. Another time, these were explained
> As ash the Phoenix left on entering
> A 'biological cycle'. And once, I woke
> *Knowing* that what had reached me was the song
> The Phoenix sings throughout eternity."

> (298–99)

The fable and the general imagery here extend throughout the entire epic. Birds include, of course, JM's own Mirabell, and the celestial M of *Paradiso* implies the grandest metaphoric progeny of Dante's line, James Merrill himself. The myths of birth and death intertwine, and Cotzias's recollection of vision under anesthetic, repeating DJ's similar experiences in *Mirabell,* prepares us for the appearance of Nature as a figure resembling Keats's austerely comforting Moneta in "The Fall of Hyperion," another woman who looks simultaneously backward through history to human suffering, and forward, in her transmission of proleptic knowledge to the eager poet awaiting a metaphoric birth to tragedy, life, and poetry. The dream of a man of science, about a dream of a mother predicting future greatness, allies science and imagination, as so much of the trilogy already has done; it also readies readers for the subsequent births and deaths throughout *Scripts.* The first session at the board in Athens brings JM in touch with Wallace Stevens, who neatly summarizes the dream references to Cotzias: "MAY I SUGGEST A CENTRAL METAPHOR: / PEACOCK TO O—to zero—AS CHICKEN TO EGG?" (300). In a book that concerns itself with its own formation as well as with the reincarnations of others, the cliché and its multifold applications come as no surprise.

Unmasking and revelation work toward the goal of the epic: the reduction of identities. From the intergalactic interweavings of human and quasi-human life, Merrill combines, eliminates, and otherwise merges entities until he alone stands before an imagined audience attending his performance. The overlapping particles appear early, as JM discusses with Chester Kallman the latter's contention that "we make our deaths" according to our lives: death and life are, ideally, complements, as are, from a Jungian viewpoint, all visions of a single symbol:

> It's random death we dread.
> The bomb, the burning theatre, the switchblade-
> Brandishing smack freak— OR ARE PENCIL & KNIFE
> & COCK ALL ONE
>           & WAVE & BREAST & WET
> SNAKY LOCKS! WE'LL SWEEP UP U CHAPS YET!
> Speaking of those breasts, Maman, the tale
> We're hearing now is nothing if not male.
> But Maya long ago said Erzulie
> Was Queen of Heaven.
>
>             (304)

An even simpler dichotomy is partly resolved when the filmmaker Maya Deren, referred to above, responds to a question of JM's:

> Is there no Ewig-Weibliche in sight?
> AN EWIG SHALL WE SAY HERMAPHRODITE?
> YOU HAD THOUGHT ERZULIE WAS FEMALE? HE/
> SHE IS/WAS RAIN SOIL SEED SUN STARLIGHT
> PHALLUS & VAGINA   OMNISEX
> QUEEN OF A HEAVEN LIKE A GAUDY EX
> VOTO WHERE DESIRE & SATISFACTION
> PEPPER & SALT THE DISH SERVED PIPING HOT!
>
> (305)

All the things of experience accommodate themselves to the capacities of the individual: the mortals come to learn that the Mohammed they "saw" was merely "A PARODY / CONCEIVED BY GABR & GLEEFULLY RE-HEARSED / OF ATTITUDES EMBODIED BY HIS FAITHFUL" (472), that Socrates was a mask that "BECAME THE FACE OF THE GOAT GOD SILENUS / WINEBAG FLUTEINVENTING COUNTERPART / TO MICH/APOLLO IN THE DAWN OF ART" (473). They are surprised, but should not be, toward the very end at their celebratory penultimate lesson when, putting on a record of *The Rake's Progress*, they find out that on the other side of the glass Robert Morse has stepped in for Stravinsky at the podium (485).

W. H. Auden makes an early statement that will ring true for JM as hero of his own poem. Speaking of his own poetry during the last decades of his life, Auden asks "IS IT NOT OUR LESSON THAT WE COME / EACH TO HIS NATURE? NOT TO ANY VAST / UNIVERSAL ELEVATION, JUST / EACH TO HIS NATURE PRECIOUS IF BANAL / LIKE THE CLICHE UNCOVERED AMONG GEMWORDS: / FOR ME, TO (COSMIC) DUST RETURNED" (308). The motif of independence, specifically literary independence, occupies much of the educational undercurrent throughout *Scripts* and the coda. When Merrill rises at the end one witnesses his arrival at the point of graduation from school, when composition is obligatory rather than merely possible. JM gains his own authority as Auden's diminishes (the disappearance/rebirths of his dead friends are Merrill's tacit homage to Dante's fate, in *Purgatorio* 27, to go it alone without Virgil). Within the space of several pages the senior poet quizzes Michael and instructs him in the nature of run-on lines (342), then works with JM to find an appropriate line for the angels' speech (they decide on "unmeasurable King / James inflections" [346]); two pages later, JM is making the major decisions, wondering how and why to have God himself speak, and whether directly or in paraphrase:

Why should God speak? How humdrum what he *says*
Next to His word: out of a black sleeve, lo!
Sun, Earth and Stars in eloquent dumb show.
Our human words are weakest, I would urge,
When He resorts to them. Here on the verge
Of these objections, one does well to keep
One's mouth shut—Wystan, don't you think? WE WEEP

(348–49)

Soon a small quarrel erupts in which JM himself clearly triumphs. Auden has been worried about Michael's lines, which are rhythmically skewed, and after his eighth lesson, the angel bids an awkward farewell:

> SO NEXT WE DON THE GLAD ARRAY
> OF ALL OUR SENSES TO MEET THE DAY.
> *Exeunt.*

WHA.    ENTRE NOUS MY DEAR HE'S NOT IMPROVING:
        NEXT WE DON OUR SENSES IN GLAD ARRAY
        & MEET HERE AGAIN ON ANOTHER DAY.

JM.     That too could stand some work, if I may say so.
        *Michael, returning unexpectedly*:
        QUARRELING, POETS?

JM.     He—I—that is, we . . .

Mich.   MY VERSE NOT METERED? NOT IN RHYME? THEN PRAY
        MAKE SENSE OF IT YOURSELVES ANOTHER DAY!

(352)

Such a sequence dramatizes in miniature the stylistic ordeal of poetic growth that underlies and parallels the larger motifs of education and evolution throughout the poem. "My characters, this motley alphabet" (454), Merrill reminds us in a delicate inlaid sonnet about the name of God, are both subject and vehicle, his tools and ultimately his own character.

That character asserts itself by correcting Auden, accepting the need for breaking the mirror, standing alone at the end, and in one remarkable passage it demonstrates through a bravura duplicity the relationship of lived life to chosen fable, or any writer's need to build a solid structure upon the fragile facts of his or her own mortality. After the last lesson, in which God B commands the poet to "MAKE A V WORK" (493) from the figures of the board, the source of his character(s) and the model of his form, JM conjures up a recollection that reflects the coherent interweaving of individual and cosmic destinies:

Friction made the first thin consommé
Of all we know. Soon it was time for lunch.
Between an often absent or abstracted
(In mid-depression) father and still young
Mother's wronged air of commonsense the child sat.
The third and last. If he would never quite
Outgrow the hobbyhorse and dragon kite
Left by the first two, one lukewarm noodle
Prefigured no less a spiral nebula
Of further outs. Piano practice, books . . .
A woman speaking French had joined their sunstruck
Looking-glass table. Fuels of the cup
Lowered to her lips were swallowed *up*.
The child blinked. All would now be free to shatter,
Change or die. Tight-wound exposures lay
Awaiting trial, whose development
Might set a mirror flowing in reverse
Forty years, fifty, past the flailing seed
To incoherence, blackout—the small witness
Having after all held nothing back?
HUSH ENFANT    FOR NO MAN'S MIND CAN REACH
BEYOND THAT HIM & HER    THEIR SEPARATION
REMAINS UNTHINKABLE. WE ARE CONFINED
BY THE PINK CARNATION, THE FERN FIDDLEHEAD
& THESE BREATHMISTED PANES OF HUMAN SPEECH

*That* was the summer my par— YR PARALLELS
DIVERGE PRECISELY HERE    I from the I
Who shook those bars, who burned to testify
At the divorce. Scales flashing, bandage loosened,
Pitiless gaze shining forth—ah cover it
While time allows, in decent prejudice!
Mine's for the happy ending. Weren't the endings
Always happy in books? Barbarity
To serve uncooked one's bloody tranche de vie . . .
Later, if the hero couldn't smile,
Reader and author could; one called it style.
Poetic justice, if you like.

(495–96)

"The third and last" is both man, God B's third experiment who comes
after bats and centaurs, and the version of JM himself who often appears in his earlier autobiographical lyrics, a third child whose parents

divorced when he was nine, who was tended by a French governess, and who *translated* his own life into a cosmic melodrama and learned, in the words from another poem about art and life, that "the point thereafter was to arrange for one's / Own chills and fever, passions and betrayals, / Chiefly in order to make song of them" ("Matinees," *FFN*, 207). Making song out of his life, he has extended parallel lines to a point out of sight, perhaps (hence the interruption above), but never out of mind. His character, formed by the characters of his speech, in turn reforms them in the spirallings of his art.

The ending of *Sandover* reaffirms the two complementary lessons that have everywhere occupied Merrill's concerns, overtly or implicitly. One is the lesson of singularity, selfhood, independence; the other is the lesson of mutuality, relationship, and tautology, or at least the indecipherability of first causes. Bound as he is to his masters' voices, JM also recognizes his superiority to them, as in this passage that follows a particularly frustrating lesson about the nature of the atom as an analogue to the history of the two civilizations before our own:

> But if it's all a fable
> Involving, oh, the stable and unstable
> Particles, mustn't we at last wipe clean
> The blackboard of these creatures and their talk,
> To render in a hieroglyph of chalk
> The formulas they stood for? U MY BOY
> ARE THE SCRIBE    YET WHY? WHY MAKE A JOYLESS THING
> OF IT THRU SUCH REDUCTIVE REASONING?
> ONCE HAVING TURNED A FLITTING SHAPE OF BLACK
> TO MIRABELL, WD YOU MAKE TIME FLOW BACK?
> SUBTRACT FROM HIS OBSESSION WITH 14
> THE SHINING/DIMMING PHASES OF OUR QUEEN?
> CONDEMN POOR UNI TO THE CYCLOTRON
> AFTER THE GREENS U'VE LET HIM GALLOP ON?
> Dear Wystan, thank you for reminding me
> The rock I'm chained to is a cloud; I'm free.
>
> (461–62)

Fact is fable, fable fact; whichever priority one prefers, JM comes to realize the control he is capable of exercising over the myths given him from without.

That he exercises this power through continual allusions to, and evocation of, principles of literary creation in a poem nominally devoted to larger acts of divine creation comes as a final confirmation of the status of *The Changing Light at Sandover* as a *Kunstlerroman* and a narrative of self-education. Correcting Auden, whose help he has everywhere solicited and valued, he proves himself worthy of his constant teacher. Toward the end, he moves beyond even Yeats, the master of Auden and JM individually and sequentially, when he plumes himself, so to speak, on his promotion (by them? by himself? can we ever know the difference?) to a quasi-stellar rank. Earlier in the final celebration, just after the music from *The Rake's Progress*, which celebrates Love as conqueror of Time, and after Maria's appearance as both Plato, her past incarnation, and a young Indian boy, her next one, Yeats himself emerges to speak:

> O SHINING AUDIENCE, IF AN OLD MAN'S SPEECH
> STIFF FROM LONG SILENCE CAN NO LONGER STRETCH
> TO THAT TOP SHELF OF RIGHTFUL BARD'S APPAREL
> FOR WYSTAN AUDEN & JAMES MEREL
> WHO HAVE REFASHIONED US BY FASHIONING THIS,
> MAY THE YOUNG SINGER HEARD ABOVE
> THE SPINNING GYRES OF HER TRUE LOVE
> CLOAK THEM IN HEAVEN'S AIRLOOM HARMONIES.

(486)

This clever cadenza: who speaks it? The question is simultaneously naive and complex because it strikes at the mysterious heart of the poem and of the greater mystery of all composition and originality of voice. Merrill's uncanny ventriloquism, his skilled pastiche of Yeats's imagery and typical rhythms, proves he has learned his lesson well. The apprentice has become the master.

The poem has always maintained the fiction of composite authorship, as even single voices may be heard as subtly varied, with inner or deeper resonances. Art is collaboration, between hand and scribe, or between master-inspiration and student-poet who has been revising, in the wording of his extraterrestrial transcripts, the messages—by dividing letters into words, words into lines, and taking general liberties with the actual constructions for JM's "tinkerings":

> I admit
> To having been up tinkering since dawn
> With Yeats's stanza, which came through a bit . . .
> MR M, I MADE A HASH. YOU'VE MADE IT CLEAR.
> THANK YOU. Oh please, Mr Yeats, you who have always
> Been such a force in my life! WYSTAN, U HEAR?
>
> MAITRE, I HAVE EVER HEARD
> THE GOLDEN METER IN YOUR WORD,

AND KISS YR HAND (This with the straightest of faces
As Yeats withdraws into the palm's oasis.)

(491–92)

So to the question, "whose voice was it?" the text will yield no answer, but it returns to the chicken-and-egg cliché (which Wallace Stevens had first used on page 300) when it grants JM an authorial dignity and independence that he has been wondering about throughout the trilogy. In the cosmic carpool, what is the vehicle, and what the driver? (Or, to use an older critical analogy, which is the vehicle and which the tenor in a well-formulated metaphor?) Dancer? Dance? Originality and ghost writers?

"The Ballroom at Sandover," the coda's final section, opens with a description of an old place (is it fictive or real in the world of the poem?) that will be the scene of the performance, the new beginning. A shock of recognition ("Great room, I know you!")—Merrill, sounding like Elizabeth Bishop ("Heavens, I recognize the place, I know it!" ["Poem"])—precedes a meditation on the way one uses one's life and is used by it:

Ah, but styles. They are the new friend's face
To whom we sacrifice the tried and true,
And are betrayed—or not—by. For affection's
Poorest object, set in perfect light
By happenstance, grows irreplaceable,
And whether in time a room, or a romance,
Fails us or redeems us will have followed
As an extension of our "feel" for call them
Immaterials, the real right angle,
The golden section—grave proportions here,
Here at the heart of structure, and alone
Surviving now to tell me where I am:
In the old ballroom of the Broken Home.

(556–57)

Merrill's lyric themes—love, loss and betrayal, time and its several directions, breakings and healings—make flickering, reminiscent appearances here, as he gathers in the harvest of his past in order to prepare for the ordeal ahead. Proportion and structure, the masonry of architecture, and the "materials" of poetry steady him for a performance in which even the audience of critics, friends, and writers assumes the number of sacred characters: twenty-six letters, therefore twenty-six listeners. Like Wallace Stevens, Merrill might well announce "stanza my stone," as he is about to reveal the edifice built out of and about his own life.

One last, seemingly trivial obiter dictum steadies the poet for his major performance. "Friends are letting me / Compose myself in tactful privacy" when a pleasantly smiling, formal young man steers his way:

> NOT THE MOMENT QUITE
> TO GOSSIP BUT THERE'S ONE THING YOU SHOULD KNOW.
> THESE WORKS, YOU UNDERSTAND? THAT OTHERS 'WRITE'
> (It's Eliot, he's thinking of Rimbaud)
> ARE YET ONES OWN    That's kind of you to say—
> NO DOUBT GRATUITOUS. CHICKEN & EGG
> AS I BELIEVE YOU PUT IT.
>
> (557–58)

So perhaps the work has been his own after all? Or ours? Having absorbed the lessons of his masters, imitated their voices and forged his own new harmonies from them, JM rises to address the imagined audience of literary judges, bringing to a close and returning to its own origin the major epic of our age. In the repetition of the performance, on both sides of the page, his education and ours will continue.

# SEVEN

# Some Speculations in Place of a Conclusion

Even those who try to evade the didactic impulse embrace it: perhaps, one might say, *especially* those who try to evade it. In his introduction to the *Oxford Book of Modern Verse*, looking back on the battles of modernism, Yeats described the revolt against his Victorian precursors as one "against irrelevant descriptions of nature, the scientific and moral discursiveness of *In Memoriam*, . . . the political eloquence of Swinburne, the psychological curiosity of Browning, and the poetical diction of everybody." Yeats, at least, managed to invent a symbolic system that would substitute for direct instruction, and to write poems that, however much they relied on the mythological-psychological constructs of *A Vision*, could be understood without explanation. The building stood without the scaffolding.

Ezra Pound is another story. As Carol Christ has demonstrated in *Victorian and Modern Poetics*, Pound came increasingly to depend on heavy doses of the didacticism that, as a young rebel, he loudly eschewed. Overwhelmed by the particulars of the *Cantos*, and increasingly obsessed with his own political and historical schemes, he succeeded in producing an epic that is not only the most didactic of twentieth-century poems but also a model for those long sequences by his American heirs who thought of themselves as rebels against a poetic and social establishment: "It is a profound irony that a poetics so bent on seeing an order manifest in things should ultimately motivate both a return to the didacticism from which it had initially rebelled and a poetry of such indeterminacy."[1]

Ironic? Perhaps, but *sub specie aeternitatis* it looks as though Pound was merely heeding Quintilian's command to the would-be poet, itself an adaptation from the lines from Horace with which this book began, that he must arrange his work successfully, "ut doceat, ut moveat, ut delectet." What was earlier referred to as the aberration of modernism might be, from a different perspective, considered merely the new bottle for old wine—or the jazzy lingo for old saws. James Laughlin's memories of studying at the Ezuversity in Rapallo[2] remind us just how traditional, in his homespun, ornery, and eccentric way, was this American autodidact, and although Laughlin believes that by the end

247

the *Cantos*, true to Pound's aesthetics, "show" rather than merely explain, most readers would agree that the didactic impulse practically overwhelms the later parts of the work. Pound retreated into silence in his last decades, as though imitating one of the Victorian masters—Ruskin, perhaps—who, for whatever reason (insanity, misanthropy, disappointment), understood the inefficacies of a lifetime's preaching. Pound tends to be remembered, however, through his work, filled with theories and prejudices that are often as distasteful as they are ludicrous. Gertrude Stein summed him up with epigrammatic justness: Ez was "a village explainer, excellent if you are a village, but if you are not, not."

I wonder exactly what that formulation might mean. Is the village the direct, or the indirect, object of Pound's explanations? Is he explaining the greater world to the microcosm of his little town, or is he explaining the village to itself? Is "the explainer of the village" an objective or a subjective genitive? As remarked in the chapter about A. R. Ammons, it is a useful fact of our grammar that "to teach" typically takes both direct and indirect objects, proving that all discourse is implicitly directed at an audience, which might also constitute the object of the discourse. As he aged, Pound found it difficult to suppress his own pedagogic impulses. He had once labeled "abstraction" the disease of the previous century and a half, but by the middle of his life his own visionary schemes overwhelmed both his intellect and his poetry to the extent that he sounded more like a free-lance lecturer, a member of the "teaching profession," whose function, he once wrote, "is to maintain the HEALTH OF THE NATIONAL MIND."[3] The man who seriously wanted to discuss his plans for world peace with Franklin Roosevelt and was disgruntled when the president would not receive him found in his poetry the perfect and perhaps the only outlet for his didactic bent. In spite of his admonition to would-be poets, "Don't be 'viewy'—leave that to the writers of pretty little philosophical essays,"[4] Pound appears, in hindsight, as certainly the "viewiest" of the moderns. In the capaciousness of his learning, the breadth of his interests, and the early confidence that he might affect society's structure and cure its defects, Pound might be the last of the Victorian sages. Even that quirky manual, *ABC of Reading*, with its classroom exercises, its mania for lists, its constant discussion of pedagogues and pedagogy, sounds like a response to Matthew Arnold. Pound happily cites his favorite lines and passages, seldom deigning to analyze or explain them, but just doling them out, like favors, to his readers. They are all moments within a chain of associations for him, allowing him to quote, savor, smack his lips, and move on. Less stuffy than Arnold, Pound has provided readers with his own touchstones.

Allen Ginsberg has stood almost alone among contemporary poets in his literary, as well as his public, efforts to affect the nation's political course. Virtually no one would presume to take the health of the national mind as the object of his or her efforts. Many have retreated happily into the quiet of leisurely contemplation. Pound's example has inspired, in other words, both emulation—in regard to poetic form— and a certain modesty with regard to poetic expectation.

That modesty is clearest in the ecological pieties of writers like Wendell Berry (in the East) and Gary Snyder (in the West). Snyder's inclination to explain as well as to describe is his largest inheritance from the Pound whom he has called his earliest favorite poet. He could easily become a central figure in the book I have *not* written, on the didactic legacy of Pound to Charles Olson, Louis Zukofsky, the Black Mountain poets, and Robert Bly. While many of the poets discussed in this book derive from Auden and the line of wit, a sympathetic critic could make a case for an equally didactic poetry coming from a source that is both more natively American (and less English), and more concerned with the foreign traditions of the Far East and Latin America. For all these poets, Pound would be what Snyder calls him in the title poem of *Axe Handles*: the axe by which a worker makes a new axe. Humans use tools to make tools, and as language is the tool for poetry, "In making the handle / Of an axe / By cutting wood with an axe / The model is indeed near at hand." It may as well be Pound, instead of the titular figure, who visits Snyder in "For/From Lew" and delivers an inspiring exhortation: "teach the children about the cycles. / The life cycles. All the other cycles. / That's what it's all about, and it's all forgot."[5]

Snyder's georgic impulse, like Berry's, combines the rhythms of the actual physical labor in which he is engaged with the poetic programs of Frost, an earlier laborer in rural and poetic fields. Both of Frost's heirs might agree that "the fact is the sweetest dream that labor knows," and Snyder, especially, mingles the factuality of work, which he describes and teaches, with the contingent dreaming that often undoes consciousness or supplements it with an oriental peacefulness: "Lao-Tzu says / To forget what you knew is best. / That's what I want: / To get these sights down, / Clear, right to the place / Where they fade / Back into the mind of my times."[6] Where Snyder sounds unlike Frost and more like Allen Ginsberg is in his reliance on bare verbs that may be understood as either present tense indicatives or imperatives. A narrative or descriptive discourse could easily be considered a prescription for "how to" perform Snyder's own labors. So, for example, the poem "The Cool Around the Fire," with its ambiguous beginning:

> Drink black coffee from a thermos
>      sitting on a stump.
>
>      piles burn down, the green limb
>      fringe edge
>      picked up and tossed in
> To the center: white ash mound
>      shimmering red within.
>      tip head down
>      to shield face
>      with hat brim     from the heat;
>
> The thinning, pruning, brush-cut
>      robbed from bugs and fungus—
>      belly gray clouds
>      swing low soft over
>      maybe rain, bring an end
>      to this drouth;
>
> Burn brush to take heat
>      from next summer's wildfires
>      and to bring rain on time,
>      and fires clear the tangle.
>
>      the tangle of the heart.
> Black coffee, bitter, hot,
>      smoke rises straight and calm
>      air
> Still and cool.
>
>                 (*Axe Handles*, 16–17)

The alternation of indicative verbs ("piles burn down," "clouds / swing low . . . bring an end," "smoke rises") with ambiguously imperative ones ("Drink," "tip head," "Burn brush") engages the reader in a quasi-sensuous participation in Snyder's foresting. He simultaneously describes his activity and his sensations and orders us to share in his rituals. Doing and teaching come down to the same thing. Repetition is the key to both. A lyric (see also, for example, "Uluru Wild Fig Song," *Axe Handles*, 95–98) may double as an instruction manual. Snyder has finely honed a poetics of learning and instructing, sharing the knowledge that he has made his own, and requiring through his soft commands our repetition of it. "What have I learned [he asks himself and us] but / The proper use for several tools?" ("What Have I Learned," *Axe Handles*, 85).

Pound and his "students" represent a tradition different from, but complementary to, the one dealt with in this book. One other didactic voice deserves to be heard. When they come to John Ashbery, many readers are so baffled by the opacity of his text, and its apparent lack of reference to any prior ones, that they despair of ever "making sense" of or deriving pleasure from discourses strangely suspended in an eternal present with neither clear antecedents nor inferable destinations. And yet virtually no contemporary poet maintains as much of a pedagogic "tone" as Ashbery does: he is a teacher in search of a subject, as the various musings of "A Wave" indicate:

> By so many systems
> As we are involved in, by just so many
> Are we set free on an ocean of language that comes to be
> Part of us, as though we would ever get away.
> The sky is bright and very wide, and the waves talk to us,
> Preparing dreams we'll have to live with and use. The day will
>   come
> When we'll have to. But for now
> They're useless, more trees in a landscape of trees.
> . . . . . . . . . . . . . . . . .
> But behind what looks like heaps of slag the peril
> Consists in explaining everything too evenly. Those
> Suffering from the blahs are unlikely to notice that the topic
> Of today's lecture doesn't exist yet, and in their trauma
> Will become one with the vast praying audience as it sways and
>   bends
> To the rhythm of an almost inaudible piccolo. And when
> It is flushed out, the object of all this meditation will not
> Infrequently turn out to be a mere footnote to the great chain
> That manages only with difficulty to connect earth and sky
>   together.
> Are comments like ours really needed? Of course, heaven is
>   nice
> About it, not saying anything, but we, when we come away
> As children leaving school at four in the afternoon, can we
> Hold our heads up and face the night's homework?[7]

Ashbery's pedagogy is both authoritative and tentative; his strong rhythms, elegiac imagery, and fluctuations between cliché, abstraction,

and enticingly original phrases engage one's attention while his cava-
lier subordinations and uncertain train of thought often make it impossible to know exactly where one might have lost contact with the
teacher's meanderings. Connections are all, and Ashbery's lines pur-
sue a random, unhighlighted, path. The poetry "sounds" discursive
although the explorations seldom reach satisfying conclusions. Coming
in the wake of Romantic and modernist certainties (or strengths that
always appear as certainties in retrospect), Ashbery can only softly
mimic the opening paragraph of "Tintern Abbey," where the "steep
and lofty cliffs . . . connect / The landscape with the quiet of the sky."
Neither religious assurance, nor cosmic order, nor philosophical system will satisfy us, "suffering from the blahs" or genuflecting ridicu-
lously to the accompaniment of "an almost inaudible piccolo." All of
Ashbery's lessons are diminished by pathos or humor; he tests hypotheses only to drop them in favor of new ones.

Even the beginning of "A Wave" promises a lesson that is not, at
least immediately, delivered:

> To pass through pain and not know it,
> A car door slamming in the night.
> To emerge on an invisible terrain.
> (SP, 322)

Like the more lucid "Self-Portrait in a Convex Mirror," "A Wave"
begins with a phrase rather than a sentence. Here, however, the epigrammatic construction promises the kind of moral lesson found in
Adrienne Rich's generalizations: "Infinitive *x* is abstract quality *y*." The
first line sounds as though it might follow the syntactic path of the last
stanza of Shelley's final lyric in *Prometheus Unbound*: "To suffer woes
. . . to forgive wrongs . . . to defy Power . . . This is alone Life, Joy,
Empire, and Victory." But what it teasingly holds out it never surren-
ders. Is passing through pain equivalent to emerging on an invisible
terrain? Does the line seek to describe the sensation of passing
through pain without knowing the pain or the fact that one has *already*
passed through it? The very ambiguity of the pronoun at the end of
the first line tantalizes. Ashbery wants to say something about the relationship of pain to knowledge, and about the relationship of experience to the understanding that comes only afterward, but he is re-
luctant to draw moral lessons in spite of the sureness of his disposition.
Lectures, discoveries, indeed all knowledge, may turn out to be merely
a "footnote," an afterthought that is irrelevant because always changing. Like a truth, a sentence can never be certain. It is as though Ash-

bery has taken upon himself the great burden of representing Yeats's tragic dictum that man may embody truth but he can never know it. Teachers perform the very truths that undo them.

Or perhaps it is Emerson's stern dictum—"the only sin is limitation"—that stands behind Ashbery's attempt to "put it all down," as he calls it in *Three Poems*. His opacities become equivalent, by this trope of power, to Ammons's and Ginsberg's democratic lists. Endless enumeration enacts a political program through a poetic practice. One understands Ashbery the way one understands a very long lecture by a speaker to whom one is only partly paying attention, as if overhearing at times, and ignoring at others, the drone of his voice. Anyone who has heard Ashbery read aloud can testify to the relative flatness of his delivery, which encourages his listeners to make their own discoveries, to infer their own instruction. It is significant, too, that most critics who discuss Ashbery choose to comment on individual lines or small units (as I have just done), items picked somehow fortuitously from the morass of his work and held up to the light of analysis for explication and sharing. Only parts seem to exist; wholes are beyond us. He gives everything and one takes away only what one can immediately make use of.

The moving last paragraph of "A Wave" insinuates the dangers of education, as the speaker moves away from the didactic gestures he has been making throughout the poem:

> And though that other question that I asked and can't
> Remember any more is going to move still farther upward,
>   casting
> Its shadow enormously over where I remain, I can't see it.
> Enough to know that I shall have answered for myself soon,
> Be led away for further questioning and later returned
> To the amazingly quiet room in which all my life has been
>   spent.
> It comes and goes; the walls, like veils, are never the same,
> Yet the thirst remains identical, always to be entertained
> And marveled at. And it is finally we who break it off,
> Speed the departing guest, lest any question remain
> Unasked, and thereby unanswered. Please, it almost
> Seems to say, take me with you, I'm old enough. Exactly.
> And so each of us has to remain alone, conscious of each other
> Until the day when war absolves us of our differences. We'll
> Stay in touch. So they have it, all the time. But all was strange.

(343)

The allure and disappointment of learning are like those of love; a naively seductive offer ("Please, it almost / Seems to say, take me with you, I'm old enough"), too much repeated, provokes only boredom, disappointment, and a slightly paranoid weariness in the middle-aged speaker, who has forgotten as much as he has remembered. The "guest" and the "question," a human and an intellectual provocation, seem to be pretty much the same thing, and the speaker turns away from both, preferring the solitary comforts of his quiet room even though, or probably *because*, he can there entertain a perpetual, marvelous thirst that he knows he will never be able to satisfy. A retreat hors de combat allows him to acknowledge the temptations of "questioning" and guests with whom he can "stay in touch" but never actually possess. The monosyllabic last line, which fades into muted cliché and unspecified pronouns, ends with a tone of agnostic wonder at the strangeness of all experience, which entices readers, and then abandons them to the partial satisfactions of what they may have learned.

By way of concluding, I return to my beginning, to the wisdom of Horace and its repetition by Quintilian. The initial division of literature into two categories—what De Quincey later termed the literature of knowledge and that of power—is a sensible but inaccurate pedagogic device that has no bearing on either the nature of literary production or the fact of a reader's experience of a text. Like all acts of definition, Horace's dichotomy simplifies in order to classify. The clarification is in part a falsehood, however helpful. But since Horace replaces the terms of his division with an idealized synthesis of simultaneous pleasure and instruction, and since Quintilian's phrasing likewise suggests three simultaneous, active processes (*docere, movere, delectare*), a more detailed exploration of the relationship of learning and pleasure is needed. The pleasure of teaching needs little explanation: it is associated in part with power, and with the erotic experience of mastering both the direct and the indirect objects of one's teaching: the subject matter, the student-objects. Roland Barthes has tackled the more devious problems of the erotics of the text and the sequence of enticement, capture, relief, satisfaction—of everything included in his resonant word "jouissance." If "writing is: the science of the various blisses of language, its Kama Sutra (this science has but one treatise: writing itself),"[8] then reading is the experience and perfection of simultaneously mastering and being mastered by the particulars of the text, the knowledge that it communicates.

Poets, of course, have always known this, and they have been utterly straightforward in acknowledging both the pedagogy and the sensuous pleasure that impel them. Recent critics have been unwilling to believe them or to take their assertions at face value. The simplicity of pleasure, in even strenuous mental exertions, seems to have required of puritanical scholars that they rename that which they wish to justify. The fear of pleasure is an old tradition, as Barthes, once more, senses:

> Hedonism has been repressed by nearly every philosophy; we find it defended only by marginal figures, Sade, Fourier; for Nietzsche, hedonism is a pessimism. Pleasure is continually disappointed, reduced, deflated, in favor of strong, noble values: Truth, Death, Progress, Struggle, Joy, etc. Its victorious rival is Desire: we are always being told about Desire, never about Pleasure; Desire has an epistemic dignity, Pleasure does not.
>
> (57)

Byron, that intelligent hedonist, once said that "there is no sterner moralist than pleasure," and the "pleasure of the text," in Barthes's phrase, shifts value to a sumptuous participation in an erotic encounter that one may be too squeamish to call "dignified," let alone "moral." But it is from Barthes and other moralists of pleasure that one must take the cue if one is to understand fully the problematic marriage of the *dulce* and the *utile*, of pleasure and instruction. Writing is play, and poetic writing, especially, might provide a middle ground between the two positions that Barthes calls, in "Writers, Intellectuals, Teachers," that of the teacher ("who is on the side of speech") and that of the writer. Barthes calls that middle creature an "intellectual" ("the person who prints and publishes his speech")[9] but it seems to me that "poet" would be as fair a label. The very fact that Barthes as a critic was always more attuned to the language of prose—whether in fictional or discursive forms—suggests his uneasiness with the possibility of a poetic middle ground between the conditions of speech and those of writing. By privileging the speaker who values his own "voice" as a principle of composition as well as a necessity for the public performance of his work, and who works to "inscribe" his language within a text that is always meant to be "listened" to, even if silently, literary theorists, practical critics, and social observers alike will be able to realign the poet with the old role as tribal shaman or historian.

What Barthes referred to, in his inaugural lecture before the Collège de France, as the two categories of speech, "the authority of assertion [and] the gregariousness of repetition,"[10] are present in all informative acts of teaching and in all poetry as well. Barthes's death three years after his lecture prevented him from exploring the paths and byways that he faintly foresaw as the desirable new direction for students of language and for teachers generally. Susceptible as he was to the breakdown of educational order and institutional power in the aftermath of the 1968 French university uprisings, Barthes spent his last twelve years seeking new ways of teaching that might minimize the perhaps inevitable oppressions of power. "All speech is a classification . . . all classifications are oppressive,"[11] he remarked, but he knew too well that classifying is precisely what teachers do, and must do, in order to make sense of the world. For Barthes the problem had become how to mitigate the unavoidable. "Floating" is his term for the ideal handling of professional obligations within an educational framework, a floating that represents Barthes's response to the happy utopianism of the cannabis culture of the late 1960s.

More seriously (and, in retrospect, since he never had the chance to test it, more sadly), Barthes proposed a way to reduce the exercise of power that language and teaching inevitably entail. Teaching, he says, must be an effort to present rather than to impose a discourse:

> For what can be oppressive in our teaching is not, finally, the knowledge or the culture it conveys, but the discursive forms through which we propose them. Since, as I have tried to suggest, this teaching has as its object discourse taken in the inevitability of power, method can really bear only on the lightening of this power. And I am increasingly convinced, both in writing and in teaching, that the fundamental operation of this loosening method is, if one writes, fragmentation, and, if one teaches, digression, or, to put it in a preciously ambiguous word, *excursion*.[12]

His final image for such excursiveness, a child playing beside his mother, tenderly updates Newton's image of himself playing by the vast sea of truth, and it reminds us again that "the comings and goings of desire" alone impel the teacher and the writer. "It is to a fantasy, spoken or unspoken, that the professor must annually return." The motifs of return and repetition are crucial to all poetry, perhaps especially to that poetry discussed in this book. Repetition is the secret not only of neurotic obsession but also of successful learning; the returns of poetry, in rhythm, sound, and troping, guarantee its effectiveness as an educational instrument, and whatever compels poets to perform their own repeated rituals in figurative language also assures their success as agents of instruction. In both cases—teacher or poet on the one hand, student or reader on the other—the demands of eros coincide with the hunger for the giving and receiving of educational nurture. "Desire," as Barthes calls it, may initially incite us toward possessing or ravishing the forbidden or the unknown, but "pleasure" is derived from something known, something capable of repetition. A child always wants to hear "the same story" rather than a new one. The pleasure of merely circulating, as Wallace Stevens put it, coincides with Barthes's image of "floating," and it is the combination of desire and pleasure that bestows the perpetuity implicit in Pound's famous dictum from canto 81: "What thou lovest well remains, / the rest is dross."

From the poet-teacher's point of view, no one has so powerfully summarized the twin ends of pleasure and instruction as Wordsworth, looking hopefully forward at the end of *The Prelude* to the joint labor that he and Coleridge might in good faith accomplish:

> What we have loved,
> Others will love, and we will teach them how.

Such confidence does not come easily to either teachers or poets; like Barthes, Wordsworth expresses within virtually the same breath his doubts and fears as well as his strength of purpose. But with the dignity of his largely monosyllabic epigram, Wordsworth, along with Barthes and Pound, attests to the legacy of poets to their students: a sharing of enthusiasms and an imparting of knowledge, but also an understanding of a process, whether in the world or in the language by which the poet represents and creates his world. Teaching, in the final analysis, does not take a direct object: the poets teach us *how*.

# ONE

Introduction: W. H. Auden's "New Year Letter"

1. *Letters of William and Dorothy Wordsworth, The Middle Years*, ed. Ernest de Selincourt, rev. Mary Moorman (Oxford: Clarendon Press, 1969), 1:195.

2. Keats's letter to John Hamilton Reynolds of 3 Feb. 1818 and Shelley's introduction to *Prometheus Unbound* are both widely reprinted.

3. See T. S. Eliot, ed., *Literary Essays of Ezra Pound* (Norfolk, Conn.: New Directions, 1954), 5ff., for Pound's early "A Retrospect." Williams's famous motto "No ideas but in things" appears in both the first book of *Paterson* and "A Sort of Song."

4. Frank Kermode, *Romantic Image* (London: Routledge & Paul, 1957).

5. Charles Newman, *The Postmodern Aura: The Act of Fiction in an Age of Inflation* (Evanston, Ill.: Northwestern University Press, 1985), 173 (emphasis mine).

6. I am indebted for this term to Anita Sokolsky of Williams College; see her essay, "The Resistance to Sentimentality: Yeats, de Man, and the Aesthetic Education," *The Yale Journal of Criticism* 1 (1987): 67–86.

7. Robert Pinsky, *The Situation of Poetry* (Princeton, N.J.: Princeton University Press, 1976), 134. The situation that Pinsky has described has been noted by many other critics as well. For example, Alan Williamson appropriates Pinsky's own terms to describe him, along with Frank Bidart and James Mc-Michael: "[they] have in common a distrust of merely decorative imagery and description, and an essayistic latitude of voice, which reaches to the scholarly and argumentative as well as to the matter-of-fact and quotidian" (*Introspection and Contemporary Poetry* [Cambridge, Mass.: Harvard University Press, 1984], 166). According to Jeffrey Perl, even Thom Gunn, a poet of a completely different stripe, now favors a poetry "of fact, not of metaphor or symbol . . . [in which] statement does all the work, and we are invited to test it only by the most general of human experiences" ("The Language of Theory and the Language of Poetry: the Significance of T. S. Eliot's Philosophic Notebooks, Part 2," *Southern Review* 21 [1985]: 1022).

8. Robert von Hallberg, *American Poetry and Culture, 1945–1980* (Cambridge, Mass.: Harvard University Press, 1985), 228–44. Von Hallberg finds "discursiveness" and "explanation" at the heart of the poetry of such poets as Robert Creeley, Charles Olson, and Edward Dorn, none of whom I deal with in this book. I am indebted to von Hallberg's discussion and his appraisals even when they do not correspond to my own.

9. *The Selected Prose of Robert Frost*, ed. Hyde Cox and Edward Connery Lathem (New York: Holt, Rinehart & Winston, 1966), 35, 49.

10. Thomas Kuhn, *The Structure of Scientific Revolutions* (Chicago: University of Chicago Press, 1962).

11. Richard Poirier, *The Renewal of Literature* (New York: Random House, 1987), 56.

12. Randall Jarrell, as usual, sounded exactly the right note in his review of the poem in *The Nation*, of 12 April 1941. He is surprised that a long didactic epistle has just been published that seems to reject everything that modernism stood for:

> The poetry which came to seem during the twenties the norm of all poetic performance—experimental, lyric, obscure, violent, irregular, determinedly antagonistic to didacticism, general statement, science, the public—has lost for the young its once obsessive attraction; has evolved, in Auden's latest poem, into something that is almost its opposite. "New Year Letter" . . . is a happy compound of the Essay on Man and the Epistle to Dr. Arbuthnot, done in a version of Swift's most colloquial couplets. Pope might be bewildered at the ideas, and make fun of, or patronizingly commend, the couplets; but he would relish the Wit, Learning, and Sentiment—the last becoming, as it so often does, plural and Improving; and the Comprehending Generality, Love of Science, and Social Benevolence might warm him into the murmur, "Well enough for such an age" (In John Haffenden, ed., *W. H. Auden: The Critical Heritage* [London: Routledge & Kegan Paul, 1983], 312–15).

13. Edward Callan, *Auden: A Carnival of Intellect* (New York: Oxford University Press, 1983), 172. Other significant analyses of "New Year Letter" appear in: George Bahlke, *The Later Auden: From "A New Year Letter" to "About the House"* (New Brunswick, N.J.: Rutgers University Press, 1970), 40–60, who even foreshadows von Hallberg's use of the term "suburban" in his description of Auden's version of Wordsworth's Earth-as-matronly-Nurse; John Fuller, *A Reader's Guide to W. H. Auden* (New York: Farrar Straus & Giroux, 1970), 131–47; and Herbert Greenberg, *Quest for the Necessary: W. H. Auden and the Dilemma of the Divided Consciousness* (Cambridge, Mass.: Harvard University Press, 1968), 99–111. None of the above, however, really treats the *style* of the poem, or the development of its argument through its poetic technique.

14. Although it is filled with mistakes and misprints, I use the first American edition, in *The Double Man* (New York: Random House, 1941) (hereafter referred to as *DM*), because it includes Auden's notes, which subsequent editions have omitted. Even the lineation in this edition is inaccurate; consequently, the line numbers given in my text are approximate.

15. Longinus, *On the Sublime*, chap. 14.

16. The title of the American volume, *The Double Man*, points toward the very fact of duplicity that is central to the poem's achievement. For a cogent, radical but not reductive, reading of the poem, see the recent deconstructive, Marxist interpretation of Stan Smith in *W. H. Auden* (Oxford: Basil Blackwell, 1985), 120–51.

17. All references to *The Changing Light at Sandover* (New York: Atheneum, 1982), hereafter *CL*, will be cited by page number.

18. Kenneth Burke, *A Grammar of Motives* (New York: Prentice-Hall, 1945), 38–41.

TWO

## The Tempered Tone of Howard Nemerov

1. Howard Nemerov, *New and Selected Essays* (Carbondale: Southern Illinois Press, 1985), vii. Hereafter referred to as *NSE*.

2. Ibid., xi. Much needs to be said about the debt of Nemerov to Burke and to Owen Barfield, his two strongest critical teachers.

3. References are to *Figures of Thought: Speculations on the Meaning of Poetry and Other Essays* (Boston: David R. Godine, 1978), 7, 100, 104, 106. Hereafter cited as *FT*.

4. *The Collected Poems of Howard Nemerov* (Chicago: University of Chicago Press, 1977), 15. Hereafter cited as *CP*.

5. *NSE*, 174. Vacillating between tones of wonder and tones of skepticism, Nemerov often sounds like a twentieth-century Pope in many of his classical prejudices ("What oft was thought but ne'er so well expressed," etc.).

6. Mary Kinzie, "The Signatures of Things," *Parnassus* 6, no. 1 (1977): 2.

7. Ross Labrie, *Howard Nemerov* (Boston: Twayne, 1980), 67.

8. Howard Nemerov, "Attentiveness and Obedience," in *Reflexions on Poetry and Poetics* (New Brunswick, N.J.: Rutgers University Press, 1972), 165–66.

9. William Pritchard, *Lives of the Modern Poets* (New York: Oxford University Press, 1980), 171–202.

10. See Dana Gioia's memoir, "Studying With Miss Bishop," in *The New Yorker* 62 (15 Sept. 1986): 90–101.

11. I think especially of such rural landmarkings as Wordsworth makes in the 1800 poems, "It Was an April Morning," "To Joanna," "There Is an Eminence," "A Narrow Girdle of Rough Stones and Crags," and "To M. H."

12. Elizabeth Bishop, *The Complete Poems, 1927–1979* (New York: Farrar, Straus & Giroux, 1979), 131. Subsequent page references in the text are to this volume.

13. Nemerov pays implicit homage to the trope of the *liber naturae* in Frost's "Time Out":

> The mountain he was climbing had the slant
> as of a book held up before his eyes
> (And was a text albeit done in plant).

THREE

## The Moral Imperative in Anthony Hecht, Allen Ginsberg, and Robert Pinsky

1. Susan Sontag, "Notes on Camp," in Elizabeth Hardwick, ed., *A Susan Sontag Reader* (New York: Farrar, Straus & Giroux, 1982), 118.

2. Jane Kramer, *Allen Ginsberg in America* (New York: Random House, 1968), 86.

3. John Hollander deserves a volume of his own, since his poetry has become a major text in the last part of our century in the same way that his commentary on others' work has proved indispensable. His recent essay, "The Question of American Jewish Poetry," *Tikkun* 3, no. 3 (1988): 33–37, 112–16, discusses, among other things, the problems confronting Jewish poets writing in English.

4. Albert Einstein, *The World as I See It* (New York: Covici Friede, 1934), 143.

5. All references are to *A Summoning of Stones* (New York: MacMillan, 1954), hereafter *SS*; *The Hard Hours* (New York: Atheneum, 1968), which contains a reprint of half of the thirty poems from the former book, hereafter *HH*; *Millions of Strange Shadows* (New York: Atheneum, 1977), hereafter *MSS*; and *The Venetian Vespers* (New York: Atheneum, 1980), hereafter *VV*.

6. Brad Leithauser, "Poet for a Dark Age," *The New York Review of Books* 33 (13 Feb. 1986), 11–14.

7. Edward Gibbon, *The Decline and Fall of the Roman Empire* (London: J. M. Dent, 1960), 1:266.

8. Joachim du Bellay, *Oeuvres Poétiques* (Paris: Éduoard Cornély, 1910), 2: 148–49, mentions the running in his sonnet no. 120 of *Regrets*, but says nothing about the Jews; Montaigne, however, in his *Journal de Voyage*, does. See *The Complete Works of Montaigne*, tran. Donald M. Frame (Stanford, Calif.: Stanford University Press, 1958), 946. Hecht conflates his sources as well as his scenes.

9. John Hollander, *The Figure of Echo: A Mode of Allusion in Milton and After* (Berkeley and Los Angeles: University of California Press, 1981).

10. W. H. Auden, *Secondary Worlds* (New York: Random House, 1968), 49.

11. All references are to *The Collected Poems, 1947–1980* (New York: Harper & Row, 1984), hereafter *CP*.

12. Helen Vendler, "A Lifelong Poem Including History," *The New Yorker*, 62 (13 Jan. 1986): 77–84.

13. Charles Molesworth, *The Fierce Embrace: A Study of Contemporary American Poetry* (Columbia, Mo.: University of Missouri Press, 1979), 38–39.

14. Quoted in Richard Howard, *Alone with America: Essays on the Art of Poetry in the United States since 1950* (New York: Atheneum, 1969), 149.

15. Kramer, *Ginsberg in America*, 115.

16. "If the mind of the teacher is not in love with the mind of the student, / he is simply practicing rape, and deserves at best our pity" ("Ghazals: Homage to Ghalib," in *Poems Selected and New: 1950–1974* [New York: W. W. Norton, 1974], 123). Rich has thought twice about this poem and has omitted it from her most recent selection; whether it was the sentiment or the pronouns that disturbed her is a question to consider.

17. *Writers at Work*, 3d ser. (New York: Viking, 1967), 295–96.

18. Samuel Taylor Coleridge, *Biographia Literaria*, ed. James Engell and Walter Jackson Bate (Princeton, N.J.: Princeton University Press, 1983), 2: 78ff.

19. Robert Pinsky, *Landor's Poetry* (Chicago: University of Chicago Press, 1969), 32.

20. Pinsky's three published volumes of poetry are *Sadness and Happiness* (Princeton, N.J.: Princeton University Press, 1975), hereafter *SH*; *An Explanation of America* (Princeton, N.J.: Princeton University Press, 1979), hereafter *EA*; and *A History of My Heart* (New York: Ecco Press, 1984).

21. Robert Pinsky, *The Situation of Poetry* (Princeton, N.J.: Princeton University Press, 1976), 152.

22. Pinsky has always been interested in the social and political dimension of poetry, areas notably scanted by literary theorists. See his recent essay, "Responsibilities of the Poet," *Critical Inquiry* 13 (1987): 421–33.

23. Harold Bloom, *Kabbalah and Criticism* (New York: Seabury Press, 1975).

FOUR

Myths of Concretion, Myths of Abstraction:
The Case of A. R. Ammons

1. E. L. Griggs, ed., *The Collected Letters of Samuel Taylor Coleridge* (Oxford: Oxford University Press, 1959), 4: 969.

2. George Santayana, *Three Philosophical Poets* (Cambridge, Mass.: Harvard University Press, 1944), 14, 25. I have dealt with the problems of philosophical poetry in "Some Lucretian Elements in Wordsworth," *Comparative Literature* 37 (1985): 27–50.

3. Helen Vendler, *Part of Nature, Part of Us* (Cambridge, Mass.: Harvard University Press, 1980), 330.

4. Harold Bloom, "A. R. Ammons: the Breaking of the Vessels," in *The Ringers in the Tower* (Chicago: University of Chicago Press, 1971), 257–90. Bloom reads the poetry chronologically, detecting a break after "Corsons Inlet," which abandons the hope for transcendence.

5. *Collected Poems 1951–1971* (New York: W. W. Norton, 1972), 146, hereafter cited as *CP*. Other poems are from *Tape for the Turn of the Year* (New York: W. W. Norton, 1965), hereafter *TTY*, and *Sphere: The Form of a Motion* (New York: W. W. Norton, 1972).

6. *The Prose Works of William Wordsworth*, ed. W.J.B. Owen and Jane Worthington Smyser (Oxford: Clarendon Press, 1974), 1: 141.

7. In his latest book, *Sumerian Vistas* (New York: W. W. Norton, 1987), Ammons uses very few colons. In the two long poems, "The Ridge Farm" and "Tombstones," each section ends punctuationless, except the last section of the former, which has a period. The remaining, short lyrics in the book all end with periods. Ammons' punctuation implies his ideas about the differences between long and short poems.

8. Virginia Woolf, *Moments of Being: Unpublished Autobiographical Writings*, ed. Jeanne Schulkind (New York: Harcourt Brace Jovanovich, 1976), 70–71.

9. Richard Wilbur, *The Poems of Richard Wilbur* (New York: Harcourt, Brace & World, 1963), 65. Wilbur's poems from the fifties and sixties, like "Love Calls Us to the Things of This World," embody the various traits that Robert von Hallberg associates with the predominant "suburban" temperament of our major poets, a modification and extension of the opulent side of Wallace Stevens.

# FIVE

"Driving to the Limits of the City of Words":
The Poetry of Adrienne Rich

1. A representative, early attack (but intelligent nonetheless) on Rich came
from Robert Boyers, disappointed by her political stridency in the late 1960s:
see "On Adrienne Rich," in Robert Boyers, ed., *Contemporary Poetry in America*
(New York: Schocken Books, 1974), 157–73. Frank Lentricchia has recently
done battle with Sandra Gilbert and Susan Gubar on the matter of feminist
stances and what he has regarded as their too-easy dichotomies: see Lentricchia, "Patriarchy Against Itself—The Young Manhood of Wallace Stevens,"
*Critical Inquiry* 13 (1987): 742–86; Gilbert and Gubar, "The Man on the Dump
versus the United Dames of America; or, What Does Frank Lentricchia Want?"
*Critical Inquiry* 14 (1988): 386–406; and Lentricchia, "Andiamo," ibid., 407–13.
Paula Bennett, *My Life a Loaded Gun: Female Creativity and Feminist Poetics* (Boston: Beacon Press, 1986), is the most recent book to treat Rich, as well as other
women poets, but with a primary emphasis on political rather than linguistic
issues. An exception to the general rule of treating Rich primarily for her political value is Charles Altieri, *Self and Sensibility in Contemporary American Poetry*
(Cambridge: Cambridge University Press, 1984), 165–90, who presents Rich
as an alternative to Ashbery, and as one who transcends what he calls the scenic mode. He defends Rich for, among other reasons, having developed a "discursive lyric speech" (166) in an age that needs discursiveness in its poetry: "In
a critical age we cannot do without discursiveness. Indeed, the contemporary
poetry most aware of the issues . . . tends to meet demands for lucidity by incorporating a good deal of discursiveness within the poetic experience" (26).
A new, Arnoldian tack—poetry as a criticism of life—seems inevitable as we
round toward the end of the twentieth century. Alicia Ostriker, "Dancing at
the Devil's Party: Some Notes on Politics and Poetry," *Critical Inquiry* 13 (1987):
579–96, distinguishes between the need for aesthetic discriminations and the
political efficacy of the poetry by women that she discusses.

2. *Adrienne Rich's Poetry*, ed. Barbara Charlesworth Gelpi and Albert Gelpi
(New York: W. W. Norton, 1975), 51. Hereafter cited as *ARP*.

3. "Ghazels: Homage to Ghalib," in *The Fact of a Doorframe: Poems Selected
and New, 1950–1984* (New York: W. W. Norton, 1984), 109. Rich's work will
frustrate future scholars because, like Robert Lowell and all other self-revising
American poets since Whitman, she is an inveterate fusser. This means that
poems appear, disappear, and reappear in various volumes. All references are
to *The Fact of a Doorframe*, hereafter *FD*; *Poems Selected and New, 1950–1974*
(New York: W. W. Norton, 1974, hereafter, *PSN*); and the Gelpis' *ARP*.

4. David Kalstone, *Five Temperaments* (New York: Oxford University Press,
1977), 135.

5. Rich could be mistaken for Howard Nemerov or Auden when she remarks that "poetry is a way of expressing unclear feelings," in her interview
with Joyce Greenberg, "By Woman Taught," *Parnassus* 7 (1979): 103.

6. Julia Kristeva, *Powers of Horror*, trans. Leon S. Roudiez (New York: Columbia University Press, 1982), 3.

7. Aristotle, *Rhetoric*, 2.2; *Nichomachean Ethics*, book 7. Jane Marcus, "Art
and Anger," *Feminist Studies* 4 (1978): 94, calls anger "a primary source of cre-

ative energy," and follows Freud in understanding anger as the ego's narcissistic defense against threats to its integrity. Like many feminist critics, she regards this narcissism as a healthy self-preservation by Rich in the late 1960s.

8. *The Will to Change* (New York: W. W. Norton, 1971), 21.

9. Willard Spiegelman, "The Ledger Sheet of Devotion: Lists as Poetic Form," *Southwest Review* 67 (1982): 381–98.

10. Calvin Bedient, *He Do the Police in Different Voices* (Chicago: University of Chicago Press, 1986), 113.

11. M. H. Abrams, "Structure and Style in the Greater Romantic Nature Lyric," in Frederick W. Hilles and Harold Bloom, eds., *From Sensibility to Romanticism* (New York: Oxford University Press, 1965), 527–60.

12. Helen Vendler, *Part of Nature, Part of Us*, 263–80; Alexander Theroux, in Jane Roberta Cooper, ed., *Reading Adrienne Rich* (Ann Arbor: University of Michigan Press, 1984), 308.

13. *Sources* (Woodside, Calif.: Heyeck Press, 1983), 23. See also *Blood, Bread, and Poetry, Selected Prose, 1979–1985* (New York: W. W. Norton, 1986) for Rich's prose meditations on her sense of her own Jewishness, a late but significant part of her poetic/political program.

SIX

The Sacred Books of James Merrill

1. All page references are to *The Changing Light at Sandover* (New York: Atheneum, 1982).

2. Peter Stitt, "Knowledge, Belief, & Bubblegum," *Georgia Review* 33 (1979): 706.

3. Calvin Bedient, review of *Divine Comedies*, *The New Republic* 174 (5 June 1976): 22.

4. Judith Moffett, *James Merrill: An Introduction to the Poetry* (New York: Columbia University Press, 1984), 196.

5. Robert von Hallberg, *American Poetry and Culture, 1945–1980* (Cambridge, Mass.: Harvard University Press, 1985), 114–15, 105.

6. David Kalstone, *Five Temperaments* (New York: Oxford University Press, 1977), 77–128; Vendler, *Part of Nature, Part of Us*, 210–32; Stephen Yenser, *The Consuming Myth* (Cambridge, Mass.: Harvard University Press, 1987). Helpful essays are included in David Lehman and Charles Berger, eds., *James Merrill: Essays in Criticism* (Ithaca, N.Y.: Cornell University Press, 1983).

7. "*Mirabell*: Conservative Epic," in Harold Bloom, ed., *James Merrill: Modern Critical Views* (New York: Chelsea House, 1986), 183.

8. "Introduction," ibid., 2. Bloom characteristically regards Merrill as a reparatory poet; Helen Vendler regards him as an elegiac one.

9. *Paris Review* 24, no. 84 (1982): 189.

10. *From the First Nine* (New York: Atheneum, 1982), 83. Hereafter cited as *FFN*.

11. For the notion of "unanxious influence" I am indebted to James Rieger, "Wordsworth Unalarm'd," in Joseph Wittreich, ed., *Milton and the Line of Vision* (Madison: University of Wisconsin Press, 1975), 185–208.

12. Yenser, *Consuming Myth*, 283–320.

13. In a 1967 interview with Donald Sheehan, in L. S. Dembo and Cyrena N. Pondrom, eds., *The Contemporary Writer* (Madison: University of Wisconsin Press, 1972), 148.

14. T. S. Eliot, "Tradition and the Individual Talent," in *Selected Essays* (New York: Harcourt, Brace & Co., 1932), 6. That "the dead . . . are that which we know" is a truth that Merrill seems to take seriously if not literally.

SEVEN

Some Speculations in Place of a Conclusion

1. Carol Christ, *Victorian and Modern Poetics* (Chicago: University of Chicago Press, 1984), 98.

2. James Laughlin, *Pound as Wuz* (St. Paul, Minn.: Graywolf Press, 1987), 34–51.

3. Eliot, ed., *Literary Essays of Pound*, 59.

4. Ibid., 6.

5. Gary Snyder, *Axe Handles* (San Francisco: North Point, 1983), 6, 7.

6. Gary Snyder, *Left Out in the Rain, New Poems 1947–1985* (San Francisco: North Point, 1986), 130.

7. John Ashbery, *Selected Poems* (New York: Viking, 1985), 325, 328. Hereafter cited as *SP* in text.

8. Roland Barthes, *The Pleasure of the Text* (New York: Hill & Wang, 1975), 6.

9. Susan Sontag, ed., *A Barthes Reader* (New York: Hill & Wang, 1982), 378.

10. Ibid., 461.

11. Ibid., 460.

12. Ibid., 476.

267